OUTSIDE of ORDINARY

OUTSIDE of ORDINARY

WOMEN'S TRAVEL STORIES

edited by Lynn Cecil and Catherine Bancroft

Second Story Press

NATIONAL LIBRARY OF CANADA CATALOGUING IN PUBLICATION
Outside of ordinary : women's travel stories / edited by
Catherine Bancroft and Lynn Cecil.

ISBN 1-897187-00-9

1. Travelers' writings, Canadian (English). 2. Women travelers-
Canada. 3. Voyages and travels. 4. Travel in literature.
I. Cecil, Lynn A. (Lynn Anne), 1967- II. Bancroft, Catherine, 1972-

PR1309.T73O95 2005   C818'.5403   C2005-904393-8

Edited by Doris Cowan
Cover design © Anne Horst/www.i2iart.com
Text design by Lancaster Reid Creative

Printed and bound in Canada

*Second Story Press gratefully acknowledges the support of the Ontario Arts
Council and the Canada Council for the Arts for our publishing program.
We acknowledge the financial support of the Government of Canada
through the Book Publishing Industry Development Program.*

Published by
SECOND STORY PRESS
20 Maud Street, Suite 401
Toronto, Ontario, Canada
M5V 2M5

www.secondstorypress.ca

OUTSIDE of ORDINARY
WOMEN'S TRAVEL STORIES
edited by Lynn Cecil and Catherine Bancroft

Contents

Acknowledgements

The journey of compiling and editing this collection of women's stories has been a long and life-altering one. To all of the contributors who have written so openly of their travel experiences, I extend my deepest gratitude and thanks. It has been an honour and a delight to work with you.

Throughout this process my family and friends have been incredibly supportive, offering much encouragement. I would particularly like to thank my husband Ben for his profound kindness and love and his unconditional support, my children, whose hugs mean more than they'll ever know, and my parents, who have influenced me in their passion for travel and whose support for my love of writing and painting began when I was two years old, and has strengthened especially over the past two years. To many other wonderful friends and relatives, thank you for your years of support, encouragement, and your friendship. You are all so very dear to me.

Margie Wolfe, Laura McCurdy, Leah Sandals, and Barbara Kamienski at Second Story Press have been unwavering in their support, their friendship, and their strength. I am forever grateful to you, and to all of the women at Second Story, for your kindness and wonderful sense of humor. You have made the publishing process so very enjoyable!

Lynn Cecil
August 2005

I am enormously humbled by the risks that all of the women have taken in order to share their stories. I believe that these stories have the ability to affect women across the world.

I am profoundly indebted to the generous support of both of my parents, Joan and Mike Bancroft, and Bill Genereux, for making this dream a reality. Thank you to my mom and my grandmothers, Helen and Jean, for teaching me about the power of spirit.

Through my travel journeys to Zimbabwe and Nepal, I was deeply affected by the presence of community and ritual in both of these cultures. Simultaneously, I struggled with the labels of developed and underdeveloped countries; although it was clear to me that our Western cultures are more economically advanced, I began to see us as more spiritually impoverished. I searched for travel literature that spoke to the spiritual, transformative journeys that women experience to assist me on my quest. As a result, I perceived a gap in this genre.

It became my dream to create a women's travel anthology that would offer a space for women to express their intimate, transformative stories. It was also my hope that the contributors would be united in community birthed by the anthology.

Thank you to Lynn Cecil for all of your hard work and efforts.

Catherine Bancroft
August 2005

Introduction

The adventure and thrill of traveling, of exploring unfamiliar landscapes, has for centuries lured many people away from the general comfort and security of their homes. From as early as the seventeenth century, women's travel writing, often recorded in the form of letters back home, focused on observations of other women, the environment, the people and culture, the customs observed, and traveling tips. Written in an expository style, women's travel stories and letters served as guides to different countries. By the twentieth century and now into the twenty-first, women's travel writing has expanded to include creative non-fiction memoirs and novels, but very few are collections of stories, and fewer still are ones in which women explore their reactions to how travel has changed their lives.

Inviting readers to imagine the excitement of travel, with its endless possibilities for change and self-renewal, and the occasion to reflect upon the past and anticipate the future, *Outside of Ordinary* provides a unique opportunity to experience thirty-two women's intimate responses to travel. In both the literal and metaphorical sense, travel has transformed their lives, expanding their vision of themselves, their communities, and other communities around the world. Opening with Kathie Sutherland's story of a new beginning, incited by being suspended above the earth in a plane, the collection contains stories that will transport readers around the world, through North, Central, and South America, Europe, Asia, the South Pacific, and Africa, as the contributors write of their elation, and sometimes trepidation, at leaving the known for the unknown, testing and stretching their mental and physical limits.

Release from daily routine often accompanies the lure of travel, and being separated from home, careers, even family, means that sometimes inhibitions are ignored, fears overcome, challenges met and conquered. Some of the women write about their uncertainty in following their impulses and dreams or facing their secret fears. Their stories reveal deeply personal thoughts on their relationships, health, families, ancestors. Sharon Butala's visit to Italy sparks intimate thoughts on a relationship that transcends language; Jane Eaton Hamilton, while on vacation in Mexico, contemplates with her partner whether to join the Canadian court case for same-sex marriages; and Jeananne Kathol Kirwin reacts to a frightening personal realization at the commencement of a family boat voyage, far from home. Alison Lohans reconnects with family, self, and her roots in Iowa, while Holly Luhning explores the idea of home being within oneself in her poetic text and poems.

Other women are psychologically transformed through accepting physically and mentally challenging quests, like Elaine K. Miller, in her cycling adventure across the southern United States, and Janet Greidanus in her risky climb to Mount Everest Base Camp. In exploring challenging aspects of their lives through retracing their family roots, or through breaking away from confining roles or situations, several women also discover a sense of inner strength. In traveling to Russia to discover links to her ancestors, Ellen Jaffe places herself in a time and a country where words and actions threaten her safety and her future, while Amanda Stevens, exploring New Zealand on her own, confronts the limits of women hitchhiking solo. Lorna Crozier's chilling account of her visit to Chile is captured in her text and poetry, and Linda Pelton faces the emotional and physical bondage of being bound to a cult in Mexico.

Several contributors investigate the power of their intuition and the experiences of personal growth that occur while sojourning abroad. Alison Pick in Saskatchewan and Charlotte Caron in Minnesota find deep spiritual connections to the landscape during their retreats at monasteries. Jan Mackie explores the power of her insight and different ways of knowing while traveling in Afghanistan, India, and Nepal. In journeys through water and mountains, Jody Wood in Indonesia, Catherine Bancroft in Nepal, and Chris Marin in Machu Picchu, Peru, explore the healing power of nature in their lives.

Working or studying in foreign countries, several of the women find themselves examining and questioning aspects of their own lives that they had taken for granted as they develop relationships with women from diverse cultures. Angèle Palmer in Taiwan, Amy Coupal in Papua New Guinea, and Christine McKenzie in Nicaragua experience shifts in their perspectives on life while traveling and working. sarahmaya hamilton finds herself attempting to impart the open-mindedness of her upbringing in Canada to her students in rural Japan. While studying in China for a year, Marion Jones learns many life lessons of her own, emerging from her former self as though from a chrysalis. Anne Sasso traveling in India, Thailand, and Argentina, Carole TenBrink in Vietnam, and Cheryl Mahaffy in Eritrea find themselves examining and questioning aspects of their own lives in relation to women from diverse cultures.

Insight into their own roles as wives, mothers, daughters, and career women allows other women in this anthology to reconnect with themselves while traveling far from home. Larissa McWhinney, in Spain, explores her connections and shifting relationships with her mother, while Gillian Steward, in Guatemala, discovers new bonds forged between her and her daughter. In Thailand and Japan, Christina Owens reflects on her estranged relationship with her father and the essence of place carried within her wherever she travels. Lastly, Aprille Janes, Shelley A. Leedahl, and Lynn Cecil, temporarily separated from their families, are able to explore more fully their lives as individual women in such varied landscapes as the Yukon, Mexico, and Bermuda.

What unites these stories is the newfound or rekindled sense of strength and empowerment that each woman experiences as a result of her travels. Through inner journeys and outward adventures, these stories celebrate women's lives and will hopefully inspire others to leave the familiarity of home momentarily behind, to be open to the transformative effects of travel, and to discover that they, and the world they live in, are anything but ordinary.

Suspended in Solitude

Kathie Sutherland

My nineteen-year-old daughter releases me from an uncharacteristically long hug, turns away and steps out through the sliding-glass door into a cold prairie wind. Little wisps of loose blond hair whip around her head, escapees from her tight ponytail. Reaching up to tuck the strands behind her ears, she looks back to grin at me over her shoulder and calls out, "Have fun, Mom!" Then, dodging a taxi pulling away from the curb, she pulls up her collar, wraps her coat tightly around herself, and scurries off out of sight into the parkade.

She's gone.

I take a big breath, scan the signs for my flight number, gate, and time of departure, and haul my rolling suitcase down a long corridor. My heart thumps a little too fast—my adult thinking brain understands that travel turns out all right in the end, but my heart can't forget the childhood experience of being swept along toward unfamiliar destinations I'd had no hand in choosing.

"Posting Out Orders" came for Army dads in May, and by the time school was out, in June, Married Quarters bustled with comings and goings. Everyone was on the move. When the men in blue coveralls arrived to pack our lives into a big orange moving van, the new kids from down the street joined up with the old regulars who were also due to move away, and everybody settled in to watch the show. Beds, bookcases, our peacock blue nylon living-room couch, boxes packed with books, picture albums, worn towels, special jewelry boxes and mismatched dishes —it all disappeared into the yawning mouth of the big truck. We kids didn't want to leave our now familiar street, but we understood that we had to go.

Leaving really started for me when the back end of our green Chevy, overloaded with six kids and camping gear, scraped the pavement at the end of the driveway, and we were off, swaying on unsure shocks down to the corner, where we waited for the Military Police barricade to rise. Then at last we were out on the highway and picking up speed. I would be tracing our route on the road map—geography was always my favorite subject—and for a little while, I would excitedly watch the center line streaming out behind the car. Then I lapsed with my siblings into a quiet, contented state of suspended reality, which settled over the family. We kids read, colored, slept, or stared out the window at the passing landscape. Silence reigned until somebody kicked someone, or moved too far over into somebody else's spot. When the squabbling began to irritate Dad, we would stop for a picnic lunch, or a bathroom break and a stretch.

Here and now, in the airport, a tiny baby is squalling in one of the waiting areas, and it sounds for all the world like a baby animal. Travelers standing in line are looking over at the young mother whose concern is all for her child. When my older daughter was eighteen months old, I took her on an air trip with me, and it was quite a challenge. Modern conveniences like disposable diapers and instant formula made it possible for me to manage it competently, but I wonder how my mother coped with food, clothing, and child care for six kids. I remember only the fun we had. She was a cruise director par excellence when it came to activities. She had us making campfire stools with sticks and twine, crafting fairy gardens of moss and small figurines set on a pie plate, figuring out the puzzle of camp cots, and scurrying about on treasure hunts. At dusk, when loon laughter echoed across the water and the mosquitoes came out, she would supervise the cutting of sticks for roasting marshmallows at the fire in pajamas and jackets under a star-filled night sky. The lake reflected the moon hanging like a reassuring beacon over the campsite.

By September, the newness of beginnings became a reality: new school, new teachers, new friends, saving paper bags for textbook covers, searching for pencil stubs and old erasers to start off the year. Embarrassed at my awkwardness in sports and too shy to talk to boys, I'd worry and feel out of place. Then gradually life in the new place brightened, and memories of the old crowd got dimmer.

Now, forty years later, I'm flying to Toronto in the midst of a SARS outbreak to visit my mother-in-law, who has been sick, lonely, and isolated. And I'm remembering what it felt like to be lonely.

For the next ten days, I will not be expected to fix meals, meet deadlines, fret over teenagers, or baby-sit the grandchildren. I will be a guest in my mother-in-law's condo, free of routine, predictable rituals, and expectations. We'll enjoy the visit as friends, a new development since the days when we clashed over her concept of motherhood and mine. I am reaching the age when I'm learning to appreciate older women. We'll catch up by talking family. I know as soon as I show her pictures of her great-grandchildren she'll *ooh* and *aah* like any grandmother worth her salt. She'll tell me how much the little one looks like her mother. We'll talk about her only son, my husband. We'll agree that grandparenting is much more fun than parenthood.

Right now, with a new journal zipped securely in the pocket of my writing bag, I'm ready for travel. I plan to live moments in my trip more than once by recording them on the page. I have a paperback of Elizabeth Berg's *Pull of the Moon*; in four and a half hours I'll be arriving in Toronto. Until then I can read, think, write, or just let my imagination float free.

I join other passengers in a long, slow Departures lineup. Once my suitcase disappears down the conveyor belt, I sniff out a coffee bar and seat myself in a comfortable spot away from the smoking room. I purposely turn my back on the closed-circuit TVs spewing pictures of frightened children in Iraq, staring wide-eyed at dusty tanks, burned-out cars, and angry faces. My dad was in a war once, and it left emotional wounds. I'm saddened to see injured eyes in these small faces.

I scan the reviews on back cover of *Pull of the Moon*, smiling to myself at the opening sentence of the *Orlando Sentinel's* commentary: "Sometimes you have to leave your life behind for a while to see it and really live it freshly again." *Coincidence?* I doubt it. It's absolutely the right book for this trip. Midlife is pushing and pulling at me, nagging me to open a few windows, sweep out the cobwebs of confusion, and let in a fresh breeze. I hope Berg has some wisdom for me.

I am oblivious to the garbled announcements on the PA system, the static of two-way radios on the belts of security personnel, and the low chatter of fellow coffee drinkers. I shut out this real world and step into Berg's reflective novel.

By boarding time, I'm on page 76. I continue to read as I stand in line at the gate. Finally, we are tramping down long corridors to the hatch of the plane. The steward is overseeing the organized confusion of stowing coats in overhead bins and finding pillows. I settle into my window seat behind the wing, fasten my seatbelt, and stow my carry-on bag. I'm glad the middle seat of three is empty, because I am ready for my first treat of uninterrupted reading. I've already decided to use Berg's prose as a prompt for my own writing.

Eventually, as the plane accelerates into a shuddering liftoff, the power of the jet's thrust pushes me back into my seat. We climb toward the clouds. Alberta recedes into a patchwork of dark squares edged with ragged gray snow, and I lapse into the passivity of being carried along like a child in the womb. I am oblivious to the people in the world that is receding below me as I climb to the edge of a new beginning.

An endless stretch of washboard cloud lies beneath the blue bowl of sky. The plane seems to crawl slowly across it, yet the safety information in the seat pocket assures me we are flying at five hundred miles per hour. I lean my head against the cool window, and a sense of undiscovered possibility spreads out like the skyscape before me. The background roar of jet engines lulls me for a time, and when the sunlight begins to slide away to the west and shadows slice long and thin across cabin, I pretend for a minute that I can see the jet stream rushing me away from my old life and stretching out the psychic threads that tie me to it, pulling them till they're ready to snap. Sometimes I just want to cut through the frayed emotional cords that tangle me in that ordinary life and those predictable marriage patterns of Friday-night TV, Saturday grocery shopping, nightly newscasts, lukewarm sex, and empty conversation. If only for a while, I want to break free, but it isn't easy. I wonder if surrendering to a new reality is as hard for other women as it is for me.

The plane and I seem to hang above the earth, supported by nothing but the air beneath us. I have no map of Canada and no watch. I feel that I am in solitary suspension in both space and time. There is only the smell of coffee brewing, the vibration of the engines, the grizzled hair of the old man in the seat ahead of me. It is the perfect time to float out of my own life into Berg's novel.

"I have felt so long like I am drowning ..." the novel's heroine, Nan, writes in a letter to her husband. I set aside the book, take pen in hand and begin, on a clean white page of my journal. *I have felt so long like I am drowning ... in busyness, rushing and doing. There is never enough time. I hurry to volunteer, hurry to work, hurry to join boards and committees, hurry to develop relationships with people, hurry to write, to get it all down on the page before it's gone.* The letters can't keep up; abbreviated words and half sentences merge into one long paragraph, as my tidy cursive script loosens and I flow through jobs and disappointments, losses and new friends, and all the dramas of my ordinary life. I end up filling three, four, five pages.

I stare at the wavy hair of a young woman two seats ahead of me. I wonder if she drives an unwashed van over crowded freeways, rushing to work and gym, speeding from home to her children's hockey games, to golf lessons, from swimming to piano lessons. Does she feel the hurry madness too? Finally, my fingers cramp and my hand begins to ache.

My journal sits open on the tray beside my empty coffee cup. *Why do I hurry so? Does it have to do with my growing up in such a nomadic way? Back then, I had to fit in quickly, make friends, and find a life before leaving again.* The stewardess brings more coffee, and I distract myself by stirring it, try to look out the window, but all I can see is the glass and my own reflection. *Friends ...* I write about a nine-year-old, dirty-faced friend, Genny, and her older brother, Ricky, on whom I had a crush. In my memory, they are still kids with marbles and broken bikes. My next-door girlfriend, Linda, the practical joker, is still my goofy thirteen-year-old pal, keeping us in cigarettes stolen from her mom. *Places ...* I write about gardens on people's farms, parks, picnic spots, and about the blue hair of a Miramichi grandmother we met once on a picnic foray to the beach and then adopted as kin. Her skin looked as soft and wrinkled as an overripe peach, and she wore blue bedroom slippers on her arthritic feet. She lives now in my memory, a gentle soul slowly sitting down to rock in a squeaky chair in the corner of the woodstove kitchen we visited on so many Sunday afternoons. As I write about cuddling my own grandchildren in my rocker, I become aware of an old longing, for someone to comfort me, someone steady, someone who knows all about me. I think about how I want my grandchildren to remember me, stirring porridge, pulling a sleigh, reading a book. I love to see the world through their new and wondering eyes, their high voices singing nursery rhymes and exclaiming over dewy spiderwebs, worms, and jet-trail writing on the summer sky. Like Nan, I am middle-aged. I need to know what it means to grow old, who I will become in this new part of my life. I am being carried forward into a new place, but this time I have no map to tell me where I'm going. I'd like to pack up my old stuff, give it away, and make room for the new. I'd like to draw together all the places that I've been to and at last know where it is that I belong.

My mother-in-law has no doubt about her place in the world—she has her community and has grown with it over a span of seven decades. She tells tales of aching hunger in the Dirty Thirties, of her brothers going off to the Second World War, of her own time in the army. She talks about the music of Judy Garland, and her delight at buying an automatic washing machine in the postwar fifties; her life, rooted deep in the past, feels permanent.

I try to imagine a state of permanent stability and rootedness. Familiarity. History. A place on the map. Perhaps if I ask my mother-in-law, she could find a metaphor for this state of being: a tree, a dandelion, a mountain. Maybe then I could understand how it feels.

I turn to a new page in my journal, and I write at the top: *Questions for Mother-in-Law*. I underline it twice. 1. How does it feel to know someone for sixty years, especially your sister-in-law? 2. Grow up in one neighborhood, watch it become a city? 3. Collect brandy snifters and Royal Doulton figurines for a lifetime and never have to worry they will be broken during a move? 4. Take your child to see

Granny at the home? 5. Attend the funeral of your grandmother? 6. Feel as if you came from somewhere?

As I dot that question mark, my eyes sting with tears. The need to feel rooted washes over me like a wave, leaving little tidepools of hurt in my chest. I let the ache sit there. I let my tears fall but do not make a sound. The yearning lies like a stone in my belly.

I don't want to make a scene here on the plane, in front of the young businessman in the aisle seat frowning over charts on his laptop. He glances up at me, then looks away, and I'm embarrassed, so I rummage in my purse for a tissue. My search for belonging, the roaming I do in my imagination, the speculating I do about other people's lives are all part of this want in me. I want to understand this *belonging* place called Home.

Outside the window the last rays of the sun have disappeared. Wiping away my tears and sniffling, I think of Nan wandering back roads, exploring small communities, talking to new people with open-hearted curiosity, asking them, "How are you?" and really listening to their answers. She does this instead of rushing on to the next place. Nan touches that deep paradoxical part of me that wants to take to the road for a while, stretch out the thin threads, risk aloneness, and hope the thread won't snap and leave me hanging. Yet I also want to come home to a safe place inside my own skin. Only I can find this place, and I can find it scribbled in every line of my journal.

The seat-belt light comes on and the pilot announces our descent into Pearson Airport.

It's funny how the darkness has come, spreading below the plane. The horizon moves up into the window, and the city below us tips on its side. The cabin lights are dimmed, and I can see strings of runway lights glittering in geometric lines. The land rises to meet us, and the jet thunders in to bump down on the tarmac.

People crowd the aisles, pull coats from the bins overhead, jostle for a spot in the exit line, reach for cigarettes, and flip open cell phones. The volume of chatter increases. As I collect my things, I feel my heart beating fast. *Aha*, I think, *there it is again. Excitement and a little fear*. I tuck my journal into the side pocket of my travel bag and carefully do up the zipper, as if I am tucking away my fear. It is still close by but now contained on the page.

I take one last look out the tiny window and catch a glimpse of a full white campfire moon hanging in the night sky. The child in me, the one who feels the push and pull of belonging and moving on, nudges me into a memory. She's the one who used to watch the moon traveling along with us in the night sky above our old green Chevy as it carried my family to our next new home. She's the one who appreciates moonscapes.

Bocca Della Verità

Sharon Butala

 I went to Italy once and fell in love with my sister's brother-in-law, fifteen years younger than me, who couldn't speak a word of English and, unlike his brothers and cousins who turned out, all of them, to be movie-star handsome, was perfectly ordinary-looking. Besides being unable to speak to each other (although my sister is fluent, I don't know a word of Italian), we had to spend every moment together in the presence of either his mother or my sister or both of them. As if that weren't enough to deter even the most marginal flirtation, I was and am married, as happily as the next person, and for a long time. And, I was to find out, although he lived in his mother's apartment still, he had a lover and they had a child—apparently—and none of what happened between us made any sense anyway.

It began when my sister and I landed at Leonardo da Vinci airport in Rome. I don't remember going through customs; I remember nothing about the airport itself. I only remember that moment when, after we'd passed through those hurdles and emerged unscathed with our luggage into a meeting area and she'd introduced me to her tall, large-bosomed and commanding sister-in-law, my sister turned to the slender, blue-eyed, balding, fortyish man standing beside his mother and said, "This is Claudio."

I turned to him, my eyes met his, and suddenly words left me— they just dried up, even a polite mumble—and in an attack of something that was like shyness but felt quite different, my face grew warm, I couldn't look at him, and I dropped my eyes to the scuffed marble floor. Until that moment I hadn't even known of his existence. I mean, my sister might have mentioned him, but if she had, I'd forgotten about it, and so his presence was a complete surprise. But in that second when our hands touched and our eyes met, though, I noticed that a faint flush appeared in his cheeks too, and he too

9

dropped his eyes, murmuring something I didn't catch but that must have been a greeting. And although I do not know what it was that happened to me at that moment in the Rome airport, I know that it happened to him too.

He drove us to the large apartment complex on the outskirts of the city that, I was told later by a Danish man I met in Addis Ababa (another long story), had been built by Mussolini for the working people of the city to live in and was a famous building. The family apartment on the second floor was surprisingly large, middle-class comfortable, and had marble everywhere—floors, window ledges, decorative trim, and all through the sizable, nicely appointed bathroom. These in-laws of my sister were working-class people, as nearly as I could make out, although Claudio had an office job (which he rushed off to on his Vespa as soon as we were safely deposited), as did his unmarried, younger sister, who also lived in the apartment.

But that evening, after he'd returned from work, showered, and had a light meal, he took us on my first trip—but not my sister's, as she had spent a lot of time in Rome over the years of her marriage to Claudio's uncle—to see this ancient, famous city where he'd been born and had lived his entire life. I think that at this point both of us had decided to ignore that peculiar, unsettling moment in the airport, and it was taken for granted that my sister would ride beside him in his small car, and I would squeeze into the back seat behind her. She and Claudio chatted steadily in Italian while he sped through traffic, took shortcuts down winding, darkened streets, occasionally making a remark about city landmarks that my sister thought deserved translating. The Bocca della Verità is one I remember in particular—the "Mouth of Truth," a large flat circular face with an open mouth, said able to bite off the hand of a liar. We didn't look at each other, or smile or try to speak, and anyway it was dark in the car.

That first night he drove us to the top of a couple of the Seven Hills of Rome. On one of them (it may have been Janiculum, but I'm not sure any more), as we leaned against a parapet in the darkness, the city of Rome reduced to a multitude of tiny white lights below us, he indicated the bulky shadow of a large building behind us, a monastery,

he said. His gesture was contemptuous or angry, or both. He said that the Church had taken all the best spots in Rome, "and that is why we are *communistas*." I understood only *communistas*. Years ago, in the late fifties, our university's only Communist student came to one of our wild undergrad parties, a rumpled, glowering, uncommunicative man in a dark overcoat that he never took off, sliding finally into a drunken stupor. I gazed at Claudio with renewed interest.

After that, he drove us down into the heart of Rome to an ice cream store—a *gelateria*—where he bought us each an enormous *gelato* cone and then, as we licked happily away, took us to the Trevi Fountain. It was perhaps nine in the evening by then, but there were many people around: tourists, ordinary Romans, and a few shabbily dressed young men seated haphazardly together watching the rest of us. My sister and I, both once art majors, walked around the space in front of the fountain, studying and discussing it, and then we threw coins into it to guarantee that, one day, we would return. Claudio stood back while we did this, watching us quietly.

We had finished our cones and for several minutes had been simply standing in silence, listening to the water's splash and murmur and gazing at the fountain's graceful marble figures, when one of the shabbily dressed young men got up from his perch on some steps, or perhaps it was a stone bench, beyond the fountain, and ambled slowly toward us. I noticed this and waited with interest to see what he would do. I was remembering Vivien Leigh in *The Roman Spring of Mrs. Stone* and thinking how disappointed he would be to find out that neither of us was an enormously wealthy, lonely, and unattached widow, when Claudio simply moved unobtrusively forward, intercepting him in his path toward us, said something softly to him, and the young man—he was long-legged, with long, black, romantically curling hair—turned and, with a hint of embarrassment in his gait, went back to his seat among the other shabby young men on the far side of the fountain.

I hadn't traveled all that much in those days, although I have since then. I began with the desire to see certain things in the world and to be a woman of the world because I had seen them—the Mayan pyramids, Prague's Old Town, the palace at Knossos. I've tried very hard to be a part of the things I've seen, but despite my best efforts only once did I ever succeed, at Tintern Abbey, and that was inadvertent, and a numinous moment. In my experience the declared objects of the journey always turn out to be the least of what we carry back home with us. Instead, it is the thing one sees by accident—the view from the parking lot at an ancient ruin on Crete; or the wedding in a Slovak village that happens to take place as one passes through; or the not-at-all famous, crumbling, inexpressibly beautiful yet unadorned, twelfth-century Norse church on Orkney; or the discovery of how overly-ornate, in fact, ugly, St. Peter's Cathedral is on the inside. The humanity of others, the little surprises, the unexpected boredom, the occasional moment of insight about oneself are what travel is really about.

So, although my sister and I did the tourist things—the Sistine Chapel (in this month before Easter the creation scene was hidden behind draperies, and we both stared in surprise at Michelangelo's newly cleaned work, the colors having turned out to be light, airy, and delicate instead of heavy and dark as our art history class slides had shown them to be); the marvelous Pantheon where, teasingly—flirta-tiously—I'd taken a picture of Claudio taking a picture of me; and the many cathedrals, one in which my sister, Claudio's mother, and I sat side by side in a pew looking silently about, absorbing the atmosphere, until I realized that my sister's sister-in-law was quietly crying.

Eventually a story emerged, although I didn't hear it firsthand, and it certainly didn't come from Claudio but from my sister's sister-in-law, who must have told her one night after I'd gone to bed. I knew that the sister-in-law was from the north of Italy—that was all I knew, other than that there is a hostility between northerners and southern-ers, that northerners feel some superiority to southerners, and that it sometimes goes so far that certain northerners will not even use olive oil in their cooking, and that certain famous Italian dishes are not, and never have been, generally cooked or served in the north.

But the sister-in-law had come down to Rome to work, and there she had met a Roman and married him. They had three sons and two daughters, and as Claudio was the oldest of the family, as in families all over the world, he bore the brunt of the parents' dreams. In this case, Claudio had fallen in love with a beautiful, dark-eyed southern woman, and his father, outraged, would not allow their marriage. Claudio chose not to defy his father, and as far as the family was concerned, that was the end of it. Unknown to them, though, it had not ended for Claudio and the woman he loved. She had married someone else, but, his mother told my sister, one day walking down a Roman street she had met her son walking with a little girl, and she had known at once that this was his child—his and that of the woman his father had forbidden him to marry. And she knew that he and the woman continued to see each other, that they were still lovers—lovers and parents as well.

During the day his mother took us through her Rome, by bus, transferring, or else walking through all sorts of interesting shortcuts in the heart of downtown Rome. In mid-afternoon we came back to the apartment, she shooed us off for a siesta to the bedroom we shared, and when evening came, Claudio returned from work, showered, ate a light meal, and took us out in his small car to see more of the famous sites of his city. That became our routine for our entire week's stay in Rome.

Elections were being held, and one afternoon at the Spanish Steps a candidate for mayor was making a speech with television cameras recording the event, and a band wearing medieval-style costumes was playing; and once the sister-in-law, on a shortcut from one church to another, led us through the stone courtyard of a university that dated back to the twelfth century, just as hordes of chattering young students, in jeans and tight T-shirts, emerged. And one night, as we sped with Claudio through downtown Rome, we caught a glimpse between a few broken, ancient pillars, of a *fascistico* rally lit by fierce white spotlights, and Claudio muttered darkly to my sister, but she didn't translate. Later, we found out that this scene had been flashed on television around the world.

For all that week that we lived in their apartment Claudio and I did not hold hands, we didn't even touch hands; we didn't sneak out

13

of our respective bedrooms at midnight and meet on the balcony and neck or maybe even make love; I for one didn't even think of doing such a thing. I felt guilty the whole week because I was—what? I can't say *in love*, but it was beyond attraction, it wasn't even in the same ballpark. I don't know *what* it was—and it was embarrassing, and wholly impossible, and especially quite ridiculous. I think now, as I write this, that the fact that we never did any of the above had not so much to do with our sense of propriety (or our bewilderment) as our mutual terror of whatever it was that had stricken us both, where it might take us if we surrendered for even a second. Or maybe that is only after-the-fact romanticizing, something I have not since indulged in because it cheapens whatever it was that happened.

Then the day arrived when it was time for us to leave Rome to go on to the family home in the north. By the time we were to rise in the early morning to catch our train, Claudio would have already been gone for an hour, and so we said good-night and also goodbye to him the night before, my sister clasping his hands in hers and kissing him first on one cheek and then the other, offering him *mille grazie*, his mother standing by watching benignly.

My sister stepped aside and it was my turn. Claudio began to murmur rapidly to me in Italian, although he knew I could not understand him, and standing close to me, leaned down and kissed me first on one cheek and then the other, then lifted his head and still speaking, he gazed at me for a moment. Then he bent down and kissed me on each cheek again. My sister turned and rushed down the hall to our bedroom; his mother turned on her heel as rapidly and disappeared into her kitchen.

I don't wonder what he was saying, nor did I wonder then. There was some strong feeling between us, had been since the first second we laid eyes on each other in the Rome airport, and now we were saying goodbye, almost certainly forever, although we had not touched, or spoken to each other, or kissed, or even pressed our bodies against each other in a moment stolen perhaps in the apartment hallway or the parking garage as my sister walked ahead of us. Nothing, *nada*, *niente*. And now, it was ended.

If I were not the age I am now (or even the age I was then), and if I did not know, although I've never seen her, that his lover is beautiful—and I am not—maybe I could romanticize what happened and lie awake nights dreaming of the perfect love that could never be. But I am too old, and romantic notions were knocked out of me a long time ago. And so I do not lie awake dreaming of his mouth on mine, of lying through a warm Roman night with him, the scent of flowers wafting upward to perfume our lovemaking. I do not dream of such things at all, although I cannot understand what happened there between us, and I have not forgotten it.

Years have passed since that adventure in Rome. I hear from my sister that Claudio's sister has married and moved out of the apartment, that his mother soon grew ill and eventually died. But before that happened, my sister told me that Claudio had at last moved out of his mother's home. She didn't know if his lover's husband had died, or if she had divorced him, or what had happened, but she and Claudio and their child were at last together. She told me that they had moved into a tiny apartment in a building owned by the king of Spain, she said, on the Campo de' Fiori. And so it is he and his lover, and not Claudio and I, who lie together in the warm, flower-scented Roman night.

Later, when we had finished our travels elsewhere in Italy—to the family home in the north below the Alps, to Florence and Venice—and had come home to Canada, after I had recovered from the illness I'd been stricken with from the lung-penetrating damp cold of Venice at Easter, I went shopping for gifts to send back to the family who had been so hospitable, rearranging their lives for our pleasure. Small things—notepaper for his mother, pictures for his sister. When it came time to find a gift for Claudio, something took hold of me, I found no small memento would do; I had to find a gift that was also a message to this man I could not speak to, and whom I would never again see. And so I looked and looked.

At last, in the gift shop of an art gallery, I found an Inuit sculpture of a seal, a piece small enough to be held in one hand, and yet weighty, and so compellingly shaped that one's very palm begged to caress it. It was carved out of that dull green stone the Inuit use, and polished to a glossy shine. But running in a graceful curve up the seal's haunch and diagonally across its belly and chest (if seals may be said to have chests) was a narrow, rough-edged fissure. It was the nearly complete break in an otherwise perfect work, an exquisite and heartbreaking imperfection that would be eloquent testimony to what we had shared that neither of us could comprehend or say.

Jaws in a Bowl

Jane Eaton Hamilton

Puerto Vallarta's mugginess is apparent even in the bottled air of the plane, and on disembarking we are hit with it, like down pillows full in the face. The Canada 3000 passengers climb into a bus that hauls us across the tarmac to the airport and Migration. We fill out immigration forms—"Family?" they ask, and Joy and I consult. Finally, sighing, we tick "single," worried that declaring ourselves as family could jeopardize our vacation. We hate—verily, *despise*—hiding, which insults and humiliates us. While we wait for our luggage, amazed tourists light up Canadian cigarettes. They look around furtively, then grin, puffing gratefully. The terminal is sultry and smoky.

A sign advertises a sports bar and café somewhere in Puerto Vallarta by announcing, "We have been established since we opened." I find this odd but appropriate, having been alive since I was born.

A stoplight decrees whether or not we'll be searched. Green for good to go. Red for stop here, *amigas*. "Green, we'll join the court case," says Joy.

It's green for Joy and red for me, offering utterly no solution.

I am bursting with energy, happy to be in the tropics again. I feel like dancing. There's a humid, moldy smell in our room and a sign on the sliding-glass balcony door that says "Prevent Entry of Tropical Pest."

Joy is reading on the couch. She says, "Water aerobics, bicycle tours, tequila parties, beer drinking contest!" Joy clicks on the color TV to Marriott Hotel information. "The spa's free. Two saunas. Seafood buffet, spelled s-e-e. Seefood. Let's go explore."

But the bed is king-sized. "Let's tussle," I say, and for a minute before curiosity gets the better of us, we do; we giggle each other around the mattress.

The sound of a billion bubbles popping as a wave explodes like Alka Seltzer. The surf spills up under our chaise longues and I can't stop laughing. Joy says, "Doesn't this remind you of the opening scene in *Jaws*?" This is because we recently saw an aerial shot of a Florida beach with four or five tourists standing in water up to their waists while, unnoticed, great white sharks tooled around the nearby water.

"That's us," Joy had said, then gripped the remote, "if we join the case." "The case" is a lawsuit against Canada's federal government to fight for same-sex marriage rights. Joy and I dearly long to marry after being engaged for years. We see the case as a means toward heightening gay and lesbian visibility, with its goal of lessening the ill effects of homophobia. Critical, this, when members of our community still lose homes, families, jobs, benefits; suffer harassment and discrimination; are denied entry to their lovers' hospital rooms; are even sometimes beaten or murdered.

"We'll be tourists?" I said.

She'd swatted me. "Shark chow."

Now surf rolls up to splash our bottoms, a tropical spanking.

I can't stay asleep. For a while, pest warning notwithstanding, I leave our balcony door open and listen to the dependable ocean roar. But it just sounds like traffic congestion on the busy thoroughfare near our Vancouver home, and I finally give up and just lie in the heat, fretting. What will it be like to sue the government? Even the thought of applying for a marriage license and being turned down, a necessary first step, is nerve-racking. I'm worried on the kids' behalf and because our extended families have never been particularly supportive. Joy has had breast cancer. What if she gets really sick and her family steps in to make her medical decisions? How can people be forced to accept what we really mean to each other without the potent symbolism of marriage to help? She's my partner, my lover, but she's not my wife.

I'm awake again at six when a room service cart crashes along the rough stone hallway. And back awake again to the incessant "bing bong" of the elevator as it duplicates exactly the first two notes of our doorbell. Who's at the door? CSIS?

We turn on the fan so its regular roar will drown out the hall, and sleep until the phone rings. It's 8:59, and fearing our children back home have been smitten dead, I start awake with my heart giving an emphatic, arrhythmic thud. But it is only Angelica, whoever Angelica is, saying, "Are you coming to the Fiesta West orientation, nine o'clock?" I blink twice while the clock hits nine and say, "I guess not." Angelica says something else in fractured English about bulletin boards and hotel hallways. When I hang up, Joy rolls over and asks who it was. When I tell her she says, "I like being disoriented."

I say, "I'm already very well established in my orientation."

Joy says, "I guess that meeting would be helpful for people who are bi-curious." When I roll from bed to open the drapes, a cockroach the size of our house hits my hand, its carapace clicking, and falls and scuttles behind the dresser. We name our first tropical pest Ben.

"Let's ask Ben," Joy says. "Ben, do you believe in same-sex marriage? Do you think we should take Canada's government to court to fight for it?"

Ben is strangely silent on this one.

I wear a towel over my suit. We traipse down the long lobby and out to the dark, deserted pool. It is a bit after nine, a clear night with a sling moon and a generous dash of stars. There isn't a soul around. All the chaise longues are evenly lined up in rows, and the Dos Equis umbrellas are lowered. Joy and I sneak down the stairs into the water. I carry her through the perfectly tepid water toward the ocean under that shimmering moon hammock. She is a year past chemo. She is made almost entirely of air and floats in my arms as easily as a balloon. Will she pop?

We buy a deep, thick salad bowl that will be perfect with the tulip salad tongs we have at home, a small bowl with a thick pewter spoon, and two picture frames.

There's a man hawking a Mexican Fiesta night. He says, "Are you Alaskan?"

"Why?" we ask.

"Because you're so white."

I look at burnished, Japanese-Canadian Joy and laugh.

We hit the pharmacy, where we want Gravol and Off. The hawker whistles for a taxi while we refuse the fiesta for the second time.

"Because we're Alaskan," I offer.

"You're not Alaskan," he says.

"Pretty close," Joy says, because, from here, Vancouver seems exceedingly far north.

"You're Canadian, aren't you? I used to work in Kelowna. That's in the Okanagan Valley." He looks thoughtful. "What's the difference between a Canadian and a canoe?"

We bite.

"A canoe tips."

We sit on the seawall, or *malacon*, in town, watching the sun set in a cloudy sky. We can't see the sun itself, but the whole sky is frothing, a mottled claret reflection on the bellies of cumulus cloud. There's a gray funnel, like a tornado, forming in the middle. The water is blood red. The sky is flushed, intense, hot, like women during sex. Bahia de Banderas curves around us. Soon the sky is magenta in a hatband across the flat horizon.

At the glassware store, all baby pink and lime green, the clerk massaged her breasts while we shopped. In the clothing store, a woman in a flowing skirt walked down a set of stairs asking me to follow, and somehow I stepped on her hem and pulled her skirt down over her bottom.

The Red Cabbage Café, Repollo Roja, has walls of keepsakes— book covers (even *The Handmaid's Tale*), postcards, sketches, photos, *Time* covers, tables with collages under glass, and silly sayings stenciled on the black legs like

> *Ten Days That Shook the Cabbage*
> *Rebel without a Cabbage*
> *Close Encounters of the Cabbage Kind*

I'm having shark soup. Jaws in a bowl. "If we join this court case," I say, "we'll eat our opposition for dinner."

"Hah!" says Joy. She knows the truth. A shark could come whipping at us in the middle of a Vancouver rainstorm and chomp us in two.

We two are one? Not for a lesbian couple. One and a half, more like it.

We hire a driver, Miguel, to give us a fifteen-minute taxi tour of Vallarta. He drives up streets that get farther away from anything to do with tourists, streets that narrow to a single lane, that climb into the mountains and offer astounding views of ocean. The streets are made of bigger cobble, now—rocks a foot round, some of them, merely buried up to their noses, with plenty uprooted. Masses of bougainvillea tumble over walls. Miguel takes us up to Richard Burton and Elizabeth Taylor's house, Casa Kimberly. It's two houses, joined above the street by a gaudy, bright pink bridge. That's what Joy and I need, isn't it, a bridge between our lesbian lives and everyone else's heterosexual ones? Our guide drives us through Gringo Gulch. Money is evident from the dark tiles ornamenting door frames and the huge terra-cotta pots full of plantain palms. Miguel stops at the crest of a mountain. Here is a sheer cliff and below, the Cuale River. Rolling up again on the other side is more Vallarta: private homes and condominiums. "Americanos and Mexicans both," Miguel says, "all mixed up." It's a lovely scene—forest dotted with white or pale houses, ubiquitous red tile roofs.

"What if someone hurts the kids?" I say.

"Let's try to change the world," says Joy. "Then they'll be safer."

I wander down to the ocean to haggle with a beach vendor, Ciro, who sells silver. Ciro says *Americanos* spend the most because the exchange rate is so good. He says conventions are best because the people have money to burn and not much time to get to town. Ciro keeps rubbing his crotch. He says it's not good that the peso's down. Beans have gone up from three pesos a pound to thirteen pesos. His white trousers—all the vendors are in immaculate white; Ciro wears a yellow scarf around his throat—are now one hundred pesos: "If you can believe that, *amiga*."

"In Canada," I say, "it's very expensive."

"*Sí*," Ciro says. "I hear that."

He tells me he used to be a migrant worker in the U.S. Five years in Michigan, Florida, and California. "Good money," he says. "Two hundred eighty dollars a week pure profit. Here on a good day I make only one hundred dollars and I have to buy all these clothes. But it's better than working at a resort. Employees get the same money no matter what the peso is doing. You know what minimum wage is here? You know how many pesos?"

"How many?"

"Twenty-five pesos a day."

"Five dollars," I say. "Or four."

Ciro scratches his crotch. I have no desire to notice this, or to consider the underlying tropical pests, which perhaps intend to breach our patio door.

"Do you live in Vallarta?"

"*Sí*."

We fall quiet. I jiggle a pair of dolphin earrings for our youngest in my palm. He wants thirty Canadian. I want to spend ten. "I'm not going higher," I say, and lower my voice into less jocular, motherhood tones, the tones I use to tell my kids I mean business. He hears this. He's going to lose the sale if he doesn't give in. He's still making a profit of probably six to eight dollars. He takes it and drops the earrings into a plastic pouch.

"Don't tell anyone," he says.

"Oh, I won't tell a soul, I promise." I'd be embarrassed to, in fact, because I'm sure I paid too much.

The days slip away in a fuzz of sun, water, and tequila. We've been using the fitness center. We schmooze in bed, admiring each other's muscles.

"You're so strong."

"You're getting definition." Across the room, Ben the cockroach leaps from the top of the dresser to the floor with a clack.

"You have peaks on your pectorals."

None of it is true, but truth is not the point.

"You could pulverize me," Joy says cheerfully.

"I could bench-press you," I say.

"Let me ask you something," says Joy, getting up on one elbow. The space where her breast once was is still a sore, raised, red scar. "Could you bench-press the Canadian government?"

It's at that point I know we really are going to join the case, no matter what terrors or satisfactions it brings. I have a woman, and I want her to be my wife. She has a woman and she wants to marry her. What we want is something every other Canadian—jailed Canadians, infertile Canadians, old Canadians, divorced Canadians, Canadians who smoke—can have unthinkingly, without anybody asking questions. I want to marry the girl of my dreams.

The flight information sign at the airport is a big white board with magic marker instructions in green, red and black. Please Wait Up Here, it says.

Planes leave for Toronto, Acapulco, and Detroit. A woman in a dark blue uniform empties ashtrays into a green plastic bucket; she doesn't use gloves.

Joy says, "We're not even out of the airport yet and I'm jiggling."

She is. Her right leg, crossed atop her left, is going faster than an arrhythmic heart.

A minute later mine is too. "Oh God," I say and slap it still. "Down, girl."

I slump in my chair. The body of a cockroach, smooth and glistening, squeezes into the light from under my carry-on's zipper. "Joy," I say, sitting bolt upright.

Joy shakes her head. "Is that Ben?"

"I'm scared," I say.

"But you've got me," Joy says.

"And apparently one gigantic court case."

"Yup," she says, grinning as Ben scuttles from view.

Sundowners in the Cockpit

Jeananne Kathol Kirwin

 Sipping sundowners in the cockpit. That wasn't the ultimate goal of our sailing sabbatical, but it was certainly one of the rewards my husband, Pat, and I anticipated after ten long years of planning and saving.

Our original reason for taking a mid-career travel leave was to ensure that we could and would fulfill our dream, not waiting for retirement—a lesson we learned from our fathers' untimely deaths. As time passed, we found the plan had even more merit as a way to be with our children while they still enjoyed being with us. Then, as the frantic pace of our urban North American lifestyle increased, we began to perceive this pocket of time as a means of jumping off the multi-tasking merry-go-round, even for just a short while.

Many a crazy evening, ferrying children to myriad activities, or dozing through yet another committee meeting, we imagined ourselves relaxing in the cockpit of our boat. We pictured a tranquil evening, watching the orange glory of sunset spill onto the million blue facets of water rippling on all sides as we sipped our drinks. Sundowners, we sailors call those drinks, no matter their contents. "Sundowners in the cockpit" became a shorthand expression conjuring up the carefree interludes we craved—niches of time holding nothing but the sunset, the sea, and ourselves, nothing else but the moment.

And now it was beginning to happen. Pat and our older son had gone ahead to buy our boat and bring it up to Virginia. The other three kids and I had flown from Calgary, Alberta, to Washington, D.C. Tomorrow we'd catch a train to Norfolk, where we'd reunite with our advance party aboard the boat. Then our adventures would begin.

"Thank you, God, for keeping us safe," my youngest said with a yawn at bedtime prayers that night in our Washington hotel room. I uttered my own prayer of thanks, grateful to have kept track of all my children and baggage, to be poised on the brink of a dream and, more immediately, to be entitled to sleep at last.

The months leading up to this moment had flown by like a fast-forwarded video, each frame dominated by an ever-scrolling, never-ending to-do list. *There's a perverse peace in knowing that what's left undone will never get done*, I mused. *The time to live in the moment has finally arrived.*

That's when it appeared to be far too soon to relax. There, lying on a strange bed on the very first night of our travels, I felt a hard little bump. Groping inside my pajama top, I found a lump in my breast.

I lay there pondering the repercussions of this find. Armed with enough vaccinations to resist every disease, supplied with enough antibiotics to last a lifetime, bolstered against injury with first aid training, our family was—ironically—unprepared for this eventuality. Back in Alberta, I'd have visited my doctor the very next morning. Here, outside Canada, accessing health care wouldn't be so easy. I had no medical relationship at all, no one to trust. Besides, I was now a sailor, not an urban landlubber. My itinerary could no longer be adjusted so readily to accommodate medical appointments. Smaller than a marble, that lump suddenly grew larger than life.

The hotel room phone rang. "Pat!" I exclaimed, overjoyed to hear his voice. "We're here in Washington!" I added needlessly.

"Well, we're nowhere close to Norfolk," he said, and went on to describe the reasons, among them the demise of one of our boat's twin diesel engines.

I could hear the despondency and frustration in his voice. This was no time to disclose my new worry, so hard and little, yet so over-whelmingly large in my thoughts. It occurred to me that it just might be a while before we enjoyed sundowners in the cockpit.

I awoke refreshed the next sultry August morning. Then, like a cloud passing over the sun on an Alberta blue-sky day, awareness of my newfound problem drifted into consciousness. *There's no point to fretting*, I told myself. *I can't do a thing about it today. Perhaps if I just ignore it, the lump will disappear.*

Each morning brought the same rationalization. Even after our crew was happily reunited and I could tell Pat in person of my worrisome find, I didn't. He had other more immediate problems on his mind. Our family was holed up at a swampy marine repair facility in Virginia, awaiting the replacement of our failed engine.

During those early days, adjusting to life aboard and bearing alone the disproportionate burden of my little lump, I longed for a confidante. I yearned for the counsel and support of my female companions back home—my sage sister, my tell-all running partners, my two wise young aunts, and the dear mothers of my children's friends. Then I met Edie, a fellow cruiser awaiting boat repairs at the same marina. A short cheery soul with deep and weather-crinkled eyes, Edie had a maternal presence I trusted. Often, as we shared a pot of tea, I'd challenge myself to speak up. *She's just the person to tell*, I'd think. Yet I couldn't bring myself to say it. To give my fear voice would be to give it reality.

The weeks passed. Soon it was late September. Neither silence nor denial had succeeded in diminishing the lump. Even worse, everywhere I looked, overt messages urged me to act. *Breast cancer awareness month is approaching*, proclaimed the ubiquitous billboards. Even the American postage stamps shouted at me. The coincidence seemed unhappily synchronous.

Late one night, keeping company with my diary, I recorded this observation. Then I stared, riveted. There it was on paper, a whispered admission. I began to scribble furiously, in profuse relief, as if recording a police station confession. *I found a lump in my breast over a month ago*, I divulged at last. *It's likely just a cyst, yet I must get it checked out just for peace of mind.* My diary had become both confessor and counselor.

Mentioning the unmentionable empowered me to act. First thing next morning, I slipped away to the marina payphone and called our extended health care provider. The clerk provided names of doctors in Washington, D.C., where we'd arrive in a month. I remained serene on the telephone, even when asked the nature of my medical problem. As soon as I hung up, though, I fell apart.

That's when Pat found me. That's how the poor fellow first learned my secret. Shocked, overwhelmed, he managed nonetheless to console me as we strolled, hand in hand, along the docks, flanked on each side by the brooding swamp.

"Why didn't you tell me?" Pat asked, his voice strained.

"I didn't want to add to your troubles," I said. Thoughts I'd never spoken aloud tumbled out unbidden. "You had enough to worry about. We've come this far with no small effort. After ten years, we're finally about to leave on this dream-come-true boat trip. How can I let a lump in my breast sabotage everything? What if I have to go home for treatment? How can you and the kids do this thing without me? What if it's cancer?"

"It's not cancer," Pat replied firmly, as if convincing himself.

We ambled along the weathered wooden pier in silence, staring bleakly at the murky water, mired in our private dark thoughts. Not until I'd blurted it out did I realize that uppermost in my mind was the prospect of ruining my family's long-awaited dream. Surgery, radiation, chemotherapy, even the possibility of death seemed remote. More real and regrettable was the possibility that after such a long wait, we'd have to abandon the boat and go home.

The only thing to do is to find out for sure, I thought. Suddenly composed, I returned to the payphone and made an appointment at a Washington clinic. I'd done all I could; the rest was up to God. That's what I told myself, but inwardly that little lump niggled relentlessly.

A month passed. We indeed set sail. We traveled the Great Dismal Swamp and crossed the mighty Chesapeake Bay. In mid-October, we docked at a marina in downtown Washington, ideally situated near the Smithsonian museums and the Mall.

The half-dreaded, half-hoped-for day of my clinic appointment approached. The night before, I lay still in my berth, yet churned within. Both the lump and my worst fears loomed larger than ever. I could do nothing now but pray, and that I did with fervor.

The next morning dawned crisp and sunny, hopeful yet surreal. Despite the crowd of commuters on my subway ride to the clinic, I felt alone, isolated, poignantly aware of nothing but how momentous the day's diagnosis would be.

The women's clinic waiting room was inundated with brochures on breast cancer. When I read about the increased risk of breast cancer among users of aluminum antiperspirants, I felt sure my brand contained that evil carcinogen. Just thinking about it got me in a sweat. *I can't stand this*, I thought.

I took refuge in watching my fellow patients in the waiting room. That's when I witnessed an amazing five-second slice of life.

A middle-aged woman swept into the room and fell into the arms of her mate. "It's okay, I'm okay, it's not cancer," she sobbed, joyful tears running down her face.

The man took her wet cheeks into his two hands and kissed her lips. "Thank God," he said simply.

Then it was my turn. Stripped to the waist, I waited for the physician in the examination room, helpless to banish my loathsome fear. At forty-two, I thought my body was much too young to betray me.

A sparrow-like woman walked briskly into the room.

"Good morning," she said, smiling pertly. "Let's see, then, what this lump might be." She moved her thin, deft fingers beneath the paper gown. "Ah yes, there it is. Well, the good news is that it's round and smooth, not typical of a tumor. Likely a cyst. But it's a good size, so you'd better get a mammogram. How about next week?"

I explained my transient situation. *Who knew where I'd be in a week?*

"Well, then, we'll have to schedule you in today," she said. "No small feat, since mammography is booked solid during breast cancer awareness month. But they owe me a favor, so I'll see what I can do." A moment later she returned. "You're all set," she announced as cheerily as if she'd just penciled me in for a cut and color. "Come back at two o'clock. They can squeeze you in then."

The intervening three hours passed with glacier weight and pace. A mild autumnal ambience graced the tree-lined streets, sun-dappled and strewn with golden leaves. Yet I felt anxious. I went for a long and aimless walk. I bought a muffin but tasted nothing. I looked at a newspaper yet found I couldn't read. My gut felt encouraged by the preliminary diagnosis, but my head cautioned against premature hope.

And then there was the mammogram to face—my first. I winced to recall those mammogram jokes women send each other on the Internet, the ones describing the best ways to "practice" for a woman's first experience. "Visit your garage at night when the cement floor is just the right temperature," the typical parody reads. "Remove your shirt and bra. Lie comfortably on the floor with one breast wedged under the rear tire of the car. Ask a friend to slowly back up the car until your breast is sufficiently flattened and chilled. Turn over and repeat for the other side."

At the appointed hour I returned to the clinic, braced for the onslaught. My credit card took the first assault. Lacking a domestic health plan, I had to pay up front. The various charges added up to more than nine hundred painful American dollars. That gave me another source of negative energy: guilt. Then came the personal hit. The mammogram was just as predicted—excruciating, even alarming. Feeling sufficiently flattened and chilled, I went for a sonogram. Finally, I visited an oncologist.

"Nothing tumorous shows up," she said. "Let me check you out myself."

Again I stripped to the waist. The doctor examined me.

"I can't find any lump," she said. "Show me where it is."

My fingers moved instantly to that memorized place underneath my left nipple, but I couldn't feel a thing. My breast was totally numb. "I wonder where it went!" I exclaimed. But I did know. That lump got squished until it popped during the mammogram.

"Then it's just a harmless cyst," the oncologist said, smiling. "Visit your doctor once you return to Canada. For the rest of your trip, though, you can just relax."

I'm free, my spirit sang, as I burst out of the clinic into the resplendent sunshine. I was grateful to the physician for fitting me into a tight schedule of mammograms. I felt greater appreciation than ever for the Canadian public health system, after paying that staggering bill. But gratitude and appreciation did not begin to articulate the sensation of sweet relief that flooded every cell of my body upon receiving the news of good health. Every possibility in the world, every adventure and dream, suddenly and wonderfully opened up to my family and me.

The marina was a few miles away, a distance I relished. Walking down Pennsylvania Avenue past the black iron rails fencing the White House, I discovered tears flowing down my cheeks. My eyes were wet not only with release but also regret. For two long months, I'd worried for nothing, allowing an imagined dark future to undermine the joy of dwelling in the moment, in this long-awaited trip. With a sigh I dried my eyes and smiled. I felt freshly washed. Raising my face and folded hands heavenward, I breathed thanks.

Back at the marina, I ran down the docks to tell Pat. "I told you it was nothing to worry about," he said lightly, yet his hug was especially tight.

Late that night, I hunkered down in the salon of our boat with my diary. *Today I learned the meaning of "a new lease on life,"* I reflected. *And now I know where the joy of that comes from. It comes from suddenly arriving at a point where you can live in the present.* Until then, I'd simply replaced the cares and stresses of my landlocked life with a new hard little worry. Learning to be in the moment—every moment, no matter what—wasn't as simple as packing up and moving onto a boat, leaving a home and setting out on a journey, turning off one switch and turning on another. The lesson of living in the present—of being truly present, of presence—may be more easily acquired while traveling, but it wasn't automatic. *Will I always remember today's message?* I wrote in my book. *I rather doubt it, but for the moment, it feels wonderful.*

The next day, souvenir shopping at the Natural History Museum, Pat asked me to choose a ring, something to replace the diamond tucked away in a safe-deposit box back home. Later, back on board, he popped in a CD. The soulful words of "When a Man Loves a Woman" wafted out to the cockpit. Pat settled me there on the cushions with my children and gave me a glass of red wine. Then, one knee bent before me, he opened a gray velvet box. There it was: the chosen amethyst ring.

"Will you marry me?" he asked.

The kids giggled. I laughed out loud. I remembered the tension breaking on that dear man's face in the waiting room and wondered if our release from that fear had any bearing upon the timing of Pat's gift.

"Yes, I will," I replied.

Then I noticed it was sunset. A million facets of blue water were tinged with orange. *Aha*, I thought, sipping my wine. *At last, a sun-downers-in-the-cockpit kind of moment.*

Roads to Iowa
(...And a Few Other Places Not on the Map)

Alison Lohans

Iowa.

My mother was born in that state and lived there until the year she turned fifteen. It was a rural upbringing in the quiet simplicity of a Quaker farm community. My mother's stories of her childhood became part of the fabric of my own childhood and left me with vivid impressions of what the countryside must be like. The "thees" and "thous" I took for granted, for my grandparents spoke to us in the Quaker plain speech—but the idea of wearing a dress while swimming in a pond (as my mother did) seemed as foreign to me in my central California childhood as the possibility of building a snowman in the backyard.

I'd always wanted to see Iowa. It was a detached kind of wanting; the distance was too great for a trip to be practical, and for years there was never a good enough reason to go that far off my well-traveled map. Even so, the imprint was strong: during my earliest adulthood years when I began dreaming of glorious sunlit cornfields beneath clear blue skies, I knew intuitively that it was time to formalize my membership in the Religious Society of Friends. Still, I did not go to Iowa.

Years passed. I immigrated to Canada, living first in British Columbia and then in Saskatchewan. I flew to Wisconsin, to Illinois, and to various other places. Once in a while a flight took me over Iowa; occasionally we even touched down in Des Moines or Cedar Rapids. I made a point of studying the Iowans who boarded, listening to their accents in search of echoes of my mother's voice. I sensed an unpretentious people, and felt connected to them in ways I couldn't quite explain.

33

In my late forties, the old lifelong pull reasserted itself. There was going to be an extended family reunion at the Bear Creek meetinghouse—the hub of the rural community where my mother, and her father, spent their childhood years. One of my sisters had attended a previous reunion with our parents, as well as various aunts and uncles and cousins. When the cycle came around again and my mother asked if I might be interested in going, I began to think of it as a real possibility.

It would mean a two-day drive each way, and I knew my partner wouldn't want to come. The maps alternately enticed, then discouraged, me. Would it be feasible to do this with my younger son, not quite ten years old? In the past I'd driven between California and British Columbia, and later Saskatchewan, several times with my first husband, who was sick with cancer, and our child. The fatigue of a more recent two-day drive back from Missoula, Montana, frightened me, however.

In the end, I decided to go. My son would have no trouble making up for lost time at school, especially in mid-June. Additionally, the trip would mean a break from intense stress: my older, teenage son, adopted with fetal-alcohol disabilities, was on the run and engaging in deviant behavior. I longed to get away. After talking with people who'd driven longer distances along the same route, I felt confident that I could handle it.

It was with a sense of adventure that my younger son and I headed out to a place neither of us had seen. He was astonished that his mother had tapes of 1960s rock music, and even (gasp!) enjoyed playing them at full volume on our Dodge Caravan stereo. Given his own free choice of music, he chose "Little Old Lady from Pasadena"; it became the theme song of the trip.

North Dakota brought a great sense of freedom as we headed east on Interstate-94 with its sunlit expanses and air that felt intoxicating with its clean sweetness. There was very little traffic. After we'd made an overnight stay in Fargo, I-29 led us into the new territory of South Dakota. The state line itself seemed to bring an instant change in humidity; it was suddenly … *hot*. We passed through Custer country, then through Laura Ingalls Wilder country. Sioux Falls (with no falls that I could see from my vantage point behind the wheel) plunged us into unexpectedly heavy traffic. This continued as I-29 flirted with the Iowa state line but didn't actually cross it until the high-speed race-track ushered us into Sioux City. My first glimpses of urban Iowa showed a panorama that had an uncanny resemblance to the old Pasadena freeway in the Los Angeles area. This was nothing like the idyllic farmlands of my childhood imagination—but I was so busy navigating amid floods of merging traffic that there was little time to think about it, let alone look.

And so my balloon popped. It was hot; the humidity was so high that we were sweltering, despite the air conditioning turned up full blast along with "Little Old Lady from Pasadena." The traffic remained dense and alarmingly fast as we and countless others con-tinued south, and then (after a stop for gas and ice cream) took the junction that headed east toward Des Moines. The rolling countryside was lush with cornfields, a deep green blanket against which the gray multi-laned pavement of the Interstate, with its cacophony of motion and drone of endless roaring trucks, passenger vehicles and motor homes, seemed a statement of irony. So this was Iowa.

It was a letdown, and yet … at some point during the tense driv-ing, I began noticing something else. Glimmering in my "inner sens-es" came bright flickers of joy. My mother was looking forward to see-ing us. She was happy, and excited. Despite the miles that still stretched between us, I could sense her anticipation as certainly as I could hear the sixties rock songs pouring from the speakers or my son talking beside me in the passenger seat. An answering joy rose inside me. The vehicles barreling along I-80 didn't fit the image of the place that had been drawn so quietly in my early childhood memories—but the Bear Creek meetinghouse was nowhere near the freeway.

At the Earlham exit I turned north. In the late afternoon light, the fields were green with growing corn and other crops, and sometimes were hillier than I'd expected. Trees were scattered here and there. Now the traffic was sparse and moved at a more sedate pace. With this change came a surprise. All around me, from the very land itself, and the air that hovered above it, there seemed to emanate a feeling of humble love. Quaker families had tended this farmland for generations. My mother was born of this land, and the place seemed to welcome me. When I tried to speak of this to my now-grumpy nine-year-old, tears of joy kept leaking through. *This* was Iowa.

We arrived just in time for supper at the meetinghouse, where family members were waiting to enfold us in fierce, loving hugs. We arrived to introductions, finally meeting people who until then had been only names in old stories, or blurred faces in black-and-white photographs. Fireflies danced above the cut grass at dusk, a first for my son. Throughout that hot weekend I saw little more of the land, for now I was drawn into the web of human love and the places of my mother's childhood. I marveled at a special shared "something" that shone in people I'd never met before, a certain sameness living on in our common genes. I felt nurtured, and enriched.

On Sunday (First Day, in the Quaker plain speech) we worshiped in the meetinghouse where my mother, and before her my grandfather, had sat in meeting as children. Sitting in silence among members of my extended family, I watched dust motes dance in sun-shafts pouring through the windows and heard human shifts and rustles, digestive gurgles, creaking benches, as humble accompaniment to the occasional spoken message. In that silence, I felt my grandfather's spirit in the meetinghouse and knew how deeply happy he must have been, with all four of his daughters present with their husbands, five of his grandchildren, and five great-grandchildren—so many generations—all of us worshiping together in this special place.

It passed too quickly, and we had to get back home. I was worried about doing another long drive so soon but was also coming to trust others' "knowings." As it turned out, one thoughtful cousin had actually considered traveling with us to help with the driving. But I sensed that everything would be all right. "You're safe in His loving arms," said one of my aunts.

So my son and I wrenched ourselves away, retracing our path along I-80 in hot, muggy weather. The Iowa part of the journey home was uneventful. As traffic thinned in South Dakota, I became acutely aware that I was heading back to the stressful world where my older son was probably still on the run and behaving in ways that traumatized others' comfortable lives. I felt the taint, the guilt, though the fetal alcohol damage occurred before his and my lives ever connected. I thought of the warm nest of family love we'd just left and for long moments was tempted not to return to Regina at all. But there was something else, too ... Between bouts of worry, there came another new sensation, something I'd remembered reading about in one of the myths narrated in Clarissa Pinkola Estés's *Women Who Run with the Wolves*. As I drove northward, my nipples seemed to be "seeing," like eyes, with a quiet kind of wisdom; I wondered what it meant. Rereading that text later, I was fascinated to find Pinkola Estés's reference to the nipples as "psychic organs."

Soon afterward, sullen clouds, driven by a buffeting wind, blotted the light from the sky. A powerful storm broke over the South Dakota prairie, with intense lightning and thunder and a heavy downpour. Wind gusts tested the strength of my hands on the wheel. The only protection available on the Interstate was the steel capsule in which we were scurrying northward. In the storm-dark, I turned on the headlights and began looking in earnest for green road signs. The closest town was Brookings, about thirty miles away, and the black clouds churning overhead made me feel apprehensive about remaining on the highway. The pavement gleamed with an eerie wet sheen, and my ears didn't feel right. There was no longer any oncoming traffic, and only three cars were ahead of us. I decided to do whatever those drivers did when they reached the Brookings exit.

Every one of those cars signaled to exit; little spurts of red light blinked through the unnatural darkness. We followed and took refuge in a Burger King that was crowded with travelers who were waiting out the storm. Most seemed not to want to look at the violent sky, yet none of us could avoid staring at the ragged clouds that dangled so low overhead, moving in the opposite direction from everything else. Every time I'd seen this particular type of cloud formation, accompanied by almost incessant lightning, there had always been a tornado somewhere. In that Burger King, tension crackled in the air as surely as the storm overhead. To the north, there was a spot where the clouds bulged down to touch the earth. People were watching it with a kind of gruesome intensity. Not wanting to worry my son, I allowed myself only quick glances. Soon afterward, I saw the bulge retreat. The atmosphere in the Burger King relaxed noticeably. "I saw that," my son told me several days afterward.

Safely back on the road, we later saw lightning flickering over Fargo. It was pink and innocuous, heat lightning without a venomous blast. And the next day, as we drove through North Dakota—back to Bismarck and Minot, toward Estevan and, eventually, Regina—it seemed as though we were already in another country, where the air felt light and the sun fell benignly on green fields.

But now I could remember Iowa, a different land, one that spoke to me of generations of tender care and a people who all shared a certain "something" I'd never seen before among so many.

Three years later I went to Iowa a second time, also in June. My destination was a poetry workshop, and I was traveling with a close friend whom I'd known for twenty years, ever since our university days in southern California. During the rites of passage of early, married adulthood, she'd moved to Wisconsin and I'd immigrated to Canada.

Driving from Janesville, Wisconsin, we encountered a different type of thunderstorm in northern Illinois. Once again we were protected only by man-made steel as the car floundered through a wind-blasted soup in varying shades of gray. The rain fell so intensely that this time it seemed we were more at risk of drowning than being caught in a tornado—or a crash, as the windshield fogged completely at the high humidity and passing vehicles splashed up heavy sprays of road-oily water. My friend clung to the steering wheel, white-knuckled, as we both swiped ineffectually at the glass. Finally we were blessed with a semi-trailer to follow, its taillights red beacons that led us through our fear.

We crossed the Mississippi River and were suddenly in Iowa. Just as abruptly, the storm was behind us. Eastern Iowa had little resemblance to the corn-growing west; the commercial buildings and businesses that were visible from the freeway reminded me of many other semi-rural areas in the U.S. There was no innate sense of recognition. I-80 took us to Iowa City, where my maternal grandmother had spent time in the hospital before the family moved to California.

The weekend poetry workshop was held at the University of Iowa. My friend and I found the sessions inspiring, intense, and far too short. On the final evening as we walked the now-familiar route between campus and the residence, a sudden sweetness drifted in the air. We'd come along this stretch several times before and, although we'd seen flowers blooming, hadn't noticed this lovely scent. "Is it clover?" I asked.

My friend shook her head. "Jasmine," she pronounced.

Right away, there came an unmistakable whiff of smoke, sharp and biting. My friend brushed at her clothes and muttered about the dorm room being a smoking room. And yet … her clothing hadn't smelled of smoke at all, for that whole day. I told her this. Joggers and skaters had gone by, but not one of them was smoking. The smell was intense and familiar: Madisons, the little cigars my husband had smoked when he was a student. Jasmine and smoke, recollections of long-ago southern California, the place where we'd all met, and each of us left, my husband later to die. We looked at each other and marveled at these spirit scents reaching from our common past.

The sidewalk led us past the Iowa River. Sunset-pink clouds hung in a pale Chablis sky; mist crept in low streamers over the grassy park. As it grew darker, fireflies blinked and darted. Lights came on in the sorority and fraternity houses nearby; voices and music peppered the night air, and students flaunted their sleek, expensive cars. Caught between times, between worlds, I stood there—receiving, *experiencing*, and feeling penetrated by layers of mystery.

Back in the dorm lobby, I stood at a payphone punching in numbers. "Hi, Mother," I said when her beloved voice answered. "I'm in Iowa … "

Traveling: Poetic Notes

Holly Luhning

When we write about landscape, travel, and place, we reveal as much about ourselves as we do about the worlds represented. The following poems take place while the narrator is traveling; they include details of physical/geographical space, and yet they often also include a reflection on the narrator's thoughts and experiences. The narrator is far from her geographical home, but ideas of home and of interpersonal relationships that inhabit domestic space are never far from the surface. Her present geographical location and her physical surroundings lead her thoughts toward a reflective, internal dialogue. The exotic acts as a catalyst to thinking about the familiar.

Travel is also a search for something: adventure, the unknown, the unfamiliar, or even home. Although we often think of home as being fixed and stable, and thus the antithesis of travel, home can also function as a place to escape to, and escape from. In these poems, the narrator is consciously displaced from her origin-home; there was a reason for leaving, a point from which she left. If one thinks of home, as Deborah Keahey articulates, as being "the powerful center—physical, imaginary, psychological or emotional—around which the individual self can orbit and, occasionally, land," one must depart from home to fully understand it and to experience what Keahey describes as the "pull of home [that] reveals itself in the tension between arrivals and departure, presences and absences, desires and fulfillments, attractions and repulsions. Like gravity, this sense of home is often visible only through its effects." This state of movement, of travel, is necessary in order to perceive the entire picture of the narrator's relationship to home. Without distance, her comprehension of home is one-dimensional, what has always been known; only while displaced is she able to re-view the place with which she's most familiar.

The narrator constructs her emotional and physical locations within the context of travel, and as she centers herself within the act of travel and movement, she inevitably must interact with, and often-

41

times trust, those she meets along the path. For example, in "Girl in a Taxi," she finds herself taking a taxi from the airport late at night in a foreign country—she does not know the landscape and has no idea about the location of her hotel. She perceives the driver as slightly menacing, yet she must trust him or else remain stranded at the airport. This sort of forced trust leaves the traveler vulnerable to any number of misfortunes; in undertaking the act of travel, she inherently must surrender a certain degree of control.

This selection of poems may be seen as snapshots of places, relationships, and sensations; however, these snapshots or fragments become part of a whole through the lens of *sinuosity*. The philosopher Jeffner Allen explains sinuosity as one mode of female existence that is "neither that of the straight line, which proceeds ... in an upright, orderly sequence, nor like that of the perfect circle, which repeats itself without variation." Sinuosity challenges the traditional ideal of a straight, ordered life path and proposes that elements or conditions in some women's (or men's) lives that necessitate a "deviation" from or fragmentation of the linear life "ideal" actually constitute a strength; cohesiveness and energy are garnered from the ebb and flow of a weaving, curved path. As Allen describes it,

> The sinuous undulates, waves, ripples, billows and floats on the breeze. It slithers silvery on moonlit nights. The waving fields of corn, the flowing of a mane, the rolling in laughter of joyous celebrations move together harmoniously. At the same time, the sinuous names the sinew, the tendon and the sinewy, tough and strong. Here anger and revolt are embedded in women's muscles, giving us the satisfaction of being able to register our feelings on the face of the world.

Much like looped or swerving routes on a map, the traveler plots a sinuous course of experience, and ultimately arrives at a concept of home as movement, rather than a fixed geographical point. (This sort of winding path is symbolized by the physical "ceramic ribbon" that the narrator finds herself standing on in "Glacier.") Instead of internalizing her experience of formerly "exotic" landscapes as emotional and intellectual fissures in her everyday existence, she embraces and challenges the differentiations between other, familiar, and self.

Holly Luhning

Girl in a Taxi

She catches her light
rayon skirt; the striped material lifts
as she swivels her rucksack into this blue
car's trunk. The driver steps back,
a better view once her hem crawls
a foot above her knee.

A glow emanates from the airport windows,
brushes the body of the car, a sack of raw sugar
left sitting at the mill, dusty. She slams the trunk;
the noise, a dog bark lunging
into the constant peal of toads,
the bleat of crickets.

The car follows the highway out of the city,
lights retreating, the broad headlamps
a single lodestar pooling into a few feet of road.
She does not know which direction
the car is moving, a dory cast off
the barbed-wire beaches, a helmsman
sunk with kava and sun.

She hopes the driver is leaning
toward the hotel address she's scrawled
on a scrap of journal paper. He turns
left onto narrow dirt ruts, an empty path
leading into spears of sugar cane.

The road is croaking,
filled with small round animals
that appear white in the headlights.

Sway

1.

The stainless steel counter reflects
cool dusk light. At Aranga Camp,
the hands of women
make tea: dried apples, cranberries,
bloated rosehips straining
against the sieve. Let it steep
like patience, ripen
into a passion fruit's gnarled shell.

2.

Golden vines of kiwifruit,
bred to be hairless, arc
along the porch, over the picnic table
where European travelers play cards
and drink, fern light finding
their throats through sienna ale.
The smooth yellow ovals hinge above;
a picker touches one, smiles at the difference
between this and the velvet
he culls in the orchards.

3.

Two pigs, corralled by the river, snort
and whine. Three girls, hair coiled like hops,
throw mandarin rinds, then trickle
toward the dock. A string
of deep orange lanterns
illuminates their passing
and feathers the water with amber light.
The girls sit and immerse
the perfect curves of their calves,
which sway, barely, in the current.

Holly Luhning

Glacier

If woman is inconstant, then I will be at home
navigating this ice; the ablation zone,
filled with dips and ditches, moraine cover
and sink holes, tattered gems. This fluctuating terrain

does me good, I am faithful
to the fluidity of water, the glacial flour
that runs under the swing bridge.
This ice flow is melting, retreating,
perpetually sliding forward, a kinetics

of ebb and flow. I fall in sync
with the jagged path, refuse a guide's offer
of a spiked walking stick. I am the first
to reach the ice cave, smooth and cerulean,
the color of juniper berries in season.

Behind me they pick their way, splintering
the blue ice around crevasses
and pinnacles. I run my fingers
over the gouges; tomorrow
they'll be glassy again. The cave
will crack and shift, move downhill,
like this ceramic mercury beneath us.

Wahike

*—the way memory will always make the best or worst of
it and knows no middle ground.*

> Diane Schoemperlen
> *In the Language of Love:*
> *A Novel in 100 Chapters*

Give me a ripe olive
from the isle of Wahike. I will roll it
down the backs of your knees,
draw a pattern like the scramblings
of a pincher crab.

Pale wasp nests in the sandy groves
mark a danger of swaying
too close, of breathing
too generously. They fade into thoughts
like bleached conch shells.

With oceans and hornets
there is no middle ground.

A sickle of sand severs earth,
ocean, just as my memory
will make the worst of
                best of
the blue veins behind your knees.

Salt to Soothe the Sting

Between Rangitoto and Motutapu we wade
to sapphire starfish and shellfish scuttling
the sand bar, a fleet of shallow words.
Every twelve hours the tide peels back
lava crust, a causeway between an onyx isle
and lemongrass cliffs.

I brush against a giant dracaena
near the shore, prickly leaves
scrawl a cluster of welts across my arm.
I cup the sea, slap it
over blossoming flesh. The starfish
are blue and beating things.

A girl on the black path plucks a single souvenir,
seals it like fruit in a sandwich bag. We pause,
then breathe, break up the truth
with laughter.

SOURCES

Allen, Jeffner. "An Introduction to Patriarchal Existentialism
    Accompanied by a Proposal for a Way Out of Existential
    Patriarchy." *Philosophy and Social Criticism* 8, no.1, (1981),
    447–465.
Keahey, Deborah. *Making It Home: Place in Canadian Prairie
    Literature.* Winnipeg: University of Manitoba Press, 1998.
Luhning, Holly. *Sway.* Saskatoon: Thistledown Press, 2003.

Shifting Gears

Elaine K. Miller

*To accept the challenge of the road is
to take a journey inside yourself.*

Connie Carpenter[1]

 A number of years have passed since my cross-country bicycle trip, and the experience, in memory, has taken on an intriguing quality of linchpin in my sense of myself. It is a physical accomplishment in a life marked primarily by intellectual ones, it has left deep tracks of expansiveness in my psyche, and it is a "lived experience," from which I draw a welcome sense of authenticity.

Reflecting on the long-ago places where this journey might have started, I think of bikes in my childhood—the magic of having the bike of one's dreams, the anguish of longing for it.

I am nine years old, and we live in Teaneck, New Jersey. We are shaped by the war years—Victory gardens, stamping tin cans, rationing. In the spirit of these times, my father has worked very hard on my birthday gift. The bike is an old one, lovingly reconditioned, with sparkling chrome and shiny black paint, a thin-tire girl's bike. My father's pride in his work is clear. I know it is a gift of love, and yet … I want a red fat-tire boy's bike, the kind my younger brother will get as a birthday gift just one year later. My black thin-tire girl's bike could not possibly lend itself to the kind of showy abandon I envision.

Years later, I do get myself a red fat-tire bike but soon realize its limitations. And many years after that, more knowledgeable still and with serious plans, I get a purple thin-tire bike, the one that will take me across the country.

Much attention has been paid to the subject of women and bicycles, from the early days of warnings that cycling was dangerous to women's physical and moral well-being, and therefore to society at large, to contemporary commentary on the psychological obstacles women must battle when they approach not only bicycling but any sport at all. A late nineteenth-century writer (in an 1895 periodical, the *North American Review*) captures well the uneasiness tapped into by opening up this psychic terrain: "chief of all the dangers attending this new development of feminine freedom is the intoxication which comes with unfettered liberty."[2]

Traditional patterns persist; women are socialized to regard their bodies as something to be looked at rather than as means to achieve our own aims, characterizing our "social existence as the object of the gaze of another," as Iris Marion Young writes in *Throwing like a Girl*.[3] With the weight of such cultural baggage, and surrounded by messages that women either cannot or should not do it, how did we— a group of forty women over fifty—ever take on this challenge? Yes, we joked about "filling public space in spandex," and "meals on wheels" as we struggled to the end of a hard day with vultures circling overhead—but it was with amused detachment, even a touch of defiance. Yes, that writer a hundred years ago had it right: "liberty is intoxicating."

The trip was organized and led by Gloria Smith, who had left a career in landscape architecture to found WomanTours Inc. and realize her dream of "spending most of her waking time on a bicycle somewhere in the world." I joined the company's first cross-country tour. Gloria, a breast cancer survivor, had joined up with the National Breast Cancer Coalition Fund (NBCCF) to make it a breast cancer benefit tour. At the end of the trip, the sponsorships for the group would exceed $44,000.

We traveled in two groups, two days apart. I was in the second— sixteen riders and three staff—a cook/driver, a tour leader/bike mechanic/sweep rider, and an assistant. In an orientation meeting the day before our departure from San Diego, each woman described how she had heard about the trip and why she decided to do it. Here's my favorite: "I was reading the paper and saw a small announcement about WomanTours. I turned to my husband and said, 'Listen to this, a cross-country bike tour for women over fifty; I qualify.' And he replied, 'Oh sure, so now I suppose you're going to want to get a bike.' " My biking companions' faces and their bikes are forever engraved in my mind. And I believe I could still identify each of them by their butts on the bike seats in front of me. On the days when we weren't wearing the WomanTours shirt, the biking outfits revealed individual tastes across the whole spectrum—flashy, conservative, sassy, modest, old and broken in, bright and new. As for me, I have always been attentive to my older sister's advice: "Never let your outfit exceed your skill level."

We dipped our rear tires in the Pacific Ocean at San Diego, California, at 5:30 a.m. on March 17, and we rode over the sand into the Atlantic Ocean at St. Augustine, Florida, at 1 p.m. on May 8 with 3,100 miles, fifty-four days, and memories for a lifetime to our credit. My bike calculator fell off the handlebars and disappeared in the San Diego surf that very first morning. Perhaps it was significant that I did not replace it until New Mexico. For an academic accustomed to assigning small pieces of time and energy to the myriad details of institutional life, including interacting with the agendas of hundreds of students a year, I found a heady exhilaration in plunging into unclocked, unmeasured, and therefore deeply enticing open space. I reveled in that sensation, giving in to the practicalities of measurements and directions only two states later. Perhaps by then, sufficiently disassociated from institutional life, they had taken on new meaning, becoming instruments of self-sufficiency, of expansiveness rather than restriction, in my on-the-road adventure.

"It is simply not true that life is one damn thing after another; it's the same damn thing over and over," the poet Edna St. Vincent Millay is reported to have remarked. Having come across this quotation in a newspaper on one of our once-a-week rest days, I was amused at how well it captured the essence of the trip. Indeed, a peculiar charm of the trip was the sameness of the routine—eat, ride, eat, ride, eat, sleep; drink water, fix some flats, see some sights; eat, ride, eat, ride, eat, sleep; eat enough to sustain physical effort, stay either warm enough, cool enough, or dry enough to continue. Same clothes, same food— but a sameness of routine that rolled across thousands of miles of a changing scene.

We rode together, and we rode alone. We rode in large groups, small groups, pairs, trios. We kept pace, stopped out, caught up, fell behind, spread out over the day's route. But whatever the spread, and whatever the space of the accidental or intentional wandering, an invisible cocoon seemed to surround us, expanding and contracting to contain us all, growing odd appendages to gather us up and, finally, by day's end, deliver us all to the same pinpoint spot on the map and our beds for the night.

Reflecting on my preparations for the trip, I must acknowledge a surprising lack of serious attention to some basics. Attention to practicalities was trumped by the emotional pull of the adventure. I knew I could ride far, if not always fast, so that did not concern me. I did pay attention to the clothing I would need for the varieties of weather we would pass through; however, I took along a borrowed tent that I had never attempted to pitch and a borrowed air mattress of uncertain size, which I had never inflated. Most shocking of all, I had never fixed a flat tire. I had hoped to finesse my sketchy sense of how to do that by managing to stay ahead of someone who did know.

The tent and air mattress worked out, and I did learn to change a tire, talked through it by a patient roommate. Early in the trip, we had joked about "shoulders to cry on," roadside scenes of an upturned wheel-less bike, dangling chain, scattered contents of a rack pack, tools, tubes, and greasy hands. But with time and newly acquired skills, the shoulders of the roads became sites for an immensely satisfying display of self-sufficiency.

I have noticed that when people ask about the trip, they are interested in not only the highlights but also the daily routines and practical concerns. A woman who approached me after a talk that I had done asked me, sotto voce, "a personal question: didn't the bike seats make you quite sore?" They did, but the group had pooled resources to make an impressive collection of remedies available to all. Our days were filled with both familiar routines and delightful surprises, an inviting mix that permitted us to feel at the same time like seasoned old hands and bright-eyed, curious children. We "listened to our tires" each morning for that barely audible hiss that meant a tiny leak would catch up to us at some point during the day. We often treated motel parking lots like our own kitchens, walking out for coffee in our pajamas and eating breakfasts sitting on the parking-lot curbs. We laughed in campsites at the day's events, our solitary voices floating out from the tents, registering aches and pains and reflecting on "just why we were doing this." We pedaled off each morning with our rack packs crammed with peanut butter sandwiches, energy bars, and bananas. On a back road in Texas, two cyclists who were traveling alone told us, when they caught up with us, that they knew they were getting closer because the banana peels along the roadside were getting fresher.

We welcomed the sight of the van at the day's halfway mark, an especially thrilling moment on days of searing heat, numbing cold, drenching rainstorms, or high head winds (which once left us straining to reach three miles per hour). Though the situation was entirely predictable, it nevertheless seemed magical that we would actually meet up with the van in the vast terrain we were covering.

We devised coping strategies for all types of weather. We cooled off by wading fully clothed into the shallow mountain streams that crisscrossed our route in the West, and we warmed up under hand dryers in convenience store restrooms. In the desert, with no modern "conveniences" for interminable stretches, we formed human circles at the side of the road around riders who needed a "pit stop," hoping to create the impression that the event was simple bike repair. We left each other messages at obscure turning spots, and we laughed at the sheer basic-ness of it as we checked to be sure our shadows fell in the right direction on the road in our trek eastward—behind us in the morning, in front of us in the afternoon.

We stopped at all possible places of interest, turning even short-mileage days into all-day affairs. We wheeled into the site of each night's lodging with smiles of relief and accomplishment. We retrieved our luggage from the support van, trekked to our rooms with bike and suitcase in tow, and walked fully clothed into showers (the simplest way to deal with washing biking clothes). A special pleasure was finding mail at the motel desk. I had wonderfully loyal correspondents, and I was the *only one* to receive a chocolate bunny for Easter!

The day's end always brought evening map sessions for the next day's route, followed by dinner on the parking-lot curb, on logs around a campsite, or less frequently, when the cook was due a rest, at a nearby restaurant. Humble as the parking lot circumstances were, the ambience that we created with candles, lanterns, and mood music was apparently so enticing that on more than one occasion other motel guests approached us asking to buy dinner. We sat in the dusk sharing stories from the day—the disasters and the delights, the flats, falls, and missed turns, and the comic exchanges with people along the way. Occasionally, someone would announce that she was definitely too tired to ride the next day, only to reappear on her bike in the morning. We discovered, one by one and to our delight, the amazing capacity of the body to restore itself. The wonder and delight we experienced at both the changing physical scene and the impromptu encounters made us want to move through it all on our own wheels, not those of the van.

We recorded the unfolding scene, at times mentally, at other times stopped by the side of the road writing in journals: the changing colors of the deserts, the grays, blues, and pinks of the sky; the blooming cacti in California, snow-covered passes through the Rocky Mountains, imposing buttes and mesas of Arizona and New Mexico, the small dusty western towns straight out of the Hollywood films, the wildflowers dancing for a thousand miles across Texas, wild grape and honeysuckle-covered fences and steaming rice fields in Louisiana, and the moss-dripping trees and sultry swamps of Mississippi and Florida.

For sheer indelible memory value, the scenery experienced at bicycle pace is rivaled only by the poignant and funny exchanges with people along the way. I was acutely attuned to both the text and subtext of these conversations. They reflected what we all, on some level, knew: that people would find it extremely curious that a group of older women would do such a thing at all, much less do it "alone"; that the sheer physicality of the adventure would challenge deeply held beliefs about women's strength and endurance; and, most interesting to me, that the disengagement from domesticity that the trip represented (some might say flaunted) would be processed by some as delightful and whimsical, by others as unsettling, or indeed transgressive. From the store owner who remarked, with thinly veiled disapproval, "Did y'all just divorce your husbands?" to the pickup truck driver who yelled to us that "the guy back there has a flat," people's reactions reminded us of the preconceptions we knew we were challenging. In many an exchange of fleeting glances, I saw the group tempted to take on the comments in their serious dimensions. But we were giddy and expansive with the excitement of an adventure, and so we moved on. Besides, we reflected, consciously sacrificing principle to practicality, perhaps there are advantages to being taken for guys out on the open road.

When a woman at a convenience store in Alabama asked if we weren't afraid, I reflected consciously, for the first time, that no, I had not been afraid. And we loved the Texan whose reaction to our story, "Well, dang!," gave us a leitmotif for the rest of the trip.

One of our biking companions, attempting later to pin down an elusive quality of the experience, wrote the following: "I'm not yet sure how hard the trip was, because it seemed so curiously easy at the same time. I know we laughed every day, laughed a lot, and I have no idea what was so funny. I still can't explain how it was that every afternoon at the end of the ride, we got off the bikes, sweaty, dirty-faced, tired, aching, sometimes wet and cold, and announced with very satisfied smiles to no one in particular. "That was a great ride!" (Nadean Wilcox, from Berkeley, California)

The challenges of the trip were physical, psychological, and also social. A key delight was breaking rules—rules mostly unwritten but recognized and lived nevertheless. In pop-culture parlance, we "colored outside the lines" and we "went over the line"—not just the state lines, county lines, highway center lines and the map lines that marked our physical route across the continent but the social lines that had shaped, contained, and constrained the lives that we brought to that moment. I think that is why we laughed.

I reflect on what has stayed with me from the experience—a sense of both physical and psychological expansiveness and authenticity. Several examples come to mind; their simplicity is compelling to me.

In addition to teaching courses in women's studies I also teach Spanish, and in my classes our activities are intended to ground the language-learning in students' real-life experiences. For example, students present bio blurbs about themselves, including one thing not true. So while they practice oral expression, they also show their sense of humor and creativity through the "lies" they invent, which the rest of the class is supposed to identify. After my sabbatical, I began to join the students in this activity, including in my description the cross-country bike trip. I discovered immediately that I loved doing it because it gave me a feeling of authenticity in a context in which that had been elusive—a non-Hispanic teaching Spanish language and culture. When I tell of the bike trip, it is a story that I *own*, a lesson I embody. I have wondered if the students notice.

I recognize also a sense of expansiveness that is now a physical as well as an emotional memory. The ease with which I signed on for the bike trip, after just one day of thought, reflected my eagerness to pursue exactly that expansiveness: the "unknowns" of the adventure made it all the more alluring. From packing and sending my bike from New York to California, to arriving in St. Augustine, Florida, seven weeks later, who knew what would fill that time and space. ? I was hooked.

And finally, am I easier on myself in physical terms than in intellectual ones? Are physical challenges, then, a welcome relief? Yes, bike trips have brought this into focus, and the cross-country tour most dramatically of all. On the bike, I cannot fail. Up and down the seaside mountain cliffs in Ireland, along the rutted trails of the Camino de Santiago in Spain, over the Apennines in Italy, and the Rockies in the Southwest—whatever the location, the overall elation is similar. Simply to have done it—"Well, dang!"

A brief exchange with a game warden in the Florida panhandle, just days before the end of the trip, left us quietly pensive. "Mercy, mercy," he said on hearing our story. We lingered a moment under the spell of those murmured words. "Mercy," we had surprised ourselves and others as well. "Mercy," we had arrived safely. "Mercy, mercy," where would we go from here ... ?

NOTES

1) Carpenter, Connie, in *Winning Women: Quotations on Sports, Health and Fitness,* Beth Mendy Conny, compiler. White Plains, NY: Peter Pauper Press, 1993
2) cited in *North American Review*, 1895
3) Young, Iris Marion, "Throwing Like a Girl" in *On Female Body Experience: "Throwing Like a Girl" and Other Essays.* Indianapolis: Indiana University Press, 1990

The Hero(ine)'s Journey

Janet Greidanus

My husband and I had traveled to Nepal to fulfill my dream of trekking to Mount Everest Base Camp. "Why do you want to do this?" he had asked me, pointing out that we had beautiful mountains close by in Banff and Jasper. It was a month before my fifty-fifth birthday. I wanted to see Everest with my own two eyes, I told him. Surprised and skeptical, many other people also asked why I wanted to do this. How could I explain it?

Gail Sheehy, a writer who studies life changes and stages, suggests that such lust for adventure is due to post-menopausal zest, "a special, buoyant sort of energy, fuelled in part by the change in ratio of testosterone to estrogen,"[1] That may be, but to me it isn't a satisfactory explanation. What I felt was a call that originated in a place deep within me, a call to begin a search for something that is very difficult to name or explain.

My first impressions of Kathmandu were overwhelming: the crowds of people outside the airport; the narrow streets with cows and goats wandering aimlessly at the sides; the noise; the cars, honking incessantly and driving on the "wrong" side; rickshaws and motorbikes weaving in and out. I was afraid that we would get run over or break an ankle in a pothole before we even began our trek! It was Diwali, the Hindu winter festival, and there were lights everywhere, including open candles on the doorsteps and windowsills.

That evening at the restaurant, another guest shared a harrowing story. A few days earlier, his guided trek to Kanchenjunga Base Camp had been cut short when he became ill with high-altitude pulmonary edema, which came upon him very suddenly. Accompanied by a Sherpa, he began to descend as soon as his symptoms were first noticed. However, he did not improve, and several times he thought he was going to die. Fortunately, they encountered an American physician in a village along the way who was able to inject him with a drug that improved his condition enough for him to make it to the hospital in Kathmandu. When we met him he was recuperating and "killing time" in Kathmandu while awaiting a flight back to the U.S.

I knew altitude-related illness was one of the potential hazards of trekking to Everest Base Camp. I also knew that many trekkers never reach Base Camp because of it and that there was no way of predicting who would succumb to it. One could climb several times without problems and then suddenly be stricken. Fitness, gender, age, did not seem to make the difference. Later that evening I wrote in my journal, *Secretly, I'm quite worried and wish now we'd signed up for a lower level trek.* But I also felt tremendous excitement. Although I did not know how, I anticipated that the words on the cover of my new travel journal would become a reality for me: "I am not the same having seen the moon shine on the other side of the world."[2]

The following day we met the other members of our group. We were four Canadians, two Americans, and six Australians. I noted that I was the oldest woman in the group. The plan was to fly to Lukla the next day in a small plane and land on the airstrip that Sir Edmund Hillary had built to lessen the time needed to bring expeditions' supplies to Base Camp from Kathmandu. The adventure was about to begin. I knew it wouldn't be easy.

I have wondered and pondered long and hard over the question of why midlife women, including me, take on the challenges they do. Some women run their first marathon in their fifties. Some, as I had, begin doctoral studies. Some want to climb a very high mountain for the first time. Marg Archibald of Calgary, who describes herself as a middle-class, middle-aged, unathletic mom, decided to go around the world on her bicycle as her grand response to turning the big five-O.[3] Ann Linnea, in midlife and deeply affected by the death of a dear friend, set off in her seventeen-foot kayak on an arduous twelve-hundred-mile, sixty-five-day journey to circumnavigate Lake Superior on a quest for self-knowledge and transformation.[4] These are fascinating stories! At one time, I considered researching such stories as part of my doctoral studies. Who or what is calling us to do these things at midlife?

According to the psychologist and author Kathleen Brehony, the bodies of women at midlife are still strong and vibrant and the physical challenge is appealing, but she sees the search for spiritual meaning as the more compelling motive for these journeys and new beginnings. There is a deep inner striving of the soul to claim a life of greater authenticity, one last attempt, so to speak, to be who we were always supposed to be.[5] I understand this. For many, many years I had been completely focused on and devoted to my roles and responsibilities as both a wife and the mother of six children. Now I am a grandmother of eleven. These roles are joyful and fulfilling, and always have been, but what about the rest of who I am? Where is she? Who is she? Brehony points out that embarking on adventures that allow for a transformation of the self is described in stories and myths from all cultures and throughout all periods of history. She refers to the mythologist and storyteller Joseph Campbell, who has described such a transformation as the "Hero's Journey."[6]

I had already made the connection between Campbell's "Hero's Journey" and the so-called extreme mountain climbers who climb to the summits of the world's highest mountains. In his book *Everest: Mountain without Mercy*, Broughton Coburn proposes that some climbers are on a quest and set out not so much to conquer a physical obstacle as to attain a new level of understanding of themselves. "Climbing a high mountain," he writes, "may be modern man's [and I would add, *modern woman's*] outlet for the classic hero's struggle codified by Joseph Campbell: approaching, confronting, and then overcoming the weakness and demons that haunt and obstruct us."[7]

Could the outdoor adventures and wilderness journeys of midlife women today also be modern-day examples of the classic Hero's Journey? *Heroine's Journey?* They certainly seem to follow the same path: the call to adventure, separation from what is familiar and safe, the adventure (facing one's fears, battling dragons and demons), and the return home strengthened, transformed, changed in fundamental ways. Such is the story of my trek to Base Camp.

Several days into the trek, on the evening of Sunday, November 5, 2000, I found myself writing in my journal in the sunroom of a teahouse with a view of Cho-Oyu out the window. Cho-Oyu is a mountain about eighteen miles west of Everest at the head of the Gokyo Valley. Every so often another load of dried yak dung was added to the stove in the center of the room, causing most of the trekkers to cough and run outside. It's not surprising that there is so much lung disease in this region above the tree line where the air is thin and yak dung is used for fuel.

To get this far had not been easy. The route was mostly a continuous uphill climb. We had crossed several suspension bridges that were missing planks and looked to be hundreds of years old. We had some frightening moments when we met two yak trains approaching from opposite directions on a narrow section of the trail. We scrambled up the side of the mountain beside the trail to allow the animals to pass. Our head Sherpa was particularly concerned for our safety because of an accident that had happened several days before when a French trekker in another group fell to his death after being knocked off the trail by a yak. Despite the danger, the sound of approaching yak bells is one of the most beautiful sounds I have ever heard. I bought a yak bell in Naamche Bazaar for seven hundred rupees, shaking many before I found the rich sound I wanted. One of the Sherpas told me I got "ripped off"! Two of the Australian women in our group succumbed to another danger and had to descend because of altitude sickness. One began vomiting and became very weak after hardly eating anything for days. Her friend felt obliged to go down with her.

The next day, Monday, we awakened at 3:30 a.m. and an hour later began our ascent of Gokyo Peak (17,519 feet) with hope that we would see the sun rise on Everest. I could eat only a few mouthfuls of porridge for breakfast, but I was thankful for the good night's sleep in spite of the fact that it was literally freezing in our room.

We climbed in the dark using headlamps to light our way. At one point we had to cross fast-flowing water in the dark using only the light of the headlamps to step from boulder to boulder across the water. It was a steep climb, and I became disoriented and dizzy. I had to stop after every few steps to get my breath and give my heart a rest. There were moments when I thought of quitting and turning back, but I kept going and eventually I caught up with the group. Most of the others had arrived a while ahead of me. But I made it! My reward was one of the best panoramas in the Khumbu. I will never forget the sight of the rising sun gradually lighting up four of the highest mountains in the world: Cho-Oyu, Makalu, Lhotse, and Everest, among countless other towering snow peaks and rock spires that filled the horizon. Many prayer flags were blowing in the wind. We sat up there for more than an hour, taking pictures and enjoying lemon tea and cookies that one of the Sherpas had carried up.

On the morning of Tuesday, November 7, the decision was made that two more of our group would have to descend. One was coughing up blood and sputum with black specks in it. Of the original twelve, eight of us would continue. I was glad I still felt well in spite of having a cold and a Khumbu cough, but I was dirty and longed for a shower. I was also sick of eating fried eggs and potatoes. Part of me wanted to go home and part of me wanted to find out how high I could go. The views were magnificent, and I reminded myself that the only way to see it all was by walking and climbing. I couldn't help wondering what else one misses in life by refusing to climb.

On Friday, November 10, we reached the famously filthy village of Lobuje described unforgettably by Jon Krakauer in *Into Thin Air*.[8] Lobuje is a small place and the continuous human traffic—trekkers and locals—continues to exceed the capacity of the conveniences provided. The small stone toilets are always full, so people simply use the surrounding area.

On the way to Lobuje we had stopped at a place where there were a number of cairns and monuments to those who died on Everest. One large one was for Scott Fisher, who died during the Everest tragedy of May 10, 1996, when nine climbers died.

There were only seven of us left by the time we got to Lobuje. We slept in a dorm with bunks stacked three high, and males and females, including trekkers from other groups, divided by a thin partition. I faced one of my biggest fears during the night when I had to climb out of my bunk to make my way alone in the cold and dark to the outhouse. After tripping over a tent peg on the way, I arrived only to find two yaks positioned directly in front of the outhouse door. Needless to say, like so many others, I found another place to go!

My husband and I will never forget November 11. The day began at 3 a.m. Even though we were wearing down-filled jackets, we were freezing while we waited to be served tea and porridge.

It was not an easy trek to get to Gorak Shep, the last little village and teahouse before Everest Base Camp. We walked through glacial moraine, around rocks, always climbing. It was so cold that the water in my bottle froze! We needed headlamps to see our way until the sun rose. One man in our group was quite sick and eventually he and his friend turned around, leaving five of us to continue. It was the most difficult and challenging day of the entire trek. Gorak Shep is well over sixteen thousand four hundred feet high. After viewing the area of Base Camp, which was deserted of tents and climbers at this time of year, and after having a lunch of hot soup and tea, we headed back down to our lodging at Periche. We arrived at 6:30 p.m., more than fifteen hours after beginning in the morning. I was exhausted.

Two days later, the trek was complete, and we were back in Lukla resting and waiting for a flight back to Kathmandu.

Our Nepal trek was the most difficult physical challenge I had ever faced. However, I saw so much that can only be seen by traveling on foot for many days. I had walked through fear, cold, exhaustion, and the threat of illness. I had triumphed over the tough demands and conditions of a trek into the Khumbu region of Nepal. What a miraculous thing it was for me to be so near to Mount Everest! I learned a lot about myself—about what happens when I abandon comfort and warmth and face difficult challenges. I learned that I can persevere and I can overcome obstacles. Knowing this will help me to carry on into the afternoon of life. Midlife is like heading into new and unfamiliar territory. Courageously and one step at a time is how I will move forward—the way I did on the trek.

I opened myself up to the spirituality and culture of other peoples. "*Namaste!*" I have been greeted on the trail by both locals and visitors. "The God in me greets the God in you." (Also translated as "the Divine in me greets the Divine in you"). How much more peaceful might this world be if we could all welcome each other with such beautiful words?

Jung believes that we have within us who we are supposed to be. The journey, then, is not really about finding something "out there" but about traveling inward to find one's True Self. I had no idea what a strong, determined, and courageous woman I really am! This is the woman I have come home to.

The words on the cover of my travel journal came true. I saw the moon shine on the other side of the world. And it was a full moon on that November twelfth of the year 2000. I saw it shine in Nepal, and I am not the same.

NOTES

1) Sheehy,Gail, *New Passages: Mapping Your Life Across Time*. New York: Ballantine Books, 1995, 221

2) Radmacher-Hershey, Mary Anne, *Blank Book Journal*. Cannon Beach: maryanne's wordshop, ltd., 1998

3) Archibald, M., *Cycling into Your Soul: A Journey Out into the World and Down into the Soul. A Triumphant Return with Newfound Wisdom*. Calgary: The Monday Communications Group Ltd., 1998, 11

4) Linnea, A., *Deep Water Passage: A Spiritual Journey at Midlife*. Boston: Little, Brown and Company, 1995

5) Brehony, K., *Awakening at Midlife: A Guide to Revivin*uer, J., *Into Thin Air*. New York: Anchor Books, 1997, 65–74

6) Ibid, 20 Brehony is referring here to Joseph Campbell, *The Hero with a Thousand Faces*. Princeton: Princeton University Press, 1990

7) Coburn, B., *Everest: Mountain Without Mercy*. Washington: National Geographic Society, 1997, 36

8) Krakauer, J., *Into Thin Air*. New York: Anchor Books, 1997, 65–74

A Russian Journey:
Cold War and Fragile Peace

Ellen G. Jaffe

Ever since childhood, I had wanted to visit Russia, so when the chance came in 1975, I took it without thinking twice! I was thirty years old, studying child psychotherapy at the Tavistock Clinic in London, England, and discovered that the nearby London Institute of Education offered a two-week tour to the Soviet Union. We would visit Moscow, Leningrad (now returned to its pre-Revolutionary name, St. Petersburg), and Riga, capital of Latvia, then under Soviet control. In addition to sightseeing, the purpose of the trip was to visit schools and children's centers and meet people involved in education.

But in reality, I had two trips planned: one, the official itinerary, the other clandestine, or at least unauthorized. I intended to explore family roots and visit friends of friends. This latter trip is what made the experience come alive for me, why these memories stay in my mind and heart thirty years later. This is the story I want to tell.

Growing up in New York City, I was especially close to my Russian-Jewish great-grandmother on my mother's side, Mary Axelrod, a warm, loving woman, active and alert until she died in her early nineties, when I was in university. She lived only a block away from our apartment, so I knew her well. Her cooking, her accent, the way she moved, the way she smelled, the plants she grew on her window-sill—everything about her was different from most other people I knew. I felt good being in her house.

Although Mary did not speak much about her early life, my mother often told the story of how Mary came alone by ship to New York in 1886, when she was fourteen, to join her parents and brothers. No one is quite sure where her family came from; it may have been near Chernigov. She met her husband, another Russian-Jewish immigrant, when they both worked in a cigar factory; he died when Mary was only fifty, so she was my principal link with "the old country."

My father's parents were also Russian Jews who met in New York City around the year 1900. They came from "Pinsk, near Minsk"— words whose sound I loved as a child. At that time, all these places were within the Pale of Settlement, a large area to which Russian Jews were confined by law (although some did live outside it). In the Pale, as Dayal Kaur Khalsa suggests in her children's book, *Tales of a Gambling Grandma,* Jews were not safe: you never knew when Cossacks might gallop into your village. Even as a child, I knew that the spread of pogroms and massacres in the late nineteenth and early twentieth century was one reason for extensive immigration to the U.S., Canada, and elsewhere. I came across Khalsa's book years after my trip to Russia, when I was looking for stories for my own son. The "gambling" grandma in her flowered housedress reminded me of Mary; how I wished she and my son could have known each other!

While my primary purpose in traveling to Russia was to connect with family roots, I was also a child of the Cold War and wanted to make the trip for that reason, too. Born in 1945, I grew up in the United States during the time when the Soviet Union shifted from being a World War II ally to an ideological enemy. My family was politically liberal and did not accept the belief that it was "better to be dead than Red." My father, a doctor, even agreed to examine a member of the Communist Party who became ill while on trial for allegedly advocating overthrow of the U.S. government, and then testify regarding his state of health; several other doctors refused to get involved because they were afraid of guilt by association.

I grew up to share their views and, in the late 1960s, became involved in anti-Vietnam War protests as well as other left-wing political activities. By 1972, I was not unhappy to leave the United States to study in England.

As I prepared for my trip to Russia, I received names of people to visit in Moscow: my former college roommate had cousins there, and one of my teachers in London had a colleague who taught English to Soviet graduate students. But the most significant names came from British friends who were in contact with refuseniks, Soviet Jews who had applied to immigrate to Israel but were refused permission to leave by their own government, then persecuted in other ways. At that time, Leonid I. Breznev was general secretary of the Communist Party of the Soviet Union; his regime was oppressive to most religious groups, particularly Jews, who were seen as dissidents for their ties to Israel, a country allied with the West.

My friends gave me the name and address of a refusenik family I could visit in Moscow, to bring Bibles, blue jeans, and a bit of hope. So I set off, packing for both cold weather and the Cold War.

We arrived early in April, when Moscow was still in the grip of winter. We stayed in Intourist hotels, ate stodgy potatoes, lumpy porridge, and unidentifiable brownish gray "meat." We visited schools and day-care centers, met Young Pioneers and old war veterans, toured museums and attended the ballet.

Late one afternoon, I met the cousins of my college roommate and gave them the jeans and lipstick I had easily smuggled in for them. I spent a morning at the graduate English class I'd been told about; after class, one student asked me to ride with him on the Moscow subway. He was a dark-haired, sharp-faced young man from Georgia, Stalin's birthplace, at the southern tip of the Black Sea. In low tones, he told me about the prejudice he and other students from outlying "non-Russian" provinces—for example, Georgia, Uzbekistan, Dagestan (he may also have mentioned Chechnya)—faced from the "Russian" people in Moscow. This was an eye-opener: I thought I was familiar with prejudice (including anti-Semitism in Europe and racial prejudice toward Blacks in the United States) but had not expected to find it among Soviet peoples themselves. Nor, growing up in New York City, had I experienced anti-Semitism myself, although my parents had encountered it at various times and places.

Finally, on our tour's one free evening in Moscow, I made my way alone through dark streets to the address of Vladimir and Masha Slepak. They were refuseniks who acted as advocates for many in the refusenik movement; they had received publicity abroad, and met other visitors from the West. Years later they were allowed to leave the U.S.S.R. for Israel, so there is no danger now in revealing their names.

To enter their apartment building, I had to pass between two elderly women sitting on the stone steps, knitting—not unlike Madame Defarge in *A Tale of Two Cities*. I wondered if they were the innocent babushkas (grandmothers) that they appeared to be or police informers. I climbed a narrow, dark staircase that smelled of cabbage and age, knocked at a door, and waited long moments while the occupants asked who I was and who sent me, then decided to let me in.

Around their kitchen table, I gave them the Bibles, other books, and blue jeans that I had brought (I had taken more care to hide the Bibles than the jeans in my suitcase) and drank glasses of tea with sugar and lemon. Gradually, I began to feel welcomed into their circle: the middle-aged couple and three or four children in their early twenties. I remember Vladimir Slepak's looming presence as he told me, in English, what life was like for his family. He had been an engineer; one reason the Soviets gave for denying him permission to leave was that he had worked with "secret" information. He and his family were not allowed to work or study and were restricted to their apartment, with ever-decreasing income. For many refuseniks, the catch-22 was that the government fired them from their jobs when they applied to emigrate, then arrested them for being unemployed! Vladimir explained that Judaism was suppressed in the Soviet Union for several reasons: suppression of all religions; government plans to assimilate Jews as a group; Jewish ties to the State of Israel, allied to the United States; and underlying, centuries-old anti-Semitism. Ironically, Vladimir's father had been an ardent revolutionary who achieved high standing in the Communist Party and survived Stalin's purges.

Toward the end of the evening, Vladimir gave me two letters, one to Golda Meir, who had recently retired as prime minister of Israel (a position she held from 1969 to1974) and one to the prime minister then in office, Yitzhak Rabin, in the first of his two stints as head of the Israeli government. (He would be assassinated on November 5, 1995, during his second term of office.) He asked me to mail the letters after I left the Soviet Union. He did not elaborate, but this seemed to be a crucial mission, potentially dangerous for me, but—more important—helpful to the Slepaks and other refuseniks. I felt honored, trusted. I took the thin, blue airmail letters and tucked them carefully into my bag.

If I had stopped to consider what would happen if they were discovered, would I still have taken the letters? Probably—even though I was aware that there could be consequences for such an action. I had acquaintances at home in the United States who had been jailed for political protests; I had also read about Soviet political prisoners incarcerated in mental hospitals, who could obtain freedom only by the ruse of saying that they were crazy, not subversive. I had seen one of these men at a meeting in London; I remembered his stooped walk, the grayness of his skin and his hair. But I was young, more naive than I knew, and did not believe any of this could apply to me on my heroic errand. I said goodbye and walked back to the hotel in the shadowy Moscow evening. The two babushkas were still knitting as I walked silently between the pair of stone lions guarding the apartment building.

I decided to hide the letters in an inner pocket of my red-leather passport holder, which I always kept with me.

Shortly afterward, we flew to Riga. I noticed that here, unlike Moscow, people on the street were actually *smiling*. Even here, however, we met people who preferred to talk to us on the street or in an outdoor café, not in a closed room.

In Latvia, we visited something I had not expected to see on this trip: the site of a Nazi concentration camp. Salaspils, near Riga, was the largest of twenty-three death camps built in Latvia. I still have the pamphlet describing the place: "this scanty, sandy heath, burnt by the sun [where] under the German occupation, plywood targets became live people." (Translation by Yves and Luba Apel, Hamilton, Ontario.) We walked among huge commemorative statues and deserted barracks, and I saw tears in the Latvian guide's eyes. Salaspils is the only Nazi death-camp site I have seen. It had a profound effect on everyone in our group, Jewish and non-Jewish alike. The air itself seemed saturated with death—the presence of people who had physically died there and the memories of everyone killed during the Holocaust. I knew that if my family had not left Russia when they did, it could have been *us*.

Our last destination was Leningrad, where we met and talked with several graduate students, including three women from Siberia. I had not realized that people lived, worked, and raised families in Siberia, and that the area included cities and towns, not just gulags and frozen wasteland. I became especially friendly with one of these women, Lina, who was missing her husband and young child back home, three thousand miles away in the city of Abakan. She was about my age, with striking silvery-blond hair, and interested in art and writing; after the trip, she and I exchanged postcards and books for a year or more. One afternoon, Lina took me out to lunch at a restaurant and then to visit museums. In an apologetic, nervous tone, she whispered to me how much she liked Russian religious icons. I realized how difficult it was for her to speak, or even think, freely.

Later that evening, when I felt slightly sick to my stomach, I didn't worry. I didn't have severe pain or vomiting and thought my symptoms could be caused by fatigue, stress, my period, or unfamiliar food and water. We had been warned about drinking water in the U.S.S.R. and were taking water-purification tablets as a precaution. I mentioned my discomfort to another member of our group, who—to my surprise and dismay—told our Intourist guide. No one on the tour knew of my extracurricular activities or the letters (dangerous as radioactive isotopes) inside my passport case. The guide scolded me for eating lunch out, then informed the hotel doctor, who decided, after only a quick look at me, that I had appendicitis and should go to hospital immediately!

Even without the letters, this would have been an unpleasant prospect: I had visions of rusty, outdated surgical equipment and unreliable sanitation. But under the circumstances, I became really anxious. I had to take my passport with me but feared it would be confiscated in the hospital. *What to do?* I finally sealed the letters inside one blank envelope, then another, addressed the outer envelope to myself, and zipped it into an inner compartment of my suitcase. Should I lock the suitcase or keep it unlocked? Which would arouse less suspicion? Looking back, I see that *anything* I did could easily have been discovered.

Too soon, I was lying in a hospital bed, picturing exile to a Siberian gulag: a Jewish-American woman with Russian heritage, ostensibly in the Soviet Union on a study tour from England, caught smuggling letters to Israel! My thoughts were spinning. What would my parents say? How far could diplomacy help me? Would I survive surgery? Had people conspired against me? I was convinced I did not have appendicitis or anything seriously wrong, and kept saying "*Nyet, nyet!*" (No, no!) when asked if I felt sick. I found an ally in the plump, motherly nurse's aide who brought me tea and treated me like a human being, not a medical case or enemy agent.

I may have slept, but it was a long, scary night. By the time the sun rose, I had convinced the female doctor that I did not, in fact, have appendicitis. Soon, our tour leader, a gentle, middle-aged male professor, arrived to liberate me. The city looked amazingly bright and alive as we made our way back to the hotel—where I checked my suitcase and found the letters intact. I guarded them close to my body until we returned to London, where I put them in the post like ordinary mail. Months later, I received polite replies from Golda Meir and Yitzhak Rabin.

I eventually left England and moved to Canada. Over the years, the story of the letters and the hospital became something I could tell at dinner parties, to impress friends and dates. I had no idea whether the letters had helped or hurt the Slepaks and their cause. I didn't know until later that my letters were only two of a large number of letters and petitions sent to Israel, the Soviet government, and the United Nations to support the refuseniks. Vladimir was actually exiled to Siberia for several years but did not give up; the Slepaks helped many people immigrate to Israel before they themselves were allowed to leave in 1987, fourteen years after their original application. (The family's story is told by Chaim Potok in a non-fiction book, *The Gates of November*).

Only gradually did I realize that my role as courier could have had serious consequences for me. I have often been someone who "leaps and then looks"; this is not a bad attitude, especially for a writer, but it can land me in difficult—if interesting—situations. I have become more cautious with age, though I still find myself exploring edges and opposing injustice.

Writing in 2005, thirty years—half my lifetime—after the event, I see why my experience in the U.S.S.R has continued to resonate. I felt that I was participating in history being made. Before the trip, as I've noted, I was aware of social and political oppression in various parts of the world; I had written poems and articles of protest, as well as participated in marches, "guerrilla theatre," and other public events. But in Russia, I undertook an action alone, secretly and unplanned, and exposed myself to danger. At the same time, I witnessed and engaged in events reaching far beyond the boundaries of myself. This was both a loss of innocence and a profound learning experience, showing how the personal and political are intimately connected.

I also became more aware of being Jewish and its meaning in my life. Meeting the Slepaks and standing on the site of Salaspils concentration camp—both these experiences made me feel more connected to Jewish history and to contemporary meanings of the journey (exodus) from slavery to freedom.

The journey also nurtured my identity as a writer: someone who works with words to explore, understand, and depict the world and one's own feelings, and someone who takes risks—emotional if not physical—to say what needs to be said. In sending the Slepaks' letters, I literally carried words from silence and secrecy to a place where they could be heard and make meaning. Metaphorically, this is what good writing always does. In addition, during the trip I found ways to talk with people living different lives from mine, a process I continue to learn.

But there can be problems with language. Words can be used to conceal, to mislead, to incite hatred and violence, as well as to communicate honestly and with love. This deception can range from the casual lie between lovers to hate-filled propaganda. In Russia, language was used against people like the Slepaks, while some years earlier, anti-Communist rhetoric in the United States led to the blacklisting that ruined many lives. It is the old story of "us" and "them," which never has a happy ending.

No matter *where*—or *when*—we live in the world, language can be used in complex ways to destroy and to create. So, in writing and in daily life, we need to use words clearly and carefully, and expose their misuse. In a sense, we are all "writers." We tell the stories of our travels through life and through love as best we can, and discover not "*the truth*" but many truths. By sharing our stories, as the writers have done in this book, we can undo the inevitable lies and lapses of memory and fear, anger and ignorance. I recall Nancy Richler's novel, *Your Mouth Is Lovely,* set in pre-Revolutionary Russia; the title comes from the Russian-Jewish phrase used when a child first speaks, to bless and safeguard her words. The narrator of Richler's novel is in a Siberian prison, writing her story for her long-lost daughter. I write this story for Mary Axelrod, my parents, and my son, as well as for readers I do not know in person and for people whose struggles I have mentioned here.

And after all these years, I still have my appendix!

SOURCES

Khalsa, Dayal Kaur. *Tales of a Gambling Grandma*. Montreal: Tundra Books, 1986.

Potok, Chaim; Leonid Slepak; Vladimir Slepak; Alexander Slepak; Maria Slepak. *The Gates of November*. New York, NY:Alfred A. Knopf, Inc., 1996.

Richler, Nancy. *Your Mouth is Lovely*. Toronto: HarperPerennial/Canada (Harper Collins), 2002.

Fear of Hitchhiking

Amanda Stevens

 A few years ago when I was traveling through California, my mom heard a story on the news about a young woman who disappeared while hitchhiking in Northern British Columbia. After telling me the story over the telephone, she made me promise that I would never hitchhike. I assured her that I never would. I had never doubted that it is dangerous for women to hitchhike, and if I ever tried it, it wouldn't be in the U.S.A., the mythical land of handguns and serial killers.

As a woman, I was always taught to be afraid of going out alone and warned that if I did ever have to be out by myself, never to trust the men I encountered, especially men in vehicles. I cannot count the number of stories I have heard throughout my life about women or children being taken against their will by men driving vans. I have never been assaulted by a man in a vehicle, and no one I know has, yet this fear was instilled in women of my generation from a young age. Of course, women do have to be careful. But the fear itself is so pervasive, that I can't help wondering whether it, in itself, keeps us from leading full and satisfying lives.

I don't drive, and some time ago I decided that not to go out walking alone at night was too severe a restriction of my lifestyle. Now I do it—usually—without a second thought. I've never had a problem. However, depending on where I am and my state of mind, I am still fearful and suspicious of the men and vehicles that I encounter. My primary line of defense is to try to appear invisible through my body language and clothing.

Hitchhiking, then, is the opposite of what good, smart women should do. A hitchhiking woman is conspicuous and vulnerable to attack. Therefore, I should never do it, end of story. Yet hitchhiking has always held a fascination for me, partly, I'm sure, because of the lure of the dangerous and forbidden, but also because the hitchhiker has always seemed to me to be the quintessence of the "true traveler," by which I mean the mythical, romantic figure of the solitary wanderer, the embodiment of freedom, a person who has escaped all conventions of time and responsibility and simply goes where her feet and her fancy carry her. A true traveler has no schedule or destination and relishes the unknown and unexpected. This myth has always attracted me, and it is the ideal I try to attain while traveling.

I have done a lot of traveling by bus and train, but with these modes of transportation I am bound by schedules, set routes, and pre-decided structures. Driving her own car allows the traveler more freedom to choose where and when she will go. But even if I had a driver's license, I would not see that as the best mode of travel for me. First, because it is not an environmentally responsible way to travel, and second, because driving forecloses the possibility of encountering the unknown and unexpected even more than traveling by bus or train. A woman driving, whether long or short distances, is alone or with selected passengers and in complete control of her environment. There will be no chance encounters. A hitchhiker, on the other hand, can travel with no set plan or schedule, and the possibilities of meeting new and interesting people and having unexpected experiences are endless.

One of the best examples of hitchhiking as a lifestyle is *On the Road* by Jack Kerouac, which takes place in the 1940s. The first time I read it, I was enchanted by Kerouac's philosophy that "the road is life." I wanted nothing more than to hitchhike for the rest of my life. However, I assumed that kind of freedom was no longer possible, because the world had become too dangerous.

Then I went to New Zealand.

Before traveling to New Zealand, I spoke to someone who had been there in the early 1980s. He said it was like stepping back into the 1950s. That, however, was twenty years ago. Arriving in New Zealand, I found that although the country has changed and has become more like Canada, a few subtle differences remain. The rate of violent crime in New Zealand is very low, and people are generally trusting of each other. People don't lock their doors at night, and hitchhiking is seen as a safe and common way to travel. The reasons for these differences are complex, but I imagine one contributing factor is that New Zealand's population is only four million.

As soon as I arrived in New Zealand, I started meeting people who used hitchhiking as their primary mode of long distance transportation—both foreign backpackers like me and New Zealanders themselves. Most were men, but I met a few women who hitchhiked with partners or alone. I was intrigued but still had no plans to try it myself. My fear was still strong, and besides, I had promised my mom that I would not.

One day my friend Alexis and I visited Tahunanui Beach in Nelson, a town on the South Island where I had been living. We walked to the beach from my house, but it was a long uphill walk back and it was a hot summer day, so we decided to catch the bus home. However, in the little city of Nelson the bus only comes once an hour, and after waiting for about fifteen minutes with no bus in sight and the hot December sun beating down on us, I thought, Now is the time to try hitchhiking. It felt like a daring idea, even though I was in the safest position imaginable: I was in New Zealand, I was with a friend, and we would only be going a short distance, on a busy stretch of road traveled mainly by tourists and locals commuting between Nelson city and the nearby suburbs.

Tentatively, I stuck out my thumb and immediately felt a rush of adrenaline. My position as a woman in the world felt suddenly and dramatically different. Instead of trying to disappear into the landscape, I was now confronting the vehicles that passed me and making eye contact with drivers. Although I was nervous, I had discovered a new feeling of confidence and control over my environment.

After about ten minutes, someone stopped to pick us up. He was a young man driving home from work. He fit our stereotype of the sort of sleazy man who would pick up two female hitchhikers—when we got in he said, "When I saw two pretty girls on the side of the road I thought it was Christmas," and he invited us out for a beer with him—but he was harmless and dropped us off where we asked him to.

Although my first hitchhiking experience had been a short trip within the city limits, I felt I had taken the first step in overcoming my fears and attaining new heights of freedom and mobility. Now that I knew I could do it, I was excited about doing it again.

The second time I hitchhiked, it was out of necessity. A friend with a car had given me a lift to an all-night dance party in a remote area with no bus service. She had left, so after the dance party I hitchhiked home with my friend Ange. She was an experienced hitchhiker, and she taught me a few fine points of the art, such as how to choose a good spot on the road and how to make conversation with drivers, which she told me is the hitchhiker's responsibility.

After this I hitchhiked with friends whenever I had the chance. I was convinced now that it was safe as long as I didn't do it alone, and I was excited that such an inexpensive, easy, and interesting way to travel was open to me. Most of the time I was picked up by locals, so hitching allowed me to learn a lot more about the history and culture of the places I visited than I would have if I had taken the bus.

I soon learned that people who pick up hitchhikers often travel alone as a part of their jobs, and they like the company. They are more often than not great storytellers, and I heard some unusual stories. One man who picked me up was a diviner, who guided people to a good spot to drill a well because he could sense where underground water was located. Another man who had suffered from mouth cancer told me about the treatment process he had undergone. Through hitchhiking, I met people I would never have met in any other way— people of all different ages, backgrounds, and lifestyles.

When I left Nelson to see the rest of New Zealand, I hoped to hitchhike much of the way, but often, because I couldn't find a suitable partner, I had to resort to taking the bus. I started to resent it; traveling by bus seemed like a waste of money, as well as boring and predictable. But I wasn't ready to start hitching alone. The idea was still too scary.

Finally, I found myself in a situation where I had to get back to Nelson for an event, couldn't afford to take the bus, and had no one to hitchhike with. I was on the South Island, which is the less populated and generally seen as the safer of New Zealand's two islands, and I was traveling through rural areas, where I always feel safer than in cities. I was also in Queenstown, the bungee-jumping capital of the world—with everyone around me jumping off cliffs and bridges for fun, hitchhiking seemed easy. I knew that by getting into a car with a stranger, or standing out on a road alone, I was risking being raped, killed, or injured. But going out anywhere alone is always risky. Going on a date, doing "adventure tourism" activities like whitewater rafting or skydiving, swimming in the ocean, or riding in a car at any time, there is always a risk of accidents or encountering the wrong person, and these are things that people do every day. I decided I would no longer allow fear to prevent me from doing something I really enjoyed. So I hitchhiked back to Nelson by myself.

All of the people who picked me up were men. My first two rides took me short distances and offered me the historical information and unique political views I had come to expect. My last ride took me all the way to Nelson, meaning we rode together for about two hours, and I got to know him better than most. As an ex-bus-tour guide, he had a great deal of knowledge to share about the area we drove through. He also confessed that he had recently ended a serious relationship and was having a difficult time meeting girls, so I listened to his romantic woes and offered him extensive advice on how and where to find a new girlfriend. This last subject of conversation made me slightly uncomfortable, but that was all. When I reached my destination safely, without any frightening incidents, I felt I had made a tremendous accomplishment and overcome my greatest fears. After this experience, I hitchhiked everywhere during my last two months of traveling around New Zealand, and I loved it.

I was able to see out of-the-way places—roads and landscapes not on any bus route. With the money I saved on transportation, I could participate in activities I otherwise would not have been able to afford. I could change my mind about where I was going at any time. I once hitchhiked on both sides of a quiet road at once because I could not decide which way I wanted to go and decided to leave it up to chance. Another time I planned to go to a particular town, but when I arrived

I decided it was not worth staying there, so I hitchhiked on to my next destination instead. The freedom was wonderful.

Every time I stuck out my thumb, I felt a mixture of fear and exhilaration. I admit that I suspected every single person who picked me up of being a murderer or a pervert. But eventually I learned that only the first five minutes of a ride is scary. My strategy is to spend those first five minutes asking the driver a lot of questions in order to get a sense of what he or she is like. Usually the person is perfectly nice and I am able to relax for the rest of the ride.

In fact, I was surprised to hear that many drivers were afraid to pick up hitchhikers and often set rules for themselves regarding whom they would and would not pick up. Women drivers often told me they did not pick up male hitchhikers or two people hitchhiking together. Some men did not pick up men either, unless they judged them to be safe, but they always picked up women. One of my rides told me he only picked up people who looked as if they smoked marijuana! I actually heard more stories of drivers who had had frightening experiences with hitchhikers than the other way around.

The few solo female hitchhikers I met shared with me the rules that they followed while hitchhiking. Some would only get in cars with female drivers. Others warned me never to get into a car with a group of men. Essentially, I realized that individual hitchhikers rely heavily on their intuition and adapt their own rules about hitchhiking depending on whether they need a ride in a hurry or can wait until another car comes along.

Probably the whole time I hitchhiked, only about 10 percent of the people who stopped for me were women, so I learned quickly that if I took rides only from women I might never reach my destination. For a long time, I avoided getting into a car with a group of men, until the day that I tried hitchhiking out to Milford Sound, where I planned to take a scheduled boat cruise. After waiting for nearly an hour, I had almost given up when three Spanish men in a car stopped for me. Although I felt leery of the situation, I did not want to miss my boat cruise, and I accepted the ride. The men turned out to be wonderful people who entertained me with Spanish songs and stories about Madrid and even went out of their way to drive me back to my hostel after the cruise.

One of the most important lessons I learned while hitchhiking is never to judge people by their appearance, as often the rides that look the most suspicious end up being the best. When a person decides to hitchhike, she steps into a space where she opens herself up to encountering the unknown and the unexpected. Once I had taken that step, I felt I had to trust in what the world handed me.

What I love most about hitchhiking is its generosity. So many relationships in our lives are based on financial exchange. Hitchhiking is based more on a karmic philosophy of giving and receiving in a continuous cycle: the driver has the privilege of having a car and extra space in it, so s/he offers to share it with a carless hitchhiker. In the future, the hitchhiker will probably remember the kind gesture and pass it on to another person in need when s/he has something that another person lacks.

I think this generosity is a big part of what traveling is all about. Friends offer me a bed, food, and a tour of their hometown, in the contented knowledge that one day I will do the same for them, or for someone else who needs it. This is the way we should all live our lives. Rather than basing our activities on a financial model, in which we pay whom we owe and only receive payment for services rendered, we should offer kindness not only to close friends but also to random strangers with the hope that one day it will be returned to us, and with the memory in mind of all those who have helped us in the past.

I found that many people in New Zealand seemed to live by this philosophy. People enjoy what they have and easily share it with others. In New Zealand I encountered little of the competitiveness and insecurity that permeates, and I believe constrains, North American culture.

Since coming home to Canada, I have given up hitchhiking. It is one of the things I miss most about my time in New Zealand. I am convinced now that my early dreams of the romance of being "on the road" were not just a fantasy; it really is the only way to travel. I believe that hitchhiking offers a person the best opportunity to learn firsthand about a different place or culture, meeting and talking with local people about their everyday lives and opinions. I plan to hitch-hike in Canada soon. I want to learn more about the people, places, and cultures that shape my country. And if I can help to dismantle the myth that women do not—and should not—hitchhike, the women I know and countless others I don't know may overcome their fears to travel where and as they please.

Chilean Winter

Lorna Crozier

Chile's most famous writer, Pablo Neruda, in poem after poem describes the beauty of his "sea-sprayed" homeland, its constellations of butterflies, and its emeralds heavy as apples. But he also writes that along the whole length of his narrow country, its nights and its rivers, "there are always bleeding ankles." On September 11, 1973, the military overthrew the newly elected government and killed its president, Salvador Allende. Within just a few years, thousands of people were tortured and murdered in Chile, and thousands of others went into exile. General Pinochet, the self-proclaimed president who remained in power until the plebiscite of 1988, continues to deny the dark time of his regime's cruelty and repression. He praises Chile's civil rights record and claims that the country prospered under military rule with big American corporations pouring money into industry and buying up the rich natural resources. Thirteen years after the coup, when my partner, Patrick Lane, and I were in Chile, *USA Today* featured photographs of Pinochet with his arm around President Reagan. The pictures bore captions like "Our Best Friend in South America."

The Writers' Union in Santiago invited Patrick and me to visit Chile to read our poems in April of 1986. The invitation arrived at an auspicious time. In the few months before our departure, the Canadian media had turned its eye on the country for reasons other than its chumminess with Reagan and its hot economy. Television cameras filmed the Montreal hospital room of a Chilean university student named Carmen Gloria Quintana. She had been part of a peaceful anti-Pinochet demonstration in the streets of Santiago. It didn't take long for the police to arrive, this time with a new weapon to add to their arsenal of guns, batons, and tear gas. They doused Carmen and a friend with gasoline, then set them on fire. Her friend burned to death beside her, but she survived and, funded by a church group, was flown to Montreal for treatment. On CBC-TV, Patrick and I watched a blackened, burned human being, the face an immobile mask. Her mouth had trouble making the shapes of the words she wanted to speak. *This is Chile*, she said slowly, then paused and lowered her blanket so we could see. *My body is my country.*

We left our own country at the start of a Saskatchewan spring. The snow had melted in our yard, and the poplar trees were beginning to bud. In the Toronto airport we met the two other poets we'd be traveling with, Mary di Michele and Gary Geddes. After a twelve-hour flight, we'd be in a different continent but also a different season. In Chile it was the beginning of winter, and for us, the beginning of a journey into a different kind of cold than the one we'd become accustomed to in Canada.

May 1, the International Day of the Workers, was our first morning in Santiago, Chile. Jet-lagged and awakened too early, we were already on the move in a rattling compact driven by a small man named Mauricio. He was hustling us to a union demonstration in the old theater at the heart of the city. As we got nearer, men with machine guns lined up on the streets, and big green buses lumbered between the curbs. They were the same size and make as the familiar yellow ones that carry Canadian children from the farm to school, but in Chile the buses were packed with dogs and soldiers, not children. I asked Mauricio what could happen this morning. "Who knows?" he said. "They're completely unpredictable."

"But what has happened in the past?"

"They've moved in," he said, "with water hoses, dogs, tear gas. They've shot people, arrested people."

"And what do we do if that happens?"

"Run."

I couldn't help wondering if we were wise to have put our safety in Mauricio's hands. He was about ten years younger than I am, a short man with a skinny mustache and greasy hair. We were told he was a punk poet and a member of a rock band. On the way into town, our topic of conversation had been his hero, Leonard Cohen, all of us singing the first lines of "Famous Blue Raincoat." He said, "This is why I love Canada!" Did he know what he was getting us into? Did he know how serious this was?

When we reached the theater, Mauricio talked to the two workers guarding the doors. They were allowing only those with union cards inside, but they were going to let us in, he was pleased to tell us, because we were Canadians and we were poets. In the dark of the theater on an old wooden bench, I sat terrified, imagining the soldiers and police gathering outside as the two thousand men and women around us sang, shouted, and stamped their feet on the floor. Just before the demonstration ended, we slipped out the back and headed in the opposite direction from the angry crowd that was pouring down the street toward the soldiers. A few blocks away, Mauricio pointed out a square, nondescript building that in Saskatoon could have been a warehouse for plumbing supplies. "That's where I was held for six months and tortured," he said.

Chile

There's one light
burning in your neighbourhood.
Is it the widow
measuring her hours,
or the baker his flour,
the yeast exploding in sugar water.

In the street
metal calls to metal.
The mongrel barks once,
then is silent
like a mouth stuffed with rags.

You cannot sleep.
A light is burning.
Is it you
who is on the list tonight?

❀ ❀ ❀

Every morning Mary, Patrick, and I took a bus from the house where we'd been billeted to the central square in Santiago, then walked about fifteen blocks to where Gary was staying with Lake Sagaris and her family. Lake was the organizer of our tour; she's a Canadian journalist and poet, married to a Chilean musician, and she had claimed this country as her home. On the way to her house, we walked by soldiers on the corners, sub-machine guns strapped across their chests. "Don't look them in the eye," Lake told us. The first few days they cast a cold shadow as we walked past, but by the end of the week we hardly noticed them. They stood on every corner like newspaper sellers, like lightposts, like trees.

Lake reported for the international press on events like the May Day demonstration, clicking her camera in the faces of soldiers and police. She equated writing with politics and action. Though she never said so out loud, one of her goals was to educate us four Canadians in the dark ways of the world. Today she was taking us downtown to the big cathedral where we'd meet the Relatives of the Disappeared and the Relatives of the Executed, both outlawed groups that members risked their lives to belong to. Since the coup, they did their quiet, necessary work in a dank, lightless room behind the pews and altars where the parishioners took communion. The first thing we saw as we made our way down the hall was a poster on the wall with a blown-up photograph of a man, one of the lawyers who had worked here. Below him hung a card with a number printed in black letters: 52. It was the sum of the days since the secret police had dragged him into a van from the street outside.

Eight women and one man sat around a table. Through a translator, they explained what their organizations were working for. When we asked them what the Pinochet regime had done to them, they told us their stories:

> My brother disappeared in 1975. He was a very good brother; he played the violin in an orchestra, and he was a worker and a union leader. One morning the secret police picked up him and two other union workers. They put them in a gunpowder store. There was an explosion and a fire. My brother was the first to

come out. "Don't worry about me," he said. "I'm fine. Please help my friends inside." But my brother was burned, bleeding. Pieces of his skin were falling off. He fell down right there and died. And inside they tried to save the others but they were charred black. I am the only one of my family left. I am fighting for them.

My husband was killed in the street about four in the after-noon, and I was arrested. They were very aggressive. They took off all my clothes. They covered my eyes. For twenty days they interro-gated me. They use different methods—blows, kicks, electric shocks. When the physical punishment doesn't work they try other things.

I have two children. When I was taken away, I was in the house with my two kids and they were left alone. So they used my children to try to get me to talk. They said the children were pris-oners too and they were going to torture me in front of them. And if that didn't work, they'd hurt them. Then they sent me to St. Miguel Prison for men. It was a very bad place.

On March 29, 1985, my husband and two others were picked up by the carabineros. They next day their bodies were found in a field near the airport. They all had their throats cut. I was one month pregnant when my husband was murdered. I named our daughter Manuela Libertad.

Grief lined the faces and deepened the voices of those who spoke to us, four strangers who had come from such a different place. I stumbled over an apology for taking so much of their time. They had better things to do, I said. A small dark woman who had lost five members of her family leaned across the table and looked me in the eye. "We are telling you this because you are poets. We want you to take our stories back with you so Canada will know us."

Later that week, at one of the private universities where the privi-leged send their children, we met the professor who was going to read the Spanish translations of our poems to the seventy or so students and faculty members who had come to hear us. She was a beautiful woman in her late forties, hair elegantly coiffed, a large emerald ring on her left hand. Standing with us at the front of the auditorium, she could barely make it through the Spanish version of Mary's poem about Argentina's mothers and grandmothers in the Plaza de Mayo, holding aloft photos of their disappeared loved ones. Her hands and voice trembled.

During the coffee break, the three of us alone in the washroom, she said, "I'm sorry I fell apart," as she dabbed away the mascara below her eyes and reapplied her makeup. Her husband, she told us, is one of the disappeared. She hadn't seen him in seven years. "He was a psychologist," she said, "and he talked too much." She didn't speak of him to her colleagues and wasn't sure how many of them knew. We'd been told that most of those who worked for Relatives of the Disappeared had lost their jobs. She, on the other hand, would be able to send her son and daughter to college, she wouldn't have her house taken away, she wouldn't give up her life for her husband's foolishness. "What have they been telling you?" she asked. "Chile is not as bad as you seem to think."

You ask me what it was like? Five children from this neighborhood were taken away and killed. The police said they were part of a Leopard Command sent to blow up a military station. But no, we saw them taken from their homes. They weren't blowing up anything. We found them later, buried on that hill. When we dug them up to take them to our cemetery, all their bones were broken. This is one of the things that has happened to us.

Digging for Bones

She dug until she hit bone
and hit bone again.
The bones began to talk.
She heard her daughter's voice,
her son's. They said
such simple things,
asked how she was sleeping,

if she was warm at night.
She could see where
they'd been broken,
where they'd been eaten by lime.

She cleaned the bones
and built a child.
There was only one arm
that worked, only one leg.
She took it everywhere.
It had to lean on her
to walk. She was its voice,
its ears, its eyes.

This child of broken bones,
of bones eaten by lime,
was born here in your city
on the hill where the eucalyptus grows
where the dead leave their shadows
among the blue leaves.

In all of the groups we met during our time in Chile, the women far outnumbered the men. They were the ones who wrote letters, made posters, kept files on the missing, and marched to the president's palace where they chained themselves to fences. One day I naively asked why it was women who did all this work. "Because our men are dead."

I couldn't help wondering what kind of woman I would have been had I lived the last thirteen years in this country. Would I have been the Spanish translator, secure in my job, angry at my husband, silenced because of worries about my children's future? Or would I have been the woman who named my daughter Libertad, at her birth setting a dangerous course for her and risking my life by working in the downtown cathedral to find proof of my husband's murder? How could I judge either of them when I knew that in a few weeks I'd be going home where there were no soldiers with dogs and gasoline, no gray cars pulling up to my house in the middle of the night, no anonymous men pounding on my door? And yet in spite of the darkness thrown over the country like a fetid burlap sack, the Chilean way of life was not unlike our own.

At first this thought surprised me. How could anyone speak of joyous things, sing, and fill a house with laughter with the taste of fear in his mouth? But such things happened. There were nights when Lake's husband, Pablo, gathered his band and we shared songs, *empanadas,* and El Diablo wine. The first weekend, he drove us to the Andes, and I delighted in watching Patrick climb the steep slopes with the grace he learned growing up in the Monashee Mountains in the Okanagan. One evening he and I danced on the long, scarred table that Pablo Neruda brought back from Paris and toasted his genius with his wineglasses, big enough to hold two goldfish. Every day there were sun-filled snapshots of friendship that sat alongside the images that burned through those terrible stories. And always, there was the reminder that poetry had been our passport to another's suffering and joy. With this came the knowledge of the responsibilities that privilege brings.

On our last day in Santiago, we walked down the avenues of the dead in the city's biggest cemetery. Gary had brought his camera, but an official stopped us at the gate, told us we couldn't take pictures, and followed us on a bicycle. The tombs of the wealthy loomed above us, miniature stone and marble Parthenons, large enough to house a family. The remains of the poor and the enemies of Pinochet were piled behind long walls of stucco, one on top of the other like drawers in filing cabinets crammed with dangerous secrets. Mary carried roses for Pablo Neruda; Patrick, carnations for Victor Jara. Like Neruda, Jara had been a beloved poet. He was also a musician and defender of the poor. Herded with hundreds of others into the soccer stadium during the coup, he moved among them, singing and playing his guitar to keep up their spirits. The soldiers tortured him, and when that didn't keep him quiet, they smashed his hands until they were flattened mitts of blood and bone. He still sang. Before they shot him, someone smuggled one of his songs out of the stadium: "How hard it is to sing/when I must sing of horror."

Without Hands

All the machines in the world
stop. The textile machines, the paper machines,
the machines in the mines turning stones to fire.
Without hands to touch them, spoons, forks and knives
forget their names and use, the baby is not bathed,
bread rises and overflows the bowl.
Without hands, the clacking of looms stops. The music
stops. The plums turn sweet and sticky and gather flies.

Without hands
without those beautiful conjunctions
those translators of skin, bone, hair
two eyes go blind
two pale hounds sniffing ahead and doubling back
to tell us
of hot or cold or the silk of roses after rain
are lost
two terns feeling the air in every feather
shot down.

Without hands my father doesn't plant potatoes
row on row, build a house for wrens,
or carry me
from the car to bed
when I pretend I'm sleeping.
On wash-days my mother doesn't hang clothes
on the line, she doesn't turn the pages of a book
and read out loud,
or teach me how to lace my shoes.

Without hands my small grandmother
doesn't pluck the chicken for our Sunday meal
or every evening, before she goes to sleep,
brush and brush her long white hair.

After our walk through the cemetery, our Chilean friends took us to lunch and then to the airport, and we said goodbye. As soon as the plane was in the air, I became violently ill, passed out in the washroom, and threw up across two continents. Patrick pushed me in a wheelchair through customs at the Toronto airport and to the gate for the flight to Saskatoon.

A few months after we got home, a letter arrived from Lake:

Dear Patrick and Lorna: There was a massacre here two weeks ago. Three women and four men were shut inside a house, then secret police agents moved in and shot them to pieces in cold blood. The floor was full of bullet holes—that is, the victims were either lying down when they were shot or once they fell, they were continuously fired upon. The atmosphere here at night is so sinister you hardly dare go out, buses and cars being stopped and searched by machine-gun toting police and soldiers in combat gear. Your visit was such a wonderful parenthesis in all this, such a break, such a breath of what life is supposed to be like, it seems unreal now as I look back on it.

My illness was more than a bug I had picked up during our last meal in Santiago. It was my body's response to what had settled in my bones, its way of speaking out when words would not suffice. One morning, I found the running shoes I hadn't worn since our walk through the cemetery. It had been raining that day, and the soles of my runners were still packed with mud. With a stick, I dug out the hard dirt and let it fall into our garden. Earth from the avenues of the dead, carried in my shoes from Santiago to Saskatoon. I expected the flowers in that one spot to come up bloody, but a month later they bloomed the same yellow as the marigolds around them. That spring, the sweet peas began their slow climb toward the sun, our cat lay in the shade of rhubarb leaves, watching the sparrows fall to the feeder, and we settled into our books and our long walks in the early evening, the trees on every corner merely trees.

I Was a Swami in Mexico

Linda Pelton

 I called my mother from Toronto and told her that I had left the yoga cult I had been living in for thirteen years. "I don't believe it!" she said. She didn't believe it because not only had I devoted a third of my life to the cult, I had recently become a swami, renouncing the world, including my marriage, to give it all to the Divine.

Now I had escaped. My mother said, "Someday you should write an article about it called 'I Was a Swami in Mexico.'" I had been sent to Mexico for two years, and that was my good luck, because it was Mexico that allowed me to wake up and realize the kind of abusive organization with which I was so intimately involved.

Mexico. The very word still holds magic for me. I was sent, with two other women, to run a yoga resort in the Yucatán. Our pretty and very pink house sat snugly in the middle of a walled garden full of fruit trees. Guests came from Canada and the U.S. to take yoga classes and to be escorted to the spectacular Mayan ruins that are so plentiful in the area. My reasonably fluent Spanish and my love of speaking the language meant that I had the most interaction with Mexican people— in spite of the restrictions placed on me by the organization—a swami, by definition, is not supposed to socialize or to form friendships. These restrictions were beginning to feel suffocating even before I left the ashram, or spiritual mother center, in Canada. Now that I was in Mexico, a country where relationships come before anything else, I was becoming acutely aware of the coldness of the life I had chosen. I hungrily—and guiltily—drank in the warmth and exuberance of Mexico. Whether I was buying tortillas at the tiny local factory or visiting the doctor, the business at hand came second. I realized even grocery shopping could be more than a tedious chore as I watched shoppers boogie and cha-cha down the aisles to the Mexican-style Muzak.

I'm not dedicated enough, not committed enough, not spiritual enough, I said to myself as I felt my heart aching to be a part of this vitality. So I stepped up my spiritual practice, getting up at 4 a.m. to do four hours of silent meditation every morning for several months—I thought that the spiritual equivalent of a seismic blast might rid me of the maya, or illusion, that I felt was drawing me away from the spiritual path.

The intensive practices worked, but not in the way I had thought they would. They dispelled my illusion, all right, but it was soon apparent that what was illusory was the idea that the problem was all mine, that I was just not spiritual enough, not committed enough. I found myself deeply questioning both the tenets of the organization— the ashram—and in particular the integrity of the guru.

One day I visited the Mayan site of Uxmál, which some say is architecturally the most beautiful site in America. It was early in the morning and raining slightly when I arrived. Hardly anyone was there. It was still, quiet, and misty as I approached the very first building, the Temple of the Magician. I walked up the steps of the temple. The stairway is lined with the faces of the rain god, Chac— with twelve images of his face on either side of the stairs. The effect is powerful and imposing. At the top of the steps is the doorway to the interior of the temple, and this doorway is in the form of the wide-open and fierce mouth of Chac. My guidebook said that this unusual doorway may have been constructed as a passageway for spiritual initiates who, by entering, were surrendering themselves to be symbolically eaten by their god. As I walked though the doorway it struck me that I had, as a disciple, allowed myself to be "eaten" by my guru. In the ancient tradition of yoga, the disciple surrenders her will to the guru's. But in my guru's hands, I suddenly saw, this tradition had been disfigured, providing an excuse for a disturbed personality to completely control and manipulate—in a sense "devour"—other people.

Then I wondered further, about the wisdom of the whole tradi-tion, the wisdom of anyone submitting to the will of another. I won-dered whether spirituality was in a sense simpler than I had thought, whether it had less to do with a guru and an organization and a set of beliefs, and more to do with how one led one's life.

I had been taking classes to learn how to speak Spanish more fluently at a school where all the teachers were Mexican. One of my favorite teachers confided to the class that he had been in the Catholic seminary for some years. He had left because he had come to believe that real spirituality has nothing to do with organized religion. As he put it, "True religion is of the heart. Some of the best people I know say that they are not religious."

In fact, in a land where Catholicism has supposedly such a strong hold, I was constantly surprised by how many of the Mayan people refused to be chained to it. One day I was driving along a country road when I saw a remarkable little building on a promontory. It was entirely covered with carvings. I stopped and spoke to the man who was cutting wood outside. He said he was a sculptor who used this building as his store in the summer, and taught Mayan art in a local high school during the rest of the year—the only place in the Yucatán where Mayan art, sculpture, and drawing were taught. When I asked about the symbolism of the carvings and told him I was a student of yoga, he began to talk. He spoke of awaiting the second coming of Kukulcán, the plumed serpent god who was to restore the lost kingdom. He revealed that many believe that this second coming will occur soon since the persecution of the Mayan religion has passed and even the government is encouraging the restoration of Mayan pyramids and temples. He said his great-grandfather had been a Mayan priest and had gone to Quintana Roo and then Belize for twenty years to escape the persecution. His family had kept a book of the Maya in secret for years. He said there were other such books in other pueblos.

Then I asked him how he sees the Catholic Church in relation to his Mayan beliefs. He acknowledged the role of the church but said that the church is "domestic: it doesn't develop the mind." He said the Maya believe that God is time and space, and that the individual gods are mediators. Mayan ceremonies are still held—there would soon be a ceremony in honor of Chac, the rain god. But the religion is no longer organized, so the ceremonies happen spontaneously and one never knows where or when they will occur.

In Mexico things merge, have no defining boundaries, are both/and and not either/or, at least spiritually. Rigid ways of thinking, straight lines, and hard boundaries dissolve in the shimmer of the sub-tropical heat. After my years of submitting to conformist thinking in the cult, these ideas burst on me like a liberation.

Not far from the town where I lived was Ixamál, reputedly once the most sacred city in the Mayan world. It had been the home of the legendary Ixamná who is said to have arrived mysteriously from the sea to create the Mayan civilization by teaching the people language, medicine, and rituals. Ixamál contains the third-largest pyramid in all of Latin America: the foundation is the size of a city block. And it's right in the middle of the modern town, with modern homes built smack up against it. It was sad to see that most of the superstructure was gone, much of it apparently used by the Spanish to build the nearby Catholic monastery. But workmen were everywhere, and it was clear that intensive work was going on to restore the pyramid. Restoration was also rapid in the ruins of Dzibilchaltún, the site nearest our house. Every time I visited it, more pyramids were rising out of the rubble.

I felt that the symbolism of Ixamál was speaking directly to me. By submitting to the guru's will, to her thoughts and demands, I had allowed my own spirituality and values, like the pyramid, to be dismantled and used to further her desires. But I was beginning to excavate my own values from the ruins; it seemed that my own identity had been there all along. I was discovering that, for me, as my language teacher had said, "True religion is of the heart."

As my involvement with and love of Mexico deepened, my dissatisfaction with my life as a swami, as a disciple, as an "ashramite," grew. I returned, very troubled, to Canada for what was to be a couple of weeks' vacation. Once back in Canada I realized the extent to which living in such a totally different culture had allowed me to see with new eyes. I saw that friends and family were often more honest and less fearful than my cult colleagues. They laughed more and didn't worry about displeasing some higher authority, be it God or the guru.

This made them able to be kinder and more compassionate and more true to themselves than my fellow ashramites, and than I was myself.

The first ten days of my vacation I spent in eastern Canada. Then I was to fly west to spend time at the ashram before returning to Mexico. While in eastern Canada, I awoke one morning to the very clear knowledge that I would leave the cult. I found it was not something I needed to consider: I had made the decision at a level of myself that simply knew. Would I have left if I had not spent two years in Mexico? I hope so, but it probably would have taken me much longer. The shock of a new culture, and the resulting new perspectives it brings, allowed me to see the guru, the organization, the tradition, and myself more objectively. But it was really the Mexican ways in particular that helped me to wake up—the lack of rigidity, the heart.

I returned to the ashram and to Mexico, but only to say goodbye. This was difficult because I knew so well the "deal": no one is allowed to speak or write to any who leave if they leave disaffected. To them I was as good as dead. When my husband left the ashram two years before me, the guru remarked that his leaving "the path" and "the work" meant that he would likely be reincarnated as a worm. She was not joking.

My husband and I reunited, and ten years later our relationship is better than ever. I took a graduate degree, and love my work. I reestablished old friendships and family ties that I had let slide during my thirteen years of cult life. I felt like a child discovering the world—full of wonder, trepidation, and excitement.

Spiritually? I cannot imagine joining any spiritual organization again. Many former cult members are of the same mind. But my spiritual life is alive and well, although less arrogant, less certain. I miss that certainty. It was reassuring to have definite beliefs. But it was not worth the price.

I have not been back to Mexico. Maybe someday. But I am grateful to its amazing, crazy, gentle, wild culture—a culture that embraces and celebrates life and relationships. A culture that shape-changes when you try to pin it down. I was asleep, in a trance, and Mexico, with great gentleness and good humor, shook me until I woke up.

The Rule

Alison Pick

"Going West?" is the title of his email. From my home in southern Ontario, I trace the blue line of highway on the map all the way out to Saskatchewan. I'm going to live and write at a Benedictine monastery for several months. I'll work on the farm in exchange for room and board. David is planning the same, he writes. Am I interested in sharing the gas?

Brother Peter grew up on a farm not far from the abbey. He sees his mother once a month; his father died many years ago. I ask if he feels that the monks have become his family. He looks surprised that I've even asked. He answers, "Yes. Oh yes."

It occurs to me that I don't know what it means to be a Benedictine monk. I can answer *some* of my friends' questions: *Do they have shaved heads?* (No.) *Do they speak?* (Yes.) But *What do they wear under their robes?* is just the beginning of things I don't know. On a trip into town, Father Douglas points out a house he owned when he first arrived in the province. David suggests he might have kept it for nights in the city, and Father Douglas says that a monk can't own property. The Rule of Saint Benedict: *For their needs, they are to look to the father of the monastery, and are not allowed anything which the abbot has not given.* There is a monk in charge of the plumbing and one responsible for maintaining the abbey's charitable status. A monk organizes the archive and another staffs the library. When my Internet connection falters, Brother Cam leans over my keyboard in tight jeans, his hair past his shoulders. Rumor has it he used to be a rock star.

The monks eat meat. Some smoke. Some tell us secrets: this is a curious development, and it happens only after some time has passed and they begin to trust us. The monks know they shouldn't be telling

101

us these things; they know that *we* know they shouldn't be doing it. Still, we seem to be prime candidates for confidences. No vow of stability binds us to the abbey forever. Brother Robert, a dark-bearded, fast-talking, pool-shooting monk: "Brother Paul loves ta shoot. Shot a *cat* the other day. Said she was eatin' our garbage. So I sez to him, I sez, '*So what? So what if she's eatin' our garbage? Plenty of that to go round in this place.*'" Later, in choir, black-robed and showered, his high voice is clear, like a bell.

The monks pray five times daily, and I join them for 5:30 vespers. Every day for several months equals more time in church than over my previous whole life. I am not Christian. My grandparents on my father's side were Jewish; they died in Auschwitz in 1943. Mine is a history of repressed loss and grief, a box of unopened darkness passed down from my grandmother to me.

We read to know we're not alone, and the same may be said for communal prayer. There is something comforting about worship sung together, the ritual of it, the habit. Vespers feels natural, perhaps because of the high value Benedictines place on words. The noon meal (dinner, it's called) proceeds in silence, with the abbot or prior reading aloud from works on theology, scripture and culture, gender and the modern church. When invited to join the monks for supper in their dining room I stop at the small podium, to leaf through the books and bibles. One of the reasons I'm here is to complete a poetry manuscript. As first books often are, mine is a poetic map: the intersecting lines of history, intention, luck. One of the map's coordinates is the Holocaust. These poems come from three generations of gestation, fully formed and bloody, hard to birth, midwived by the great-grandmother who survived. She taught my father that it is not the specific religion that is important but what it leads to: people in community depending on each other, a sense of the sacred in the everyday. This is what vespers gives me. The Rule of Saint Benedict: *Let us sing the psalms in such a way that our minds are in harmony with our voices.*

Our usual job: sorting vegetables into pails according to size. We sing to pass the time, all of the songs we can think of with the word *blue*, or *river*, or *child*. When Brother Peter joins us we sing Christmas carols, though it's only October, our voices wobbly in the long light.

Silent night, holy night ...

David holds up two carrots that have grown together in the earth, spiraled around each other so it's impossible to pull them apart.

"Seeded too close together maybe," says Brother Peter.

Under the trailer, David passes it to me.

Father Douglas gets back from his bone marrow operation at one, hobbling slightly, leaning on his cane. He is the monk responsible for the monastery's guests, and despite his convalescent condition he chairs a board meeting, then heads downtown in the communal truck to pick up twenty-two new beds for the guest wing. I sit down with him for a coffee at four. He tells me about a woman from a nearby village who has asked him to translate her life's journals from Slovak into English. He's just finished the first box—at four hours a night it took him eight months—and is worried he won't live long enough to finish the project. His last will and testament is in an envelope, taped to his office wall.

The phone rings and he excuses himself. The Beef Producers of Regina want to book a weekend retreat. It rings again: a group of Jungian analysts from Alberta. Again, and it's a youth group leader confirming this afternoon's arrival. Sixty teenagers will take over the place: discussion, Ping-Pong, rowdy sing-alongs until three in the morning. The Rule of Saint Benedict: *Let all guests be received as Christ.*

Brother Robert, David, and I are cleaning the machine shop: stacking chairs, pulling sheets of plastic from piles of springs and pulleys, extracting the guts of an old typewriter from several inches of dust. Tom the janitor comes in the side door. Robert jerks his head at an engine in the corner of the shed.

"Hey Tom," he says. "This here engine bigger than the one you got at home?"

Tom sizes it up.

"Naw," he says, "mine's *way* bigger."

Brother Robert spits on the floor.

David and I exchange glances, trying to decide if they're joking. They're not.

Brother Robert must not have noticed my shoulders because when it comes time to move the heavy equipment he jerks his head at me. "You sand that there piece of wood," he says, motioning to an old scrap picture frame shoved in the corner of the shop. "David, you come with me."

"She's just as strong as I am."

I fight off the urge to kiss David right there.

Robert looks at both of us a little sharply.

"*Men*," he says, "have stronger upper bodies than *women*."

This is not up for discussion.

I rub a flimsy piece of sandpaper across the wood, peel back the varnish like skin off a sunburn. David helps with the bureaus and then Robert shows him two pieces of a fence that need to be welded back together. David in coveralls and a visor, a shower of sparks in a high arc over his shoulder. I long for Brother Peter, who expects me to lift metal pipe, haul scrap wood through mud, back up the tractor with a trailer hitched on.

When the job is done David tells Brother Robert that I've been on a one-hundred-day canoe trip, that I've portaged and paddled the width of three provinces with all my existence on my back. Robert lifts his mask. "Wow," he says. "I hope she didn't take that thing I said about upper body strength seriously."

I love being a hermit. A single bed, a simple gas stove, two windows facing the prairie. My cabin, traditionally reserved for monks in deep contemplation, is at the edge of the forest at the south end of the property. On my way here I pass between two rows of pine trees, planted only a few feet apart. They have grown strong and high, a natural corridor with branches for walls and a bed of needles for a floor. On a small knotted branch at the entrance hangs a wooden sign that says "Silence."

The Rule of Saint Benedict: *There are times when good words are to be left unsaid.* When David and I approach the woods, no matter how involved in conversation we are, we stop speaking. I like to think of the many pairs of feet that have walked this path through knee-deep snow, through the long light of late afternoon. Through a silence in which the sound of a heartbeat is the loudest sound there is.

Saturday is free, and David and I drive into town to do errands. Brother Peter has to pick up a lock, so we invite him to join us. "We'll just be a few minutes," David says.

Three o'clock. Our first stop is the locksmith, a man in an undershirt who hands over a small paper bag. Next, the post office. I buy a book of stamps, three big envelopes. David buys postage for a package to Ontario. Then the photo store, where I reach for my wallet and realize I don't have any cash. I need to run to the bank machine. Brother Peter waits on the sidewalk.

Three forty. I take out a hundred dollars, throw the slip away without looking at the balance. We pay for the photos and cross the street to the grocery store. Luxury items: oranges, broccoli, bok choy, dark chocolate, all this despite an abundance of food at the abbey. Our plastic bags strain their handles. Brother Peter holds his lock, tells us he's going back to the car. Four thirty. For the next forty minutes we troop up and down the remaining streets buying vitamins, Walkman batteries, printer paper, ink cartridges, potato chips, tampons, licorice. Solemn vows mean that monks give up personal property. They get a small allowance each month, and room and board is provided. Other than that, they live on what they harvest from the land. When we get back to the car Brother Peter is waiting patiently. We load bag after bag into the trunk. "Brother Peter, teach us!" David says.

Skirting the monk quarters I hear a voice: "Ouch!" I peer around the corner, expecting an emergency. Instead, I see Father Lance clinging to his bedrails. A bib, his white hair thin and baby fine. Father Lance has reached the place in life's circle where old age returns to meet infancy. Sometimes in vespers there is this same sort of scream-ing, his head snapping up like a child from a nightmare: "I can't move!" he'll yell, chin to the heavens, or, "Who's there? Who's there? WHO'S THERE?" The first time I heard it I wanted him quieted. I wanted to absorb the palpable silence, the rows of monks lined up like blackbirds on wire, the psalms that seemed to be singing themselves back and forth between the pews. But Father Lance has been living at the abbey for seventy years—he's almost a hundred years old, and this is his home. When the service is over Father Adam pushes his wheel-chair to the dining room, feeds him dinner like a mother with a new-born. The Rule of Saint Benedict: *Care of the sick must rank above and before all else.*

Brother Peter works with us in the afternoon. Standing on the lawn behind the car garage, we sort through a trailer of carrots, divid-ing them for the cooks into small, medium and large. I pass David three carrots that have grown together, like a braid.

"A family," I say.

David asks Brother Peter when he knew he wanted to become a monk. He tells us that after a long period of waiting and listening, God's intentions simply became clear to him.

"Did you ever think about marriage?"

"Weeeell, noooo," he says in his characteristic drawl. "Not reeeeal-ly." Although he does tell us a bit about a girlfriend he had in his early twenties …

Then he asks, "Have *you* ever thought of getting married?"

David and I sneak a smile.

"Too soon to tell," I say.

When the vegetables are done Brother Peter drives us back to the college. Past the gymnasium, the old priory, the chapel's gold bell, the truck bumps over gravel. Past the pump house, the greenhouse, the machine shop, alongside the rows of newly cut corn. Brother Peter stops beside the tap and David hops out, grabbing our water bottles from the front seat. Peter and I wait in the idling truck. It's the first time I've seen him sit still.

"What about the novices who didn't stay on at the abbey after their three-year trial period?"

I'm imagining them going out into the world with dreams of families, children, a house to themselves, a bathtub with jets, a car. Instead, Brother Peter says, "They felt the Lord calling them in another direction." His faith is as refreshing, as strangely clear, as the water David brings back for us to drink.

In November, Diane, an author I love, comes to speak at the college attached to the abbey. After two months in a community of men I am overjoyed to see her at the dinner table. She's talking about a group of young nuns in Japan who use their spirituality as a springboard for social activism. I am deeply interested; I am also content to close my eyes and simply listen to another woman's voice.

She reads from a novel about World War II and the distorting influence of time on memory. Then she reads from a new manuscript of poems: intensely ecological, the language runs from her tongue like the last pristine river. She reads as if words are on the verge of extinction.

Afterward, during the question-and-answer period, hands fly up like finches from a field. *When did she know she wanted to be a poet?* (When a university professor told her she'd never make it as an actress.) *How does she write a poem?* (Writing is mostly waiting, feeling where the poem wants to go. She tries to "thoroughly scrub content from the fabric of a poem.") *Does she take notes before beginning?* (No, unless it's a sequence of poems in which case she might take a few. But no.)

A young man with a plaid shirt and a cross around his neck raises his hand. "I have a question about your first reading," he says. "You said the heroine was named Susan. And her lover was Lucy. Am I correct in thinking that the characters are both *women?*"

"Yes," she says clearly, and waits for the next question, which is about the intersection of politics and writing and her experience as a feminist writer in the Canadian publishing market. She describes a close group of writers who have supported, mentored, and been mentored by her. She stresses the importance of finding a community to share writing with, and of reading the literary tradition out of which you are writing. "Find your foremothers and read everything they've written," she says to me later, over tea. Her words are like water on a dry, dry prairie.

At the edge of the parking lot, we're trying on hip waders, preparing for an afternoon in the dugout. Brother Andrew, no more than five feet tall, emerges from the kitchen wearing yellow plastic kitchen gloves, a framed photo under his arm. He has shown us, on a map, his home in Vietnam—he and his family were "boat people" in the mid-1980s. The sixty-five-foot waves would have drowned them if the ship's captain had not known to follow the swells, diving into them instead of fighting back.

A good philosophy in general, he told us.

Peter: "Whatcha got there?"

Brother Andrew bashfully lifts a painting of the Virgin Mary.

Peter rolls his eyes and winks.

"Oh, *her* again!"

We've been here three months and my thoughts on the Catholic Church haven't changed much: hierarchical, patriarchal, prescribed. I won't find one to go to back home in Ontario. But we're here, and I'm grateful. I go.

Afterward, I walk the trails at the forested end of the abbey. The woods are thick, deciduous, and clouds of mosquitoes are billowing out of the trees like black pirate-ship sails. I slap them off my neck and hands, staining my clothes with my own blood. Deep in the woods there's a green plastic armchair, almost invisible from the trail. A small man in a baseball cap and sneakers is perched there, staring down at his belly. He lets the bugs land on him, only occasionally brushing them away.

"Hello, Alison!" he says, and he must see the confusion on my face because he introduces himself. "Father Roman. Easy to remember because I'm *Roman Catholic!*"

He hoots with laughter, as if it's the first time he's said this.

THE RULE

Alison Pick

This is the man who said mass this morning, in a purple robe heavy with gold trim, his height enhanced by several feet of pulpit. Now, at perfect ease in the swarm of bugs, he motions me over and points down at his stomach. A small potbelly strains his buttons. Several mosquitoes biting through the shirt. And then I see what he's looking at: a transparent insect with tracing-paper wings, a thin line of green through its delicate body like ink through the shaft of a pen.

Father Roman smiles up at me, careful not to disturb the wisp of life balanced on his stomach. "It's a miracle," he says simply. And I see that he's right.

The Rule of Saint Benedict: *We believe the divine presence is everywhere.*

A Healing Beauty

Charlotte Caron

 If I were to write this essay as a travelogue, it would be very short. It would begin with something like *I drove from Saskatoon to Collegeville, Minnesota*. It would describe a trip across rich prairie farmland, across a border, across a culture. I would name the towns we passed through: Lanigan, Mozart, Foxwarren, Gladstone, Ste. Agathe, Fergus Falls, Montrose, and a hundred others. It would tell of the shift from fields of wheat and canola to fields of corn. It would record the tiny Canadian churches—Protestant and Orthodox—gradually giving way to enormous American Catholic churches that dominated the skyline. It would note the flags I saw everywhere south of the border. It would describe the stops for meals and nights along the way. That would be it: one paragraph to spell out the trip.

But the trip was something more. Perhaps one fact—that if you look on most maps for Collegeville you won't find it—gives a hint about our Eden-like destination. Slightly mythical, slightly mystical, real and yet timeless, a space marked only by beauty and the ringing of the monastery bells. I traveled to a new home for a year and to new ways of being at home for the rest of my days. The exterior landscape changed. The interior soulscape opened.

I like subtlety. Anything noisy, blatant, or crass irritates me. I notice little things, the nuances of my environment. I need space for that kind of osmosis. That is why sabbaticals work for me. They provide time to sleep, to dream, to find again creative cracks, to follow passions, to discover difference, to discern futures, and to follow body and spirit rhythms. Traveling into unknowing: unknown places with unknown people, writing without knowing ahead what you will write, never knowing what revelations will come but trusting they will. Living in openness. Valuing the moment at hand.

The Canadian Oxford Paperback Dictionary defines *sabbatical* as an adjective, "(of leave) granted at intervals to a professor or teacher for study or travel, originally every seventh year." As a noun it means "a period of sabbatical leave." A period of study or travel. Or both. The word sabbatical relates to Sabbath, both in its religious sense and in its meaning as a time of rest. So sabbatical: travel, study, spirit, rest.

Travel

I do not like traveling at the best of times. I don't like being out of Canada—different money, miles instead of kilometers, no medicare. Going across the border with a carful of possessions. So I am grateful when we arrive safely in Collegeville after an easy and uneventful border crossing and trip.

The Institute for Ecumenical and Cultural Research in Collegeville offers space for sabbaticals. Each year about ten scholars are invited, from varying places around the world and from varying religious perspectives, to live in community. Housing and offices are provided for the scholars and their families in a rural setting in central Minnesota, at the site of the world's largest men's Benedictine monastic community. St. John's University, a private Catholic men's university (now with nineteen hundred students) has been in this location since 1857. Just down the road, in St. Joseph, the women's College of St. Benedict, with its two thousand students, is operated by Benedictine women.

Our apartment living room has floor-to-ceiling windows looking out on a lake about ten yards away, parquet floors with area rugs, a dark brick fireplace that separates the living room and kitchen, two bedrooms, and a study with a couch. Our unit is one of ten in the Ecumenical Institute complex, which also includes a building with offices for the institute staff, a lounge and reading area, and a small chapel. Scholars' offices are a twenty-minute walk away on the campus.

The move goes smoothly. A few days later someone asks me if I am settled in with all my boxes for house and office unpacked and organized. I say that all my belongings are settled—but I'm not! It takes a while to ease the unreality and lostness that always surround traveling to a new environment. Yet I am happy to be in retreat this year in this idyllic little place. It is amazing how removed from the noise of traffic, the busy days of work, and the multiple interactions of daily life this place is.

Occasionally I am reminded that I am here as a foreigner, a guest in another country whose views are not my own. As a feminist, I thrive on social analysis and visions of a peaceful world where all people live with sufficient resources for well-being, but I have to learn when to speak out and when to bite my tongue in a country that envisions itself as the most important in the universe. No news is reported in depth, and people actually appear to believe the minuscule news clips that seem designed to frighten them with the creation of new enemies. A week is given to remembrances and memorials for September 11, 2001. Americans think I have gone mad when I suggest that the real disaster was not September 11 but October 5. I have to explain that the U.S. attack on Afghanistan on October 5 ultimately brought much more destruction and devastation to the world than the loss of two buildings and twenty-seven hundred lives in New York and Washington.

In February we listen to endless news reports about how bad the Iraqis are and watch President Bush's glowing face on TV as he pontificates about how good Americans are to take care of the whole world. Now the propaganda on North Korea, in need of an American "cleanup," is under way. I have no illusions about either the Iraqi or North Korean governments being perfect, but waking up to a half-hour each morning on public radio about the latest threat from Iraq (even though there has been nothing new for days) is very difficult.

On March 19, 2003, I write in my journal, "The war against Iraq is likely to start tomorrow. It is disturbing to be in U.S.A. at the moment. The media are all full of war with no alternative voices allowed, and there is not a sniff of news about anything but the war. As if the rest of the world does not exist. The obsessiveness is very distressing. I can hardly write about it because it is so awful. It was good to be in Canada for a few days last week and to hear what is going on in the world with a little more clarity. We are in rural Minnesota, but the fear is present even here."

The world went on while we were enjoying our safe haven. And the war will continue long after we return to Canada. One of my American colleagues tells me she is surprised. She thought Canadians were all wannabe Americans. She never knew that we have different values, politics and culture. I was not far from home: to travel from Saskatoon to Collegeville is a matter of only a few miles, but to travel to a different mindset is a very long trip.

Yet voices for peace are present. The monks and sisters have the same prayer ritual, day after day after day. Wars do not change it. They take a long view and pray for peace. They engage in iconoclastic acts to break the pervasive molds around them. Brother Paul's act is small in light of the world. He has a fish house out on the lake each winter, as do thousands of Minnesotans. Most people use their fish houses for fishing, drinking, and escape. Brother Paul serves sliced oranges and tea in china cups with a red tablecloth and reads poetry to guests in his fish house. He models a different way of life. Brother Paul's fish house represents a way for monks to defy the culture around them and offer grace.

Travel. Crossing borders. Dwelling in a climate of the creation of fear. Finding the grace of tea and poetry on cold winter days. Sabbatical: travel, study, spirit, rest.

Study

During each sabbatical, I write. This time I am writing about loss in women's lives and the spiritual resources that emerge. At the Ecumenical Institute, scholars have no teaching or institutional service responsibilities; we devote ourselves to full-time research. We are required only to be part of a focused community of scholars and to participate in some seminars and public lectures. The university provides office space for scholars. Each day I retreat to my little office two floors underground. Some people do not like being in "the dungeon," but I love the protective cocoon without interruption or distraction. I enjoy days of no meetings and no disturbances, days when I can choose what I am going to do when I get up in the morning. The open, unstructured time is a treasure. It is a great contrast to the busy work life I lead back in Saskatoon.

I love having time to think and putter and get into creative states. I go down the road to an Episcopal House of Prayer to a retreat on writing spiritual autobiographies. The leader's morning pun is that we would start with a prayer *to compose ourselves.* The remarkable amount of art on campus arises from the Benedictine beliefs, which advocate of a mix of work, worship and beauty. The mix creates an environment of sacred space. Mythical and mystical. Freedom to follow one's passions—to work hard and to relax. It fosters an identity not based on work. I write *to compose myself.*

The days find a rhythm. I spend hours watching the birds and animals. Slow pace—no stress. I have menopausal symptoms: anxiety attacks when I wake in the night—but in the end they make me laugh because I have nothing to be anxious about. In ordinary life I could always come up with something to fret about if I wanted to.

As the days go on my heart shifts. For many years I have worked happily at the same place. I have filled many different roles in the college and have seen the institution through many changes. It is hard work trying to keep a small school going as a vibrant and creative educational center, with pressures from every side to do more with less. The sheer volume of work is too much. This sabbatical becomes discernment time to sort out the next phase of life. The Collegeville days of little pressure and low stress make clear how much energy I give to work, and I do not want to gear myself back up to the pace of meetings and negotiations for institutional survival the job demands. I send in my resignation.

Life with the monks and the beauty of sun on winter snow and bright red cardinals, chatty blue jays, and ever-hungry woodpeckers keep me grounded. My work goes well—chapter by chapter to completion.

Sabbatical: study, spirit, rest, travel.

Spirit

The time in Collegeville is about *being* rather than *doing*. It is true that I have a book manuscript to show for my time. But what we will remember is our state of being. The pleasant rhythm of the days, with no need for alarm clocks or daybooks. Watching the birds while eating breakfast or supper; laughing at the squirrels; walking to the office noticing the blueness of the sky, the circling of the eagles, the frosty air of winter and the fresh green of spring. Emerging from protective and quiet office spaces at the end of the day, surprised that the world outside looks different than when we entered in the morning. Happy evenings at home without papers to mark or classes to prepare. Visiting. Playing with the neighbor children. Being still. Having naps. Absorbing hospitality. Being present to the moment. Being present to the self. Being present to God. Being restored by the beauty of the days and space: being. Being underlies the experience, and long after the books are published and daily life resumed, it will be the cell memory of being that holds us.

A friend, Anne Marie, noted that we had made our place homey. We did it very simply—a few small touches of beauty. But it is our home. This is our life. We have awareness of life and of wanting it to be full and beautiful. Life will be shorter than we want. So we need this year to be as perfect as possible. As full of healing beauty, of healing from the bruises of our last few years, of renewing work and deep love as is possible.

The beauty restores. We watch the reds, oranges, and yellows of autumn leaves give way to white blankets of snow. Then slowly the temperatures climb and dandelions pop out and the loons dance on the lake waters. The leaves hint green, ready to burst forth.

In my project, I read about a woman's cancer treatment. Tears well up for Gwenna. I try not to cry too much—after all, I am in my office with the door open, but the tears are there. The sadness that comes from reading other people's stories, and the sadness of knowing that the future will be worse. We wonder if we should be doing something else—eating better, organizing our lives differently, planning something. Yet I believe at a deep level that just watching the squirrels and birds is as healing as it gets. Not putting too much effort into the days. Letting them flow with healing energy. Bathing in beauty, living in gratitude for each day with her, loving fully and richly, and being present seem right. We do those things she wants to do with her life. I watch her walk, play her flute, talk to the squirrels, and enjoy the sunshine. The days are good.

Sabbatical: spirit, rest, travel, study.

Rest

Early in the year, I wake in the night with a great deal of anxiety. I have started to think about my writing project on the subject of loss. I have re-read all the interviews and material. In the night I begin to grapple with the losses I have experienced since my last sabbatical. And of course there have been many. I know the writing will come. I need to trust that it will be published because it will speak.

It is a gift to be in a community that has hospitality as one of its missions. The staff people at the institute itself, as well as the monks, are very clear about what it means to welcome people and offer hospitality. The welcoming luncheon sat everyone in just the right place—foreigners at the head table, Gwenna beside the center's director. Food was unobtrusively provided for me that was appropriate for my dietary needs because of allergies. The hospitality is not accidental—institutional care is given to send a strong message that we are welcome here as a couple, and I am respected as a person with special needs. They offer me a rest from the usual fight to be sure that my food is safe to eat and to convince others that it really is necessary to provide food for me that I can eat. I am grateful. Grateful to be reminded that it is not too great an expectation of a place to do these little things and to honor people's lives in clear and subtle ways. It is refreshing to be reminded that institutions can actually set behavioral norms and live by them in decency and respect. It restores the soul for us to be treated like ordinary people, like anyone else, as worthy of respect by our existence.

We could go to a friend's home for the holidays as we often do in winter. I resist. We do not go. Our days in this mythical, mystical home in the holiday season are spent watching cardinals, woodpeckers, and squirrels, enjoying the sun, and doing jigsaw puzzles. I do not push myself. I need the chance just to be—to rest and absorb the beauty and to recognize the heaviness of the years.

One spring Sunday morning we do not go to church. Gwenna has a cold and is tired, so when the alarm goes off, she nestles back down. I listen to the rain on the skylight and drift in and out of sleep. I snuggle around her back thinking how I love that space. It is my safe space to return to in dreams, in memory, as well as each night. Such a perfect morning—no reason to get up, no pressures, just pleasure in the moment. Drifting in and out of sleep. Safe and beloved.

We love the beauty: the stillness of the lake at suppertime and just before dusk; the blue heron, wood ducks, teals, frogs, and muskrats. The red-tailed hawks and eagles fly high; nuthatches, sparrows, juncos, and wild turkeys come to the lawn. Deer feed on the acorns. Gray squirrels chase each other wildly, storing food and just scurrying. Chipmunks live in holes in the tree. Mudhens one day—they have become so rare that I could not believe I was seeing a flock of them. Crows and blackbirds, too, flocking and squawking. The beauty calms and restores.

For some reason Gwenna's cancer seems less threatening in this environment of beauty and love. Each day is a gift and each day is full of love and beauty. It is agreeable not to be present to the inevitability of death at every moment. Presence and love are much more real.

Sabbatical: rest, travel, study, spirit.

The trip was something more than a few miles across the prairie. Most maps do not show Collegeville, with its mythical and mystical quality, real and yet timeless, a space marked by beauty and the ringing of the monastery bells. Travel to a new home for a year and to new ways of being at home in life. The exterior landscape changes. The interior soulscape opens.

Ways of Knowing

Jan Mackie

Traveling. Did it change my life? There is really no way to know the answer to this question, as I now know no other life than this one full of travel that I stumbled upon. The life I'd known before traveling was quite unshaped, unformed, determined largely by family and societal expectations. A life that in retrospect did not seem to me to hold the potential to include the mind-altering experiences of being immersed in other cultures, other landscapes, other ways of understanding the world.

I cannot recall the moment or event or feeling or dare or escapist thought that catapulted me out of the community of higher learning in which I was struggling and into a new world; a vast world, in which I could begin to reclaim my trust in my intuition, a world that would permanently reinforce my sense of awe for the earth and the creatures that inhabit it. I do remember a challenge by a friend who once said to me jokingly, and with a touch of disdain, "You'll never leave this place." This place was suburban Windsor, Ontario, and we were eighteen (or thereabouts) in the mid-sixties. Perhaps it was that scorn ringing in my ears that pushed me over the edge into territories that I could not have imagined. Perhaps it was simply meant to be. Thirty-five years later I have a clearer sense that by traveling I gained the only education that was possible for me. Information, knowledge, understanding enter *through* the body and by tasting, touching, hearing, smelling, and sensing the world, the full range of life, from horrific to ecstatic, I gained the knowledge I needed. My body inhaled it like a hungry wolf.

Europe, and then Turkey and Iran, gave me new tastes to savor, but it was in Afghanistan, India, and Nepal that I was transported to another mental space, wakened to other ways of knowing. Thirty-five years later, I am still embarrassed when I remember having to ask a companion to show me where Afghanistan was on the map as we sat waiting for our Afghan visas in Munich. I knew so little, and I understood virtually nothing.

After much hard travel overland from Munich to Tehran and onward, we arrived in Afghanistan in the middle of a cold December night. Our weary bodies had been jostled about in the back of a lorry, and we finally laid them down to rest in the kind of simple and bare hotel room to which those who travel with next to no money become accustomed. It was the beginning of the holiday at the end of Ramadan. We had been desperate to make it to Herat and not be stuck in the tiny Iranian border town on the other side of the forty-mile-wide no-man's land that separated Iran and Afghanistan. The holiday lasts for three days, and all commerce and transport across the border ceases during those days of festivities. We slept deeply and awoke at mid-morning, groggy and cold in the dark, bare room. Hearing much activity in the streets below we pulled open the shutters to have a look.

It was as if the pictures in my childhood Bible had sprung to life. I was pitched back in time two thousand years. The horses were decorated with lush weavings. Elaborate tassels swung from side to side as they trotted along, pulling newly painted carts ready for passengers. Everyone was out, dressed in the finery that had been meticulously stitched by clusters of women in courtyards during the month of fasting that preceded the festivities. The bright reds and deep burgundy of the fabrics, the mirrors and gold braid spoke in incredibly sharp contrast to the dusty brown of the dwellings and the landscape. We wandered about the streets fascinated, transported.

In retrospect, I see the moment of walking out into that celebration in the streets as the first experience that both connected me to and disconnected me from my past with the jolt of new awareness. I was in a place that I had absolutely no prior knowledge of, in the midst of a people who were unlike anything my previous experience could have prepared me for. I was delighted and at the same time terrified. I understood nothing of the details of what was going on around me. I could only take it in through my senses. I understood none of the spoken language, the body language only a little. On the other hand, the spirit of the moment, the music, the smells of freshly prepared special foods, the hustle and bustle—all of these resonated in a joyful place in me.

I find it is often the awareness of some small detail that opens doors to a world previously closed to me. On this day it was the scribe sitting on the ground beneath the tall thin poplars at the front of the post office who stopped me in my path. Suddenly that word, *scribe*, a word that I knew but had no real understanding of, had a face. The man sat cross-legged on the ground with a small podium in front of him. People (always men) would emerge from the post office. One with a letter in hand would come to sit with the scribe and hand him the letter, which the scribe would then read aloud to him. There would be some conversation between the scribe and the man, or silence; then the man would dictate a letter to the scribe. Some coins would be exchanged, and the man would return to the post office with his reply. In the telling, this moment seems so mundane, yet in that moment so many stories, concepts, history lessons, glimmers of understanding of the culture before me fell into place. Here was a man whose task it was to hear, consider, and advise on the affairs of the entire town and very likely those of many parts of the country. Suddenly, before my eyes, I was witnessing a time-honored way of communicating, a way that existed in history books and in my Bible stories, for which I had previously had no context, and of which I had only the most superficial understanding.

That first long journey took me next through Afghanistan and Pakistan on crowded, noisy, cold buses and overcrowded trains where I was the *only* female, to the border of India. At this point we were almost beyond weary. Our bodies were struggling with the changes through which our adventurous spirits had put them. Our psyches were reeling from the pace that, in our naïveté, we assumed we could handle. As we made our way on foot from the border crossing to the train station on that New Year's Eve, entering into the year 1969, I experienced another of those startling moments of awareness. Road-weary and bedraggled as I was, I felt an amazing and surprising sense of elation—my entire body, my entire being, felt suddenly and total-ly "at home." In that moment there were no words to define that sen-sation, only a bodily calm, of a kind of contentedness that allowed me to look up, look around, look out and see this new world into which I had stumbled. During the next six months as I traveled in India, and even to this day, that sensation of being "at home" has been an anchor, a still place to which to return, a knowing of some place in me that does not need words.

In India the opportunity arose for me to travel alone. At first I was quite afraid—of what, exactly, I did not know. I had traveled on my own in Europe, but I was afraid because my upbringing and precon-ceptions of myself in the world affected trust in myself. That distrust often translated into a distrust of others, a cycle that could easily esca-late and at times was truly paralyzing. What saved me was India, and that particular time in India. It allowed me to learn, to listen more openly and attentively to my intuitive voice: it was phenomenal. When I needed help, someone reached out or gave me shelter. When I paid attention to the signals in front of me I remained safe and found, to my amazement, that people treated me like their sister or their daughter. Dangerous people and places were there, yet I seemed able to walk by them or around them. I seemed to become almost invisible to them. Daily, I was able to employ an intuition that I had previously been exceedingly tentative about. I found privacy within myself, not in my surroundings. I had long conversations that did not depend on language as I rode the trains, traveling in the women's car. The women fed me from their containers of home-prepared food when they ate with their children, and I fetched tea and water at the train stations for all of us. The women were astounded that at my age—twenty-two—I did not have children.

As my journey continued, acts of kindness and openings seemed to flow to me with little or no effort on my part. They came because of an openness and a trust in me that was being continually nur-tured—a self-reinforcing cycle. I was offered a ride on the back of a man's bicycle when the caves I had gone to visit turned out to be a long way from the center of the town. I slept in a huge men's dormitory where the older men, without any outward indication, or prompting, simply took on the role of my guardian angels. I found myself a guest for ten days in the simple, shady courtyard of an amazing community artist, an older man around whom the local elders, poets, philosophers, and religious scholars gathered two or three evenings a week for discussion, debate, and exchange. They seemed to find me as fascinating as I found them.

It was two years before I was able to begin to incorporate these experiences into my being and a lifetime before I could see how they shaped me. Through them, I was given a broad range of entry points for understanding differences in the world; each of these moments of opening I have written about here is deeply etched in my memory. I suspect that putting them into words does not do them justice. Nor is my remembering "accurate," yet they are clearly there in my senses.

Moving from the plains of India to the roof of the world in Nepal, I rejoined my companion. Time has little meaning when there is no itinerary, no plane to catch, no job to return to. I cherish the good fortune that allowed me that rare opportunity: to wander free of time frames, to have so many encounters, to be given so much space to practice being in the moment.

When I arrived in Kathmandu, my companion had met a number of other travelers, one of whom he suggested we visit. We walked the few miles to the village where his new acquaintance was living in a simple room, researching, learning about Tibetan *thanka* paintings. We arrived and had the usual welcome cup of tea as we exchanged ideas, stories, and information, a much-appreciated habit and necessity when travelers met. There was a sound at the door, and there stood his teacher, a Tibetan monk. I had seen many such monks walking along the street, always laughing when they were with companions. The monk smiled, bowed gently, and entered the room. When he sat down on the floor, it was as though a wave of energy preceded him. As the wave washed over the room, the quality of light was transformed. A clarity and peace settled into the room, holding us. Again, I was—fortunately—completely unprepared for such a moment. I have no memory of what came next, what the conversation was about, what we did afterwards. Etched in my being is the experience: I had not known it was possible for a human being to be so entirely present, unquestionably in the moment. Later I was told that this monk had three times completed the three-year, three-month, three-week, three-day fast in a cave in the mountains, living on only *tsampa* (barley gruel), butter tea, and water provided by his monastery.

Much of what I thought I knew at that time may well be untrue or incomplete or misconstrued. I only know that I was offered a gift that became a point of reference to which I would return, that has always been there to remind me of the beauty in appreciating each moment, each sensation, each new layer of understanding that is offered to us when we are open to it.

What does one do with such experiences? How do they translate into the actions of a life? I believe they have enabled me to cross through the boundaries, the frames that our society creates, to look and to live both within and outside these frames, the frames that both allow and exclude many possible ways of thinking, knowing and being. There are many paths to this end. Mine was reinforced by the richness of travel, travel with no agenda, travel with no funds, travel inward, travel into the unknown. I am grateful for the opportunity I was given at a young and impressionable age and also for the people and places that helped to bring me home to myself.

Lautan

Jody Wood

 "Isn't the ocean magnificent?" Theresa said softly. We were sitting on a weathered wooden bench on the shore of the Indian Ocean. We could hear the rest of our team off in the background playing games in the camp. I chuckled to myself. We knew we should be participating, but instead we had wandered away together and were just sitting, neither of us really speaking, just watching the waves, the clouds, and the colors of the sky.

Feeling a great sense of peace I whispered, "It is absolutely beautiful. I am so glad to be here."

"Here" was Ujong Kulon National Park on the Javanese island of Indonesia. We had been invited to take part in a trek across the south end of the park as an endurance quest. Theresa and I had met ten days earlier on the plane to Jakarta. Never were two women more different. Theresa was tall and healthy with beautiful long golden wavy hair. I was instantly drawn to her laugh— hearty, infectious, and constant. I, on the other hand, have a sardonic outlook on life, my hair is shorn, flat, and mouse colored and I am not tall. Some have commented that my picture would make a good illustration for a text on anemia, or perhaps a poster showing the plight of refugees. Despite our differences, Theresa and I had become fast friends. We connected in our deep desire to explore the meaning of life and spirituality, and we shared a passion for personal growth and connectedness. Theresa was a learned person who studied languages, the arts and sacredness in all its forms. I had dabbled mainly in psychology, but recently I too had embarked on a spiritual quest. Over the past week our nights in the steamy Indonesian jungle had been spent discussing theories and experiences in our lives. Indonesia had become a blessing.

Gazing out at the ocean now, I commented, "Last year I traveled through Nova Scotia and I was struck by how many

memorials there are to the dead who have been killed by the ocean."
Always the cynic.

"Really…?" Theresa was always curious to know more.

"Yeah, all along the shore were tall statues with name after name
of men who had been killed by storms at sea either with the military
or in fishing boats. The ocean has killed a lot of people. I came away
with a strong sense of the way man challenges her power."

"Men will challenge power," said Theresa and quipped, "Look at
what they do to women." Suddenly she sprang to her feet, her gold
anklets jingling. "That's it! The ocean is a woman," she proclaimed,
raising her arms above her head and waving a fist. "Look out there! See
how beautiful she is?"

"Yeah," I said, slouching down on the bench, "but what about all
those dead people? Apparently she can be quite miserable when she
wants to be."

Theresa began to prance around, kicking up sand. "She is the
power. She is the great force of power. Her voice is the music of the
lapping waves …"

I began to get into the spirit. I jumped to my feet too. "Or her
yelling and raging in a torrential storm."

"She is warm," Theresa chanted.

"She is cold," I shouted, leaping in the air.

"She is soft, she is bold," she sang on.

We grabbed hands, leaping in circles, chanting our declarations
playfully, whirling and whirling.

"She can sparkle, she can shine!"

"She sends a tingle down my spine," I rhymed back.

Theresa flung herself onto her hands in a feeble attempt at a cart-
wheel. Sand flew up into my face. She collapsed on her back, panting
and laughing while I lunged toward her and crashed on my belly next
to her.

We lay on the sand for a moment, collecting our breath. Then
Theresa whispered, "And her tides, they rise and fall like the very
breath we breathe."

"Ahhh, well said." I rested my head on her thigh.

"Hey, I can't hear anyone in the camp any more."

We scrambled to our feet, giggling like children. "Yikes … we better move it." Across the sand and down the path to our beds we ran.

Much later that night I found myself still awake. Theresa was sprawled out on her mattress, her blanket twisted around her, breathing deeply. I thought about our evening, the dancing and silly fun we had shared on the beach. I felt that Theresa and I had made a connection with the ocean, and that I now understood, at least symbolically, how important she was to our survival. I wanted to see her again so I climbed out of my bed and left the tent. The air was thick and humid under the trees. I wanted to run away and breathe the clean air of the beach. I stepped carefully along the path that led to the water, ignoring the sharpness of the pebbles on my bare feet.

Emerging from the jungle onto the beach, I came upon a sight that was almost too beautiful for words. The moon was full and high in the sky, casting a soft light on the lapping waves. *Her voice,* I thought. I perched myself on the bench we had sat on earlier, bringing my knees up under my chin as I absorbed the scene.

"*Salam,*" said a voice from behind me.

Startled, I turned around. There on the soft grass of the bank was a little woman, perhaps four feet tall.

"Hello?" I was instantly alert and cautious.

She moved toward me, shimmering in the light. As she came closer, I saw that she was carrying fireflies in the palms of her hands. She sat beside me on the bench. Her feet dangled, not touching the ground. She seemed ancient: her face was dark and weathered, her hair long and silver in the bright moonlight. Her eyes were heavily outlined with thick black charcoal, and they looked old, watery, and dark as the ocean itself. She was wrapped snugly in a deep blue sarong and a coat of the same deep blue and silver; on her head was perched a tiny fuchsia cap. The color of her clothes glowed. Her feet were bare, but each of her toes held a tiny silver ring. Her arms were laden with silver bangles that jingled when she moved. She smelled of salt.

"Are you English?"

"I am Canadian."

"Are you with this group that has been walking my beach?"

My beach? Perhaps she was a local person, a tribeswoman who lived in the forest nearby.

"Yes, I am. The beaches here are gorgeous. I mean, look at this one tonight."

"Ahhh yes, just what I thought you might say," she murmured, delicately playing with the fireflies that were dancing in her hand. She spoke again, with a rhythmic intonation. "Do you like fireflies?"

I smiled at the flashing creatures. "I have never really seen them before."

"Put out your hand," she whispered.

I obeyed and she gracefully put her palm under mine. The insects bumped right along from her skin to mine, making my flesh tingle.

I watched in amazement as the pins of light danced around my palm.

"I have noticed you," she said slowly with a soft, sad smile on her lips. "You and your friend. You love each other. You are so lucky to have that kind of friendship. My name is Lautan," she continued. "The world is filled with misunderstanding people who seem to like to hurt Lautan. Who won't see Lautan for who she is … to see her beauty, to see her gifts. You see her beauty, I can tell."

I sat in disbelief. I had never seen this dear soul in my life, yet I began to have the strangest sensation that I had been with her before, very recently. "Why do you say this about me?"

She looked down at her hands folded neatly in her little lap. "You and your girlfriend, you are connected to the earth." She craned her neck to look directly into my eyes and whispered "Lautan loves you." Her eyes welled up in tears. "Lautan loves all people and wants to give her gifts to people, but people seem not to be able to handle the gifts that Lautan gives." She paused, sighing deeply. "Many people cry to Lautan because her force and her fury are too harsh. You must know that Lautan feels deeply sorry when she catches and cradles their dead. You must know that she comforts them. So many people use Lautan and so many people are afraid of Lautan, but you are not. I can see that you respect the power in Lautan. Will you help Lautan to be respected?"

I thought for a moment. She seemed nice enough, but whose respect was she seeking? I didn't know. But perhaps I could help. "Well, yes, I can try to see that you are respected."

Perhaps sensing my trepidation and confusion, or possibly having received the answer she wanted, she slowly slipped down from the bench, painfully placing her wide old flat feet back on the sand. She turned to face me, putting her withered hands on my cheeks. Her sad old eyes looked deep into mine. "*Teman terima kasih.* Thank you, my friend. Lautan loves you. And she will watch for you. She will see you again very soon." She turned ever so slowly and wandered off toward the edge of the sea. She was humming a sad sort of tune that melded perfectly with the melody of the lapping waves. I glanced down into my open palm. The fireflies were gone. When I looked up, the old woman had disappeared.

The sun was penetrating the walls of the tent. Theresa had awoken first and was unzipping the door. Outside, the camp was bustling with activity. I could hear Martin, our master guide hollering to get that last remaining tent down—our tent. I was still lying in my bed and Theresa had only been awake a few minutes. We burst into giggles. Here we were again, last, late and probably missing breakfast.

Once our belongings were once again stowed in our backpacks we hefted them onto our shoulders and set off. As we passed "our" bench in the daylight, I said to Theresa, "Last night I met an amazing old woman on the beach."

"Really? When?"

"I couldn't sleep, and I got up and came down here to see the ocean. A woman came out of the trees and sat with me. Her name was Lautan. She told me how she was sad and hurt and that people were mean to her. She had fireflies that danced in her hands."

"She said her name was Lautan?"

"Yes, and she said that people didn't see her beauty."

"Do you know that *Lautan* in Indonesian means 'ocean'?"

"Really?" I said pensively, and I looked out over the water. I had not seen Lautan leave. I saw her walk to the edge of the sea, but I did not see her leave.

Theresa, her voice filled with awe, said, "I think you met a spirit. I think you met the Spirit of the Sea."

It was true. As the realization washed over me, I said, "She said that she had noticed you and me. She said that we respected her." She had seen us playing in the sand, calling out her virtues. She knew that we understood her role in the world, her place in our survival, and was sad that so few of us understood that. The meaning of her message began to dawn on me. It was from the world at large that she was seeking respect. She wanted humanity to be kinder to her: to stop polluting her with garbage and oil; to fish her waters and pillage her depths less.

Theresa and I both stopped and stared at the horizon. For the first time I really saw her. *Lautan*, beautiful shining Lautan. I saw how she rolled and sparkled, waving hello and beckoning us to come and play in her surf. Theresa turned to see if we were both sensing the same thing—the need to be near her, to accept the invitation of our new friend Lautan. In a single movement we dropped our bags and, hand in hand, ran shrieking with delight into the waves.

Passages

Catherine Bancroft

Galileo's head was on the block
The crime was looking up for truth
And as the bombshells of my daily fears explode
I try to trace them to my youth

—"Galileo," The Indigo Girls

 Traveling away from the familiarity and security of my home, and away from the city I grew up in, has shaped important transitional points in my life. The act of traveling has broadened my comfort zones, altered my perceptions of myself—of who I am and where I belong—and enriched my understanding of the world. From the time I was six weeks old, my summer always included a month at my grandparents' cottages on Lake Winnipeg, and it was in those childhood days that I learned to love traveling. The excitement of being embraced by the generous love of my grandparents, the eager exploration of new places and people, and the illumination I gained from myself in different contexts all helped to develop a thirst for travel that has led me to many destinations around the world. My travels have brought me both a tragic personal loss and a profound sense of rebirth.

At the age of twenty-one, I spent a summer working at Lake O'Hara lodge with one of my closest friends, Jana. This lodge is tucked in along the Alberta and British Columbia border, sixteen hundred feet above sea level, in Yoho National Park. Lake O'Hara lodge is a gem, known to only a few. There are countless trails leading into the mountains and gorgeous vistas everywhere you look. The colors in the lakes range from bright turquoise to dark blue—unusual shades produced by the natural

131

chemicals of the glaciers that feed them. This was one of the most gorgeous places I had ever seen. Here, Jana and I, both from Ontario, felt such freedom, such potential to explore life, to live every day to its fullest.

Jana and I sang the Indigo Girls' song "Galileo" from their CD *Rites of Passage* at our staff parties every Saturday night at the lodge. We sang it with an exuberance and joy inspired by the mountains, and the feelings of immortality and youth that their ancient, eternal presence awakened in us. "Galileo" was our song that summer; it expressed our vitality, our energy, and our love of life. We never talked about why we loved the song, we just did. The music itself seemed to overflow with the sheer joy of living. I had never listened to the lyrics carefully enough to know that Emily, the lead singer of the Indigo Girls, was singing about death and reincarnation.

When you are traveling, everything can change in a day, an hour, a minute. You may meet up with someone unexpectedly, there is a sudden change of plans, someone makes a decision to try something unplanned, and your life takes a new direction. It's the openness to explore such possibilities that often attracts the traveling spirit.

Jana, my soulful, spirited partner, was half the adventure. Without one of the halves, the exploration could not happen. We had experienced the rugged and scarred terrain of tree planting together the year before, an adventure that taught us mental, physical, and emotional perseverance. This journey was different; the sheer beauty and embrace of the mountains led us to believe we were safe, and we lived life to the fullest without fear. We explored the mountainous terrain together, and in doing so, explored ourselves. We sang, with the Indigo Girls:

> And then I think about my fear of motion
> Which I never could explain
> Some other fool across the ocean years ago
> Must have crashed his little airplane

The haunting image of our song, of a crashing airplane, didn't seem to apply to us. The fear of death didn't exist for us that summer. We all know that sometimes airplanes crash, and other accidents happen, but it's a distant notion. Those things usually happen to someone else.

One Saturday in August, after we had been immersed in the community at the lodge for three months, Jana went out climbing on her day off. That evening, she and I were scheduled to entertain the lodge guests, and we had been preparing a couple of songs. When she left, she promised to be back by 7 p.m. so we could rehearse. At seven, the show started without her. At nine, I looked at the back door through which she was supposed to enter and had a horrible feeling in the pit of my stomach that she was not coming back. I had an image of her on the mountain. I felt a sense of fear, urgency and shock I had not experienced before.

Later that night, she died.

When she fell, it was dark; we were sixteen hundred feet above sea level, and no helicopters could reach her to take her to the hospital. Once the team of men bushwhacked their way to where her body was, she was already dead.

After climbing all the way up the mountain peak called the Watchtower and back down almost to the base of the mountain, she had fallen thirty feet from the ground.

Thirty feet, dark, no helicopters.

I felt as if my left arm had been cut off and I could not find a place to reattach it. Death is as permanent as it gets.

The airplane of her life had crashed, and so had mine. I began to have fears I could not explain. My youth had been hit by a bombshell, and I definitely did not believe in reincarnation.

For all their beauty, their enclosing, embracing comfort, the mountains had failed her, by not catching her or softening her landing when she fell. I felt torn in half, betrayed by nature, betrayed by life. The next morning, as I watched the helicopter carry her body away, I threw myself to the ground in shock. The thoughts racing through my head were ideas that I had never considered before. *Why her, why not me? I should never have found us the jobs; I should never have let her go mountain climbing.*

> And then you had to bring up reincarnation
> Over a couple of beers the other night
> And now I'm serving time for mistakes
> Made by another in another lifetime

I wondered, was I serving time? A life with so much potential, so much to offer. A life that brought so much beauty to those around her. I was left to travel alone, searching for a part of me that I could never replace. *Had she been in pain? She died without warning. Would anyone else close to me die so unexpectedly? What happened to her once she died? Did she experience light? Could I speak to her, call on her resting soul?* I was completely unable to rationalize her death or be comforted by any belief or possible explanation. I felt too stripped, too vulnerable and emotionally raw.

> How long till my soul gets it right
> Can any other human being ever reach that kind of light?
> I call on the resting soul of Galileo
> King of night vision, king of insight

We would never sing "Galileo" again. "King of night visions, King of insight," we had sung, but we never would again.

> How long till my soul gets it right?
> Can any human being ever reach that kind of light?
> I call on the resting soul of Galileo
> King of night vision, king of insight

Do we need death to value life? Experiencing tragedy drew me into a deep struggle. I questioned everything I knew.

This questioning, confusion, and disorientation led me to experience different parts of myself, where I sought new levels of understanding and insight. Through travel out west to a lodge sixteen hundred feet above sea level; through experiencing the death of my friend and a part of myself; and through travel to Nepal, where I experienced the rebirth of parts of me, each time the mountains were the force that drew me there. This force asked me to let go of things that were previously precious to me, whether it was my friend, beliefs that I held, ways of perceiving the world, or parts of myself. Each time, I needed a spiritual sanctuary and a catalyst. Each time, I experienced an awakening process.

Like an elastic band, I was pulled, stretched, and lengthened. Jana's death led me to search deep within to seek answers to unanswerable questions about life, death, my life, the purpose of life. Keeping a journal recorded my struggle and called me deeper into it. The writing and self-reflection helped me to find my voice, clarity, and courage. Pain broke the shell of my understanding of everything as I knew it.

There are two journeys to make through life. There is the outer journey, with the milestones of youth, marriage, middle age, old age, along with births, deaths, and the transitions of life that occur with jobs, relationships, babies, families. There is also an inner spiritual journey, with a secret history of its own. Allowing myself to journey through my grief offered me a path of transformation as I was led to new understandings, new visions, and new insights. The mountains were the cause of the death of my soul sister; during my journey through grief they became the catalyst, transforming my views of myself and my life. At the time, my love of mountains was completely overshadowed by her death.

Eight years after Jana's death, I embarked on another trip through mountains that would once again act as a passage on my spiritual journey. During the first journey I had experienced the awakening that death and deep loss bring to the spirit. During the second, I gained a sense of rebirth and discovery. Both came by chance and were unexpected: one a cruel accident, the other a fortunate opportunity. In both cases, I unexpectedly found spirit, beauty, courage, and transformation. It was while I trekked on the Annapurna Circuit, located amongst the Himalayan Mountains in the north central region of Nepal, east of Everest and just south of Tibet, that I experienced a sense of rebirth.

Before I began the twenty-one-day trek, I spent time at a Hindu temple. I am drawn to places of ritual, and I found the burning of the dead out in the open particularly fascinating. The smell was strong and took me off guard. I was struck by the dichotomy between my culture's way of concealing death and the Hindu culture's way of revealing death. In this ritual, the body is burned on a pyre out in the open with all of the deceased's loved ones there to witness the disappearance of the physical body and then to watch the ashes float down the river. This ritual was very significant for me to witness, as it showed me a way to accept death openly rather than fear it. We might be repulsed by this, but I believe we have something to learn from it.

In Nepal I was again surrounded by mountains, walking among them and taking in their beauty, vastness, and immense power. This one hundred and fifty-five-mile, twenty-one-day trek was a circular route, through a pass that stood at 17,770 feet. We spent approximately ten days climbing steep terrain to reach the pass. The circuit became a symbolic journey of transition for me: a passage from death to rebirth in the part of my spirit that had been severed when Jana died.

I fell in love with the mountains again. I didn't experience the sweaty, dizzy feeling of panic I'd grown used to feeling every time I approached them or looked at climbing gear. I had to surrender myself entirely to the transformative experience of being in a mountainous area again, like my journey through grief. I spent ten days climbing to reach the pass, or bridge; a symbolic bridge to understanding and meaning. Such a climb presents hard physical challenges: managing fatigue, pacing oneself, knowing one's limits, coping with nausea, headaches and difficulty breathing from the altitude. The emotional challenges can also be overwhelming, including self-doubt and fears of the unknown.

The views were incredibly beautiful along the way, but because of the physical strain of the days climbing to the pass, I was unable to fully appreciate them. I doubted whether I would have the strength to cross the pass, as I had doubted that I would ever get through the grief journey. But once I was over the pass, the beauty I saw in the landscape was unlike anything I had ever experienced. Once I moved through grief, I found parts of me that I didn't know were there. I found reservoirs of strength.

This sacred place on the circuit was filled with the presence of the beauty and intensity of the mountains; the spirit of the people and their culture was blessed, and here I found a safe space for new beginnings for me. I knew I was coming full circle. The sacredness of the journey through the mountains came from the desire to experience transformation. I was very aware of our modern Western malaise of alienation from ourselves, from each other, and from the rest of creation. Going on a sacred journey reconnected me with the possibility of transformation.

My body was opening up to vision and insight. I could feel the meaning of the song "Galileo" coming full circle, returning to its beginning. On day six of the trek, we went from one small village, Pisang, to another called Braka. When we stopped for lunch, there was a woman sitting on a mat with her beads in one hand and her prayer wheel in another. She spun her wheel, she repeated *Om nom me pad me hom* over and over. Her image is still etched in my mind. I was overcome with the feeling of how she spent her days: putting her energy into prayer. I began to think that her culture's rich gifts are disguised, by poverty whereas North American culture's spiritual alienation wears a disguise of wealth, making us appear better and them more impoverished.

I began to experience the spirituality of this culture as interwoven into their society. Here people don't enter a building like a church or synagogue to experience spirituality; it's interwoven into the people, culture, and land. When you live in such an austere climate, mystery and magic accompany spirituality.

We walked and walked. When walking, you enter a meditative state and the normal barriers of life break down: *us and them; who does what; what your roles are.* Even the most competitive person doesn't go untouched. I had a sense that the people are the mountains.

Sometimes our soul gets it right. I had the feeling that my soul was getting something right. The personal transformation I had experienced after Jana's death led me through a rite of passage. The transformation I experienced on my trek in Nepal was leading me to extract meaning from death and to accept new visions and insights. On day thirteen we crossed the pass. Our next stop was Muktinah, a place of pilgrimage for the indigenous Nepali people, who visit it once in their lifetime. There is a temple, where there are seven spouts of water to wash away your seven deadly sins. I was struck that the indigenous Nepali people often have to wait their whole lifetime to do this pilgrimage. They walk for seven days from the east side of the pass in order to wash away their sins and remember their ancestors, whereas I had flown to this country and after twenty-one days of walking from the west side of the pass I had arrived.

How long till my soul gets it right?
Can any human being ever reach that kind of light?
I call on the resting soul of Galileo
King of night vision, king of insight.

I was called to the mountains, and in both cases a passageway opened up. It was my choice whether I wanted to go through the passageway, over the symbolic bridge or over the physical pass to the experience of transformation: of myself, of my views of myself, and of my understanding of the world.

Night vision and insight were always available.

After I left Asia, I went to volunteer at a camp in Eugene, Oregon, for bereaved children. I flew into Portland, and on the first night I went to meet some people to listen to music in the park. On my way, I stopped for a tea. I talked with a few of the guys in the shop who told me that the Indigo Girls were playing next door. I went next door and walked up to the box office to inquire about tickets. The woman said, "Yes, we have one ticket left in the front row."

That night, as I danced in the front row to "Galileo," energy ran through my body. This was the completion of my circle. Jana and I had sung "Galileo" every week at the lodge. That night, I sang it alone with a renewed sense of love of the song and of life.

The Edge of Risk

Chris Marin

We sat in a circle, and one by one, we explained why we wanted to go to Peru. Machu Picchu was the dream of most. Visions of Incan ruins had attracted me since childhood. There was no doubt in my mind that I had to go, and when the moment came I unhesitatingly signed my name to the list of prospective artists to take a "Spiritual Journey to Peru" in May 2001.

As I left the meeting I was asking myself, *What have I done?* How could I hike through the Andes at approximately ten thousand feet above sea level, and climb hundreds of stone steps, when most days it was a challenge for me simply to walk from the chesterfield to the refrigerator? Since 1977, fibromyalgia, with its chronic fatigue, pain, and severe sensitivities to almost everything, had dictated how I lived my life. Although I was much healthier than I had been in the past, I still could not walk around the block without pain.

The goal of traveling to Peru with fellow artists, many of whom were friends, was a powerful motivator. I immediately began Nia and Pilates classes to try to condition my body for the adventure. Nia, a series of body-mind-spirit dance routines, gently reintroduced my body to movement. At first I had to stop periodically because of fatigue, but eventually I could complete the whole class except for the yoga-like stretches at the end. Pilates on the floor hurt my back and neck, but Patti, the instructor, was kind, and encouraged me to do only what I could. She purchased a special banana seat to enable me to try the core exercises without straining myself. I asked her if she would help me to exercise at home twice a week, and we began a routine of walking around the block with my dogs.

I was making progress. The stretches for legs and feet that I learned to do during and after the walk were crucial. A variety of other stretches for the back, light weights, and exercises on a Swiss ball strengthened me. There were days when the pain was too forbidding, and other days when the exercise was actually easy, and even on the bad days I knew that I was accomplishing more than I had in decades. I could now envision myself climbing the steps of Machu Picchu.

On the overnight flight to Lima, Peru, I was extremely proud of what I had achieved just to get to this point. I felt a deep responsibility to myself to take each day of the trip one step at a time, at my own pace. I did not want to jeopardize the glorious prospect of Peru by forcing my body to work too hard.

A short morning flight took us from Lima to Cusco, an ancient city high in the Andes, and we began our journey into the Incan world. The twelve-thousand-foot elevation was a challenge for most of us. When we visited the ruins at Saqsaywaman, I left the group early and rested on the bus. On the hike down the mountain from the Incan salt mine, I was in a group of four women. We were the slowest, bringing up the rear, but we talked, laughed, and took photographs for the entire one and a half hours it took us to make our way down the dirt path to the valley. Afterward, I stretched in the yoga room of Willka T'ika, where we stayed in the Sacred Valley.

I was still out of breath and sweating at dinner an hour later. It didn't matter! "Jubilant" best describes my mood that evening, and when I awoke the next morning, I had no stiffness or soreness. That night, however, we joined Julianna, a local medicine woman, to make an offering (*haywarikuy*) to Pachamama, Mother Earth, and receive a healing (*humpa*) from her. Smudge and incense filled the room. In the past I had reacted badly to these allergenic inhalants, but I persuaded myself that I would be fine this time.

The next morning I was very weak and was helped to bed after nearly fainting. There would be no excursions for me that day. I was crestfallen and went to bed that night feeling very sad. I slept fitfully, and at some point, half awake and half dreaming, I saw in my mind's eye a trapezoid portal, the architectural shape of windows and doors preferred by the Incans, and was drawn to glide through it. In this place beyond the portal, Hanakpacha, the Incan spirit world, I felt utterly accepted by mother and father, by *All-That-Is*. Pain and worry slipped away. Early the next morning I awoke and was surprised to see the three visiting coca leaf readers from a remote mountain village sitting outside the window of my adobe cottage. I had met them the previous day, and they had talked about "healing me during the night," but I thought that I had misunderstood their words in the translation from Quechua to Spanish to English. Now, as I stood shivering outside, watching the sunrise, the pink-tinged morning mist (water symbolizing the feminine) separated to form another gateway and exposed the golden sun (masculine), painting the mountainside in broader and broader strokes of light. My sense of being embraced by my mother and father grew stronger and was affirmed in this moment. It was a turning point on the trip, a vital pivot in the span of my life. I have had no significant fibromyalgia pain since.

The remainder of my first journey to Peru slipped by in a euphoric haze. Machu Picchu was beautiful, heart-wrenching, and inspiring. Sitting in the grass in a secluded area, we meditated while Hebert, a Peruvian shaman, played ancient drums, flutes, bells, bowls, and condor feathers. We could hear the birds in the surrounding trees responding to the haunting music with an answering call. After the meditation ceremony, six of us took our painting materials to the sun-warmed rocks looking off toward Wayna Picchu and worked there until dusk. The moon rose in the indigo sky. In the solitude and silence and elegance I was completely happy. When we realized that the gates to Machu Picchu, "our" City of Light, would soon be closing for the night, we ran like giddy schoolchildren down the stone steps and across the grassy terraces without a care in the cosmos.

The feeling of creative, life-affirming energy lasted for many weeks after my return to Canada. I painted with a gusto previously unknown to me. I worked every day, and the textures, colors, symbols, shapes, and cosmology of Peru entered my paintings and collages, reflecting my journey. I begin most paintings by pouring yellow, red and blue paints onto paper and allowing them to react with salt, rubbing alcohol, waxed paper and/or stretch wrap. The lines, shapes, and colors that emerged were intuitively created, without conscious control. While on the trip I had poured paintings at the Incan sites of

Saqsaywaman, P'isaq, Circles of Moray, and Machu Picchu, and also at Willka T'ika. Now, out of those pourings came snakes, pumas, and condors, symbols of the three Incan worlds, trapezoid portals, spirals, earth, mountain and moon, Incan faces, and the vibrant flower gardens of Willka T'ika.

I experimented with new media and techniques: one piece, *The Feel of Peru*, is a collage incorporating textiles, crinkled paper, semi-precious stones, silver and gold, bay leaves (to represent coca leaves, which I did not dare bring across the border!), and other materials that would convey the touchable textures of Peru—its chenille mountains, patchwork fields, ancient stones, woven Incan rag dolls, silky-smooth calla lilies, and more.

After the artists' trip, our leader Jill Segal, an artist herself, organized the "Celebration of Creativity" art exhibition in November 2001. There were over ninety paintings, all created by the eighteen artists on our trip. I had sixteen pieces on display; it was my first show, and I was very excited and nervous. It was a success! My painting *Gateway to Hanakpacha*, poured onto trapezoid-shaped watercolor paper, attracted much attention and was the first of mine to sell. When I told the purchaser how the painting began by pouring the paints and letting the images appear on their own, she shivered!

When Jill confirmed that she would take another group in July 2002, I knew that I had to return. I was not finished yet. There were more hurdles to face. The previous year I had not had the stamina (the day after my near-fainting experience) to walk up the mountain with the others to the sun temple in P'isaq. But it was not only a lack of strength that stopped me. All of my life I have had nightmares about height ... being stuck on stone landings where the stairway has collapsed below me, clinging to the edge of balconies, walking across narrow bridges without railings over consuming chasms ... terrifying and paralyzing. This time I wanted to conquer my fear.

The path that went up the mountain was wide enough for only one person. The intermittent stone steps were not easy for me to negotiate while I was carrying a heavy backpack full of art supplies. But, it was the sheer drop of hundreds, maybe thousands, of feet on the left side of the path that I feared the most. I kept my eyes straight ahead and clung to the rock face, at times to the point of bleeding knuckles. Jill stayed right behind me, gave me hard candies for my dry mouth, and encouraged me throughout the climb. She took a photo of me entering a long, narrow tunnel in the rock, "like a birthing canal," she said, and then another of me coming out, reborn like the phoenix after surviving the ordeal. To sit at the top of the mountain and pour paints in the presence of the sun temple was such an enormous achievement that tears ran down my face, as they do now at the memory.

My painting *P'isaq Sungate* was inspired by my successful climb; it is full of life, movement, and strength and drew much attention from viewers at the exhibition after the second trip. It now hangs in the purchaser's home in a place of honor. Another painting of this episode is *Phoenix*, which adorned the invitation to Jill's and my joint exhibition, called "Everlasting Visions," held at the Davenport Gallery in Toronto in October 2003. My accountant recently purchased *Phoenix* for her office.

I found an uncredited saying in a magazine once: "It is only at the very edge of risk that one finds the energy to transform one's life." Those words are now my mantra. I plan to join Jill's group again, with hopes of next time also staying on the Island of the Sun on Lake Titicaca in Bolivia. For me the edge of risk is the path of creativity, and images recurring in my poured paintings are leading me back to South America again, with more energy than ever before.

Made in Taiwan

Angèle M. C. Palmer

To me, Taiwan was once a distant Asian country where many of the products I used daily were manufactured. I knew little else about Taiwan until, like many other Canadians, I ventured abroad to explore the tiny island for myself. After graduating with a bachelor of arts degree in 2000, I spent almost a year teaching English in Taichung, a small but densely populated city on the coast of Taiwan, where I learned about culture, racism, capitalism, sexism, and myself with a newfound understanding. It was a year complete with mixed blessings for which I am eternally grateful.

With the help of a friend who joined me on this adventure, and the other teaching recruits who surrounded me, I adapted relatively unscathed to life as a foreigner on the island. Finding out where to eat good food, where the hot night spots were, and where to buy a cheap scooter were all immediate goals that initially distracted me from the subtle dynamics at play in the culture of teaching English.

I admit that I was disappointed to discover that the traditional dishes in Taiwan were not the same as the food served in Canadian Chinese restaurants. I sought sanctuary from my culture shock at pubs that catered to foreigners with Western-style cuisine. The smells and sights were constant reminders that home was only a distant memory, and it was here that I learned the nurturing qualities of food. Lost, and straining to carve myself a space in this foreign existence, I longed for the familiar.

The children I taught to pronounce English words and to count to one hundred were adorable, but this story is not about them. It is about the cross-cultural systems of power I discovered, a constant source of unpleasantness and even pain, like a needle pricking my skin from inside. I came to see how my physical self—my Western look—

was unavoidably connected to every word, thought, and action, constantly altering my sense of self and my understanding of the world around me.

My first clue to the complicated social undercurrents I intuited in the foreign-teacher scenario was the photo that was required along with my degree and résumé. I speculated that this might have been to ensure I was indeed white. Though I had no proof of this suspicion, I doubted it was merely a coincidence that all the foreign teachers I met were white (there were many Taiwanese English teachers). After all, many Chinese Canadians are surely qualified to teach English in Asia. Why weren't there any? I didn't take these speculations any further at the time, but my experience in Taiwan greatly increased my understanding of my role in the game of foreign exchange. In Canada, I had thought myself wise to the intersecting barriers of race, class, gender, sexual orientation, age, and ability that crisscross each person's lived reality. But my experience as a white female Canadian English teacher in Asia challenged me further yet.

Although some parents paid, as mere pocket change, the expensive fees required to attend the English private school where I worked, I learned that others worked sixteen-hour days in order to provide their children with the same promise of opportunity. I grew intensely frustrated with the educational and socioeconomic structures that propped up an unequal system, but at first I was able to ignore my gut feeling that my role as English teacher was contributing to a grand hierarchy. Instead, I attributed the noxious taste in my mouth only to the diesel I inhaled daily on my commute.

In my first couple of months teaching, I befriended a Taiwanese colleague whose English name was Ellen. She worked as an English teacher as well as doing administrative duties and anything else our employer asked of her. Our communication rested on her strong command of the English language, and through our interactions we uncovered our similar interests. Ellen eventually informed me, subtly and ambivalently, that she was being paid one-third of what I was earning. I acted surprised, but I had guessed, or felt in my bones, that she would be seen as less valuable, even though she began working at the school before I arrived in the morning and stayed long after I left for the day. I was benefiting from the color of my skin and my Canadian citizenship; she was paying for it.

Although Ellen and I feigned a surface friendship, the inequality of our professional situations, my guilt, and whatever she felt about me, possibly resentment, remained barriers to the formation of a genuine relationship. My loneliness grew.

I resigned myself to the most Western lifestyle I could achieve, living among the other foreigners and trying to exist in a sort of bubble until my bank account was healthy enough to justify my return home. It didn't work; I couldn't help knowing where I was. Even though close friends surrounded me, every morning I dreaded the thought of facing yet another day. I lost myself in books every night in an attempt to escape my surroundings. Fiction was a distraction from my complicity in the twisted structure I found myself in. I wasn't comfortable with this sense of being a powerful player in any game. I struggled with my personal understanding of my position, so in conflict with the spiritual progress that I craved.

My colleagues and I did talk about these matters, and I knew they had some of the same misgivings. We comforted ourselves by saying we weren't just there for the money. Not like the other foreigners we'd met who talked of nothing but the thousands of dollars they pulled in each month. We told each other we were there to learn and experience a different culture. I ignored the unease that lingered, blaming my unhappiness on cultural differences and my inability to adapt to my surroundings. If I had faced the fact that my depression was actually related to the guilt I felt, I would have had to return to Canada, like a dog with her tail between her legs. My internal struggle to stay in order to achieve my goal of saving a certain amount of money was in conflict with my observing self, which nagged me daily to acknowledge the internal processes wreaking havoc in my gut. I remained steadfastly in denial. Depression was an inevitable outcome.

White privilege was rampant in the workplace and infiltrated personal relations. White men were recognized to have sexual prestige. These men, then, were not only well paid for minimal work, but were also tempted with the opportunities to experience the "exotic Other." For example, when I asked one male acquaintance why he had no plans to leave Taiwan, he said (about his Taiwanese girlfriend), "I would never get a hot chick like this in England." This was a common attitude, and it made my blood boil for reasons I couldn't even begin to articulate. I didn't want to say anything about it and be told I was just a bitter, jealous white woman whose criticisms stemmed solely from her own loneliness and lack of male attention. My opinions, though, were undoubtedly colored by this embarrassing probability. I was lonely and in search of a relationship to ease my unhappiness with my life in Taiwan. I had to admit, if only to myself, that I was troubled by the fact that the available foreign men seemed to be available only to Asian women.

My dislike of the situation, however, was far from being merely personal. I did not like the attitudes of many foreign men toward the Taiwanese women. There was a covert but undeniable connection between the power dynamics being played out in sexual relations and those operating in the workplace. Sexual exploitation and cultural consumption of the exotic Other by foreign men made me despair of the structure of heterosexual relationships in general. I was offended by the displays of arrogant machismo and the submissive response of the Taiwanese women that I constantly witnessed. I began to question whether my ideal of a heterosexual relationship was even possible, given the pervasive imbalance of power that was so pronounced in these interracial pairings. Were same-race relationships any more likely to be free from these intricate power games? I doubted it.

I rarely witnessed a white woman with an Asian man, and that prompted me to wonder why I hadn't been interested in any Taiwanese men. Their brown betel-nut-stained teeth were not the only reason I felt no sexual attraction toward them. Asian men had simply not been sexualized for me the same way that Asian women had been eroticized for male foreigners. What men of "other" cultures did I find attractive? Perhaps I was guilty of seeking only men who fit the masculine ideal of tall, dark, and handsome, and of course white. My narrow ideals of masculinity seemed connected to the consumption and colonization of women of color by the white Western men. These thoughts picked at my brain like my chopsticks at my teppanyaki. While sitting at the bar some evenings with a pint and cigarettes and observing the interracial flirtations around me, I wondered whether I was the only one haunted by such thoughts.

When I learned about the prevalence of body image issues among the Taiwanese women, I realized that I had assumed this problem was typical only of the West. The common physique of Asian women is very tiny and thin. However, I discovered that even they wanted to be thinner! I observed a colleague one day with a bandage on her ear and asked whether she had hurt herself. She responded that beneath the bandage was a small acupuncture needle her doctor had inserted so that she could press on it to suppress her hunger whenever she was tempted to eat. When I protested that she was beautiful just as she was, she responded with nothing more than a vacant smile.

White skin was another characteristic the Taiwanese sought; an entire aisle at the grocery store was devoted to skin-lightening creams. I was aghast at the irony—while white people were buying tanning creams to darken their skin, others were spending their money on creams to be whiter. I cringed when I saw ads for these products, pointing my finger at corporations that profited from this self-loathing.

Troubled by learning that women's value in Taiwan was attached to physical appearance, just as it was in North America, I wondered where in the world women are deemed beautiful by their own standards. I, too, had no immunity to the standards for slenderness. The only stores where I could buy clothes that fit were "American," and even there I had moved from a size small to an extra-large in the Taiwanese fashion market. Much as I'd wanted to deny and resist it, I was unnerved. In this respect, there was little difference between me and the Taiwanese women who felt inadequate if they didn't fit the perfect physical ideal.

I wanted so much not to care about the fact that I looked large compared with the women, or that my students considered me fat. I wanted not to care that I was making more money than I ever had playing games with children for six hours a day, while my Taiwanese colleagues were working twelve. I tried not to be bothered by the fact that white men weren't interested in me. Except that I did care. I couldn't deny it, but still I refused to acknowledge how I felt. I didn't want to have to convince myself to leave, to stop profiting from the exploitative system. I was accountable for my reality, and yet I fought it like a warrior.

I remembered Canada as perfect, thinking of the open spaces, the beautiful expansive forests filled with delicious fresh air. I blamed my discomfort in Taiwan on the horrible food that I could neither pronounce nor digest. I blamed the limited nightlife, the bad music, and the surplus of ecstasy that I was determined not to sample; I blamed the putrid-smelling hot weather that drained my energy after eight in the morning; I blamed anything I could see with my eyes. I foolishly asked the Universe why I was sinking into a depression. Why was I drinking more than what was good for me and smoking cigarettes, a habit that I had previously given up? What I thought I had known about myself and life in general was being undermined on a daily basis; I felt directionless, fake, and ignorant, especially within a frame of societal norms that excluded my own knowledge. Once a month, on payday, when I received a large stack of money, I felt temporarily content and deluded myself that it was a worthwhile compensation for my struggles and the reason that I needed to stay. The truth remained suffocated within by my greed and desire for privilege. My bank account guiltily expanded.

I wish I could say that these were the reasons I ran to the airport one month before my contract ended, but in truth I gave in to my desire to return home to the nurturing love of family and friends and the scent of sweet clean air. I had anticipated a euphoric homecoming but never found more than a nice return and a stream of tears that overtook me at the Winnipeg Folk Festival two days later. Painfully, I realized that Canada too had dirt and stink and bad drivers and isms and its own set of prescribed norms. Canada was not the glorious haven transmitted by a Molson Canadian beer commercial. I realized Taiwan was not to blame for my depression. The same inequality and power dynamics were just as pervasive in Canada as in the small, over-populated island from which I had just flown.

When I returned from Taiwan I was a different woman from the one who left; no other experience could have caused such a transformation. When people asked me about it, I told them the truth. I told them that it was hard, it was trying, and that I would never do it again. I also told them that even though I hated Taiwan when I was there, I wouldn't have missed it for anything, because I had learned valuable lessons from my experience. Now that I was home, my view was different. I no longer "hated" Taiwan. In fact, I realized I was grateful to the country—for being my teacher.

Journey

Amy Coupal

 From the plane, we could see untouched mountainous highlands. There were few signs of roads, homes, or industry. People were waving before the plane even hit the ground. As I stepped through the gate that separated a makeshift airstrip from the small town of Goroka, in Papua New Guinea (PNG), I couldn't help thinking of the rumors I had heard about the presence of cannibalism on this South Pacific island. The welcoming onlookers were smiling, but their lips, teeth, and gums, all dripping with cherry-red moisture, gave me pause. As I looked down, I saw crimson patches all over the dirt at my feet. Surely those stories weren't true! I hadn't wanted to believe them before arrival. Now that I was here, I felt a greater sense of urgency and curiosity about those rumors. My assumptions, fears, and best intentions were already being challenged.

Seeing the local contact waiting for our group of twelve volunteers helped alleviate my anxiety. As foreign English teachers living in Japan, we were enthusiastic about exploring yet another culture and making a contribution through the Habitat for Humanity build we were about to embark on. Fundraisers and planning meetings had allowed our almost exclusively female group to get to know one another, but this new experience was still daunting.

It was a relief to learn almost immediately that the red tinge to the locals' mouths and the patches on the ground were the result of chewing betel nut. This popular and easily procured stimulant does unpleasant things to one's oral hygiene and is much favored by South Sea islanders.

From the very first tired and frazzled day, it was clear that my journey to PNG would be a life-changing experience. I wanted to learn new things about the world, encounter different people, engage with other cultures, and, hopefully, share what I learned with others. What

I didn't know was that I would have to face my own misconceptions about another culture and myself and reexamine my assumptions about working as a volunteer in another country. But as we began our journey into the highlands, it was time to open my eyes and begin to take it all in.

Passing through Goroka and into the highlands, I was immediately aware of an extreme clash of urbanity, poverty, untouched wilderness, indigenous culture, and westernization. Perhaps it was the Larium, my antimalarial medication, but my new surroundings appeared surreal: concrete buildings sat next to thatched huts, locals in Western-style clothing drove by us in pickups, and the small town seemed like a stain on the sprawling, untouched, forested highlands all around us. I also struggled with the blending of Western objects with tribal tattoos, piercings, and ritual scarring. I was unsure if one man's septum piercing adorned with a Bic ballpoint pen was meant to be beautiful, political, or utilitarian.

Partway through our journey, we transferred from a small bus to a large pickup. It was overcrowded with about a dozen locals and our group of twelve volunteers. The second part of the ride was much bumpier and more harrowing than the first as we passed over extremely rickety bridges and navigated huge ruts in the muddy road. I could have stood waist-deep in some of them. Despite the possible danger of the ride, I continued to enjoy the scenery and felt my excitement increasing.

Arriving at our final destination, the village of Ontenu, we were greeted with a powerful and emotional welcoming ceremony. The villagers sang for us in English and their native tongue. We passed through a huge procession of villagers, tribal dancers, and curious neighbors. The ceremonial garments were beautiful, as was the face paint. Most interesting, though, were the Western undergarments peeking out from underneath. The juxtaposition of traditional dress with sports bras and boxer briefs was striking. I couldn't help thinking they would have looked better without them, and why they were wearing them at all? I worried about the impact previous visitors had made, how Western values might have altered their own. It was a reminder that my own presence here and these new relationships came with unasked-for power, potential, and responsibility.

We were the first Caucasian people that many of the villagers had ever seen. For others, it had been many years since Australian missionaries arrived in their village and converted them to Christianity. Their fascination was obvious, as was their happiness in having us there. The feeling was mutual. I felt charged by their beauty, smiles, and energy. It seemed ironic that I was ostensibly there to give something to them: short of openness, kindness, and hard work, I couldn't see what I could possibly give. I feel blessed to have my life, but on that day I felt blessed to be part of theirs, to see other people's priorities in motion, to see happiness in the face of what looked to be poverty. Their savage reputation seemed incongruous.

The road that had filled up with eager strangers on our arrival was empty the following day. I came to realize how few people actually lived in the immediate area. The village contained fewer than a dozen thatched, round houses, each one home to several members of an extended family. The peaks of the nearby hills displayed similar groups of dwellings, where I assumed some of the previous day's participants lived. But there had been so many; some people must have traveled a great distance to join in the ceremony.

As we approached the building site, we discovered that the frames and roofs of the two houses had already been constructed. It was obvious that our physical contributions would be minimal. The local men were much stronger and more experienced than we were. Thankfully, they had (I suspect) been told that they should make/help us to feel useful. They would start hammering nails, and we would finish the job. As members of both groups gained confidence, we began to work together more productively and with greater harmony. We focused on our strengths and established a cooperative approach that allowed all parties to feel confident of their contribution and the durability of the construction. I quickly realized that the most important gifts we could offer were the money we had raised and our friendship.

I particularly enjoyed making jokes with Ontie, the new "hauspapa" and head carpenter. He was a good-natured fellow who didn't hide his excitement or sense of responsibility about the whole project. He shared his observations on my "weak skin." It was hard to disagree; his skin, and everyone else's there, was much tougher than mine. This was especially true of their feet, which were also wider and flatter due to their never having worn shoes. The signs of exposure were evident not only in the condition of their skin but also their bodies, leading me to overestimate their ages greatly.

After the first day of work, a group of young girls informed us that it was bathing time. With my bikini under my clothes as a precaution, I followed them down the path to the river. Knowing that they bathe communally made me nervous, but they had set up the most beautiful-looking makeshift shower, made from a bamboo shoot tapped into a running stream. The water was bone-chilling, but my relief at being surrounded by a dirty canvas tarp overshadowed my discomfort.

Surprisingly, it was the girls who were bold enough to observe us from atop the hill. It was clear that the differences between our bodies were as fascinating to them as they were to us. Theirs were seasoned, reliable machines, attuned to the traditional demands of living in a hilly, subsistence community. They relied on few external supports for strength or vanity. In contrast, our bodies looked and were much weaker. We wore shoes, socks, and gloves when we worked. Sunscreen, bug spray, hats, and sunglasses protected us from the environment. All our tools, designed to make life and our jobs easier, suddenly seemed counterintuitive.

During the work process, a lack of organization, planning, and safety precautions often hindered our progress. There were long lulls waiting for supplies, people, or a meeting of the minds. We also learned that most work was done before lunch. On some days, good work was even undone by our bleary-eyed hosts, who appeared to have enjoyed more than just sustenance over their lunch break. Despite misgivings, we followed instructions, such as measuring floorboards in sequence. If they didn't fit, my job was to trim them with an enormously blunt saw while balancing on the meager framework of the house some ten to fifteen feet above the ground. I straddled the beams as best I could and sawed the boards toward myself, all the while trying to dispel the worrisome image of sawing off my own leg!

When I needed a break, I would visit with the local ladies, who brought water and food to support the workers. They would invite me into one of their round, thatched houses, which were small and dark even during the day. The fire in the centre of the hut and the absence of a chimney made it quite smoky, though some fumes escaped through the gaps in the thatched roof. At first, I thought I should not accept the women's offers of food and drink. I was there to help and didn't want to take more than I needed. Later I realized that accepting these tokens of appreciation was an important part of the relationship. Just as I was, they were giving what they could. Embracing and appreciating their desire to come together and share with us strengthened my relationships and understanding of who they were and how they lived.

The villagers of Ontenu did everything they could to promote exchanges between us. One Saturday evening, we were ushered into a round house to "story" or chat. Well into the evening, a neighboring pastor, who had grown up in the village, addressed us. He expressed his happiness that we were there and actually staying for a while. He emphasized how important it was for both the community and PNG that we were learning about them as individuals. He concluded by saying he hoped that we would tell people that no one tried to eat us! It was shocking and amusing to hear him talking about what people outside of PNG thought about them. He had a keen awareness of and connection to the outside world that the villagers of Ontenu didn't have. I shared his sentiments and looked forward to telling others about my experience.

Despite these positive feelings, however, I couldn't deny my growing suspicion that our presence was actually doing more harm than good in the community. The following morning brought evidence of the confusing effect of our visit. Our group was invited to one of the visiting pastor's services. His passionate message seemed, in many ways, to be directed at our group of visiting non-parishioners. The two-and-a-half-hour affair was manageable enough, but the subsequent personalized speech felt like too much. The pastor told us he hoped coming here would help us to accept Jesus Christ. He explained that money, possessions, and education often led people to abandon religion and hoped that seeing people who had nothing, but had accepted Christ, would inspire us to accept him too.

I had not expected this sort of preaching. As foreigners coming in, we worked hard to keep our respective religions and values to ourselves, yet this local leader clearly disagreed with our values, telling us to repent and see the evil of our ways! It was also upsetting that he seemed to feel that the fund-raising, volunteering, friendship, and new homes that had come out of the process were insignificant. Instead, the message seemed to be that it was all for naught if we didn't accept Christ. This lack of acceptance of difference was disappointing. The pitfalls of colonialist and missionary assumptions that I had been trying so hard to avoid seemed to be happening in reverse. My efforts to form collaborative and respectful relationships felt thwarted as the missionary zeal was turned on me! I had welcomed the possibility of transformation as a result of this journey, but I didn't want it to be forced or expected. I didn't want others to lecture me on how I should change or why. If my values, ideas, or feelings were to change, it needed to be from the inside out. I saw how the impact of this experience could go both ways.

While I was still trying to reconcile my feelings about this encounter, my concerns about our impact on the people of Ontenu were growing as well. One of my new friends, Betty, invited me to her house and presented me with a *bullum*. It was a touching gift, as I knew she had made the bag herself, but when I read the note that came with it, my heart sank. She wrote that she was happy to be my friend and happy to give me the bag. In return, she expected three things: my sleeping bag, my green sarong, and a pair of my footwear. The note seemed genuine and not intended to be hurtful, but the list of demands had that effect. Instantly, the relationship we had developed felt false to me. I felt used and conflicted. Our group had been given strict instructions not to give individual people our personal goods, as it could result in jealousy and theft. The villagers had been told the same thing. I began to question the relationships I had developed and the kindness people had extended to me. What were the villagers' motives for bringing us there? Had people been nice only because they wanted things from us? I also struggled with my indignation over Betty's failure to realize how hard we had all worked to go there. Shouldn't knowing that people care enough about you to come across the world to help you fund and build a new house be enough?

While questioning their motives, I also had to question my own. What had I truly wanted from the people of Ontenu? Was it fair for me to judge Betty's request as self-interested when I could simply have given her those things and replaced them? Would the value of the project outweigh any damage done? The excitement, enthusiasm, and pride I had felt at being a part of this seemingly positive contribution dwindled. My misgivings felt justified. I was overwhelmed by the loss of control.

My concerns about bringing my Western ideals and goods (however modestly packed) began to feel justified. I felt guilty having a knapsack filled with more items than my new friends had in their homes. My goal of leaving no trace on this journey had failed. More painful was the realization that it had never really been possible. I had been so concerned with not leaving an impact that I hadn't really considered the inevitability of doing so. I had assumed I was in control of that outcome, but now I saw that I was not, and couldn't be. I was forced to recognize how my expectations for this experience and these new friendships had impaired my ability to respond to unforeseen challenges or voluntarily let go of control.

In my naïveté, I had desired a friendship with no strings attached, an idyllic connection that would transcend all borders. My assumptions about the people of Ontenu had distorted my understanding of how they saw themselves and us, their relative wealth or place in the world. I had placed them on a higher pedestal because they live more simply, more organically. I came face-to-face with the Western, patronizing, noble-savage perceptions I didn't even know I had!

This awareness allowed me to see all of our lives in a much broader context than this project. Each of us brought an individual life experience, perspective, and motivation to the situation. For both my new friends and me, our contact—each interaction and contribu-tion—could have a potentially great impact: it was volatile but could be beneficial. How we would absorb, process, and respond to what we had learned would be up to each of us.

Our departure from Ontenu was bittersweet. It had truly been a life-changing experience. New friendships had blossomed, new skills had been developed and many lessons learned. Perhaps these things were on everyone's mind as we took the bumpy, dirty, hot journey out of the mountains, the air filled with the songs of the village leaders rid-ing with us in the back of the pickup truck. The undulation of their voices was the perfect soundtrack for our transition back to the increasing levels of civilization we would encounter.

As we rode, I realized that my goals for this experience had been more than fulfilled. I had learned as much about myself as about oth-ers. I continue to believe we all have a responsibility as citizens of the world to make positive contributions to our communities, large and small. This experience taught me to examine very carefully how I do that. Certainly organizations realize that people will be more likely to fund-raise/donate money if they are able to take part in something. They are right. I wanted a unique experience, to meet new people, and to support others. The local group welcomed the new relationships and contributions to their community.

Yet, despite the fact that these goals were fulfilled, I continue to wonder whether the personal growth and benefit to all parties out-weighs any damage our visit may have done to this community. I may never know the answer to that question, but I am nonetheless truly grateful for the experience. I discovered so many dimensions to my worldview that I didn't know were there. Perhaps the most important lesson for me was about how much—or how little—power each of us has. This personal power comes with a tremendous responsibility. I appreciate that it must be used wisely.

I'm Not Just Here to Take a Walk, You Know...!

Christine McKenzie

 The women of the small community on the Caribbean coast of Nicaragua where I was living were my salvation. They did everything they could to make sure I was okay: they "minded" me, and in fact competed over who would have this role. I am not sure how I would have been able to live there and do my research if it had not been for them.

Even though they were busy with the daily demands of fetching water, scrubbing clothes, cooking over their fire, and taking care of their kids, the women of the neighborhood made a point of checking in on me often in the little home I rented there. They cooked for me, made sure I had clean clothes, called out as they passed by my porch, and often wandered through the house for brief moments of exchange between chores. They kept me up to date on the wind direction and what this implied for drying laundry and the possibilities of catching fish, both of which affected me, but were rarely at the forefront of my mind... and of course, they caught me up on gossip about the others ...

One day when she breezed through to see what I was up to, my neighbor Miss Cynthia, who was my main "mother figure" and a woman I had grown quite close to, picked one of my participatory methodologies and research books off the shelf. She always seemed curious about my books, and I was pleased that she picked up this book in particular. Having a chance to talk with people about what I was doing there was important to me, and a natural opening like this was like a blessing!

I said that the book was about the kind of research I wanted to do—that would involve the people in saying what their problems were

163

and would allow us to learn and work together to improve people's lives. I said I did not want to just ask a bunch of questions and then take off. I wanted to share power with people.

I said a few words about this, but I had hardly started before something in the book made Miss Cynthia explode into laughter. She was too hysterical to say anything. All she could do was point to the title of the chapter, which I remember as having been written from the perspective of a community person who was "being researched."

The chapter was titled "What do you know about my life anyway?"

She continued laughing and I scrambled for a response, a question, something. Before I could say anything, one of her kids called for her from next door and she was gone.

The moments I shared with the women of the community frequently involved telling stories and laughing together, but other moments, like the one with Miss Cynthia, were uncomfortable. These moments of exchange, especially the uncomfortable ones, were rich with significance.

I entered a new dynamic when I was able to have my neighbors accept my participation in doing my own laundry. It may sound trivial, but within the complex system of loans, favors, and paid work between neighbors in this fishing village, I was never permitted to do manual labor, and this troubled me. I like physical work, and when I could, I wanted to be able to give support and share the burden. As a young single woman who spent most of her time consumed with research that was often carried out with the village elders (read *men*), I had a role that was both contradictory and different from that of the other women. One thing was clear to my neighbors, however—I was "from the North" and therefore I was wealthy. In this instance, at least for an afternoon, I had turned my back on this identity, taken my monetary contribution out of the equation of the local economy, and gone with some of the young girls to the creek behind the community to do the wash.

While we had an important task to do, it was also a time for play. For a good portion of the afternoon, we were alone at the creek under the hot sun. We teased, pushed, and splashed one another as we stood waist-deep in the water, scrubbing on the plank of wood suspended over the creek that acted as a washboard. When we had nearly finished the last bunch of clothes, an older woman whom I did not know approached the creek with a huge basket of wash balanced on her head, one hand on her hip.

"Not done yet?" She scowled at us. "I'm not just here to *take a walk*, you know!"

My seven-month stay in Nicaragua as a student researcher was a new experience for me. When I had traveled before, it was out of the desire to gain a new perspective on the world, like many women who travel.[1] This time, however, my reasons had shifted. Now my interest was not so much in getting a new perspective on the world as it was in thinking more critically about the perspective I already had. I was now thinking about how that perspective had been shaped and what it meant for the way I moved and interacted in the world.

Miss Cynthia's laughter and my afternoon washing clothes in the creek were among the memories that stand out as strong catalysts for reflection.

This trip was different from those I took as a tourist or an NGO development worker. This time, being a student, I took more time than usual before my journey to consider the British and Afro-Caribbean historical legacies and the political repercussions of the Sandinista revolution on Nicaragua's Caribbean/Atlantic Coast. Also, living the majority of my time in a small community, without the company of expats who might have sheltered me from the unfamiliar rhythms of daily life in a culture that was new to me, I participated more fully in my present community; I was immersed in it and in the joys and pain that came with it.

Within this context and with an embarrassingly large pile of critical theory on my bookshelf, I focused my attention on the investigation I had come to carry out. However, there were also things nagging at me from the periphery, stuff that crept in, demanding to be looked at, that took me longer to name. It was where the personal and the theoretical merged. My experience of Nicaragua was challenging me to consider who I was in the world, primarily through my struggles with the contradictory nature of the closeness I shared with the women in the community and the issues of colonialism that these tensions pointed to.

For me, it was important to trust those niggling feelings and follow up on my discomfort. Reflecting on feelings and analyzing them to see what they point to is essential, as considering things from a feminist perspective means taking emotions seriously. This means not treating emotions as secondary or merely "subjective" reactions to "real" experiences but rather as something substantial to pay attention to on its own merit.[2]

For instance, I was distressed that Miss Cynthia seemed entertained by the thought that I could be interested in working toward a common cause despite our different realities. I had to acknowledge that though I had developed strong bonds with many of the women, mutual support and the intention of solidarity were not going to be enough to eliminate our divisions. Likewise, I was uncomfortable with the suggestion that I was "taking a walk," or hanging around idly, that my participatory action research with the community made a pastime of the Creole woman's daily chores and life's circumstances. This forced me to question the belief that my effort to participate, or "give back," would be of value simply because my intentions were good.

Miss Cynthia and the woman at the creek confronted me, at a very personal level, with my erroneous assumptions. My individual actions could not be transformational, particularly if I failed to situate them within a deeper historical context. Many travelers may not consider that colonization is a practice that is structurally reproduced around the world in the present day. The local community was grounded in a complicated history of outsider intervention, conquest, slavery, and "emancipation" by the British, followed by the continuous exploitation of land and resources, a system that was embraced by the locals because it provided needed employment. My presence, in view of these factors, was experienced in complex ways.

Colonization was not a one-time transaction that took place when the New World was violently "settled," but a practice that continues in ways so subtle and pervasive that they are often invisible. Historical beliefs and structures that began with colonization have been normalized over time and have created unearned privileges based on race, class, economic, or "development" status. These are then transmitted as rights that are seen as just "the way it is." Systemically, as a white person I am taught to be blind to the perpetuation of colonialism because I profit from it and therefore can easily dismiss the privileges that it grants me.[3]

How was it I could choose to take a break from my research to do laundry, or define myself as someone working in solidarity with the women of the community, or travel to their country in the first place?

It is continued colonialism that grants these privileges, basing them on the accepted notion that distant countries and their less advanced people are there to be ruled, or in some way assisted.[4]

Travel unfortunately often reinforces such stereotypes. It has been noted that for white women, contact with Others, often non-white women, allows them to position themselves as modern and enlightened, and reinforces the imperialist idea that they are more liberated than their sisters in the South.[5] By taking advantage of their privileged ability to leave their home environment and elect to "be someone else" in another space, white women can escape the need to confront and challenge oppression such as the sexism, classism, and ableism (among others) that they may experience in their daily lives in their own countries. This aspect of travel is rarely questioned in travel literature. Similarly, the extent to which women in the North and the South support gendered oppression, as some women exploit and others serve them in our globalized economy, is also largely made invisible within the context of travel writing.[6] Travel can ideally enable conversations across differences, illuminating these issues to create new understandings, meaning and action for change. These exchanges, however, cannot be divorced from the way that colonial history and stereotypes have shaped what we each believe about ourselves and one another.[7] Understanding this is a good place to start.

Within these structures of colonial power, I do have the individual choice to try to be an ally,[8] acknowledging the injustices that exist and exercising the personal agency I have within these systems to alter them. However, understanding and acting responsibly *from* who I am and not in *opposition or denial* of who I am is central to working to change things.[9]

Although I, an outsider, could not fully understand the particular lived experience of oppression, it is not necessarily the case that I can *never* come to share insights or know others.[10] This understanding takes courage, humility, a sense of humor, and above all patience. To work on the basis of assumed solidarity will never be as meaningful or lasting as remaining open to uncomfortable moments when they arise and following through to question one's assumptions about relations of power and the unearned privileges that these moments reveal.

These questions may never lead to neat, packaged answers. The world is complex, and we travel whenever we move into a new setting, whether at home or abroad. These movements can facilitate transient disconnect, and they can illuminate critical questions and build self-recognition, which leads to new decisions about our actions and new forms of change. Each time, there are choices about how we will be *taking a walk*.

NOTES

1) Jansz, Natania and Miranda Davies, eds., *More Women and Travel: Adventures and Advice from more than 60 Countries*. New York, NY: Rough Guides, 1995. Jansz and Davies summarized that many women "have launched themselves abroad as a means of escaping a rut, relishing the chance to free themselves from the usual reference points, find new stimulation and a new perspective about the world in which we live." I think it is important in this case to question which women we are referring to, who have the luxury to travel and "escape from reality" and why.

2) Narayan, Uma. "Working Together Across Difference: Some

Considerations on Emotions and Political Practice," *Hypatia* 3, no. 2: 31–47

3) McIntosh, P. "White Privilege and Male Privilege: A Personal Account of Coming to See Correspondences through Work in Women's Studies," Anderson, M. and P. Collins, eds., *Race, Class and Gender: An Anthology,* 2nd ed. Belmont, CA: Woodsworth, 1995, 438–44. McIntosh notes that "unearned" is "liked an invisible knapsack of assets that I can count on cashing in each day, but about which I was meant to remain oblivious.

4) Said., E. *Culture and Imperialism.* New York, NY: Vintage Books, 1994, 10. Said explores how imperialism is portrayed and perpetuated through art and literature.

5) Razack., S. . *Looking White People in the Eye: Gender, Race, and Culture in Courtroom and Classrooms.* Toronto, Ont.: University of Toronto Press, 1998.

6) Ibid, 13.

7) Frankenberg, R. *The Social Construction of Whiteness: White Women, Race Matters.* Minneapolis, MA: University of Minnesota Press, 1993, 5. Frankenberg says that, "there is a direct relationship between 'experience' and 'worldview' or 'standpoint' and that a system of domination is seen most clearly from the subject positions of those oppressed by it." In other words, not being one who was oppressed in the situations I describe here (based on racism, classism or my Western status), it was more difficult for me to see my own position of power in my relationships with the women of the community.

8) Bishop, A. *Becoming an Ally: Breaking the Cycle of Oppression.* Halifax, N.S: Fernwood Publishing, 1994.

9) Narayan, "Working Together Across Difference," 36.

The Missionary and Her Mission

sarahmaya hamilton

 In an episode of the television series *Six Feet Under*, Ruth asks her co-worker, Robby, what happened when he came out to his parents, and Robby is affronted by the question, suggesting facetiously that Ruth share something deeply intimate from her own past with him. Before this, it hadn't occurred to me that a person might not want to share her coming-out story with any curious straight person who asked. Curious straight people, I figured, were an asset in the effort to expand societal awareness on all matters queer. Why wouldn't every queer person want to strive toward that, by divulging histories on request?

Assumptions such as this can become distorted with the crossing of borders, much like seeing your own hand through a glass of water. Since August 2002, I have been living in a small town in rural Japan, teaching English with the JET (Japan Exchange and Teaching) Programme, where my mandate is both the teaching of English and the amorphously defined "grassroots internationalization"—which might just mean living day to day, exposing the conservative (but earthy) people of my town to the Amazing Life of a Foreigner.

I chose Japan because one of my mothers, Joy, is Japanese Canadian. Her grandmother, Chieko, is still alive but speaks no English, and I had wanted to study Japanese to learn the story of her life. Unfortunately, because of Chieko's cultural background and Joy's sexual orientation, I am not certain whether Chieko recognizes me as her great-granddaughter.

Likewise, in contemporary Japan, it is frequently the case that queer identities are not disapproved of—they simply don't exist. Outside larger cities, queer people tend to enter into straight marriages for the sake of their families and careers. Thus, they avoid distinguishing themselves from their straight co-workers and further their chances of promotion. In the conservative *inaka*, or countryside, prefecture of Ehime, straight Japan seems only dimly aware of the possibility of queer orientations—as yet another odd, foreign importation.

In September 2003, at the gentle urging of my co-worker Ohno-sensei, I spoke with each of the classes in my junior high school about my mothers' marriage and their battle to get there. It was a matter of chance that I happened to be living in Japan at the time that the Canadian marriage law changed to include same-sex couples, that I was the daughter of two of the pioneers who had fought to make it so, and that I was co-teaching English with a man who had a passion for expanding the minds of his students. When one twelve-year-old asked, incredulous, "Are there gay people in Japan?" he answered quietly and firmly, "Of course there are. Of course!" Perhaps one of the students needed to hear this. As a catalyst, I was a convenient cog in the right place at the right time, with a ripe opportunity to strike a chord with one of my students—in my own small, grassroots way. Maybe this would open a dialogue about queer issues in small-town Ehime and make it easier for a teenager to come out.

Opportunities to discuss queer issues in English class came up sporadically after that. For example, one day Ohno-sensei chose "Born to Love You" by Queen as a warm-up song for the third-year students. Mid-song, a pair of lines piqued my gaydar: the lack of gender references suggested a deliberate omission. I soberly remembered that Freddie Mercury was gay and had died of AIDS. But I was excited to make a link between his life and the song, since "Born to Love You" had enjoyed recent fame in Japan, as the theme of the immensely popular TV drama *Pride* (a show about a Japanese NHL player; the word doesn't have the same connotations in Japan). Here was an opportunity for me to relate something queer to something that was familiar for the students. We sang the song, and then I asked Ohno-sensei if we could speak to the students about Freddie Mercury. He agreed. In Japanese, he told the students that the now-deceased singer of the song they loved had been gay.

While admirable, this was not the conversation I'd had in mind. "Is it okay to talk about AIDS?" I pressed. I was concerned that the topic would now be couched in the context of queerness; maybe the students would think my warnings didn't apply to them, as ostensibly straight people. But then again, they probably hadn't had enough exposure to the topic of AIDS to make the fallacious assumption that North American teenagers might—that only gay men are at risk for contracting HIV. Although the students had been given lessons on genitalia in elementary school and would this year learn about heterosexual sex and sexually transmitted diseases, I still felt that the rising rate of HIV infection among both gay and straight youth in Japan made it imperative to talk about Freddie Mercury's death from AIDS.

When I was in the eighth grade in rural Canada, I was impressed by the frankness of two sex educators who demonstrated how to unroll a real condom onto a stand-up wooden dildo. My parents were open to discussing sex, but it was this lesson that impressed condom usage on me. Now in English class, I was hoping to give a similar shock to my students, to speak frankly and respectfully with them about this "adult" topic. They were likely to remember the lesson if it was delivered by a foreign teacher. Maybe it would save their lives someday.

Ohno-sensei nodded his assent, hesitant, perhaps fearing that I would speak too explicitly. The roomful of fourteen- to fifteen-year-olds watched us expectantly. I asked if anyone knew how Freddie Mercury had died. After a silence, they began to call out illnesses.

"HIV!" said the ever-stylish boy at the back.

"Right! He had HIV. And HIV can lead to AIDS. And AIDS can kill you." My words had to be simple. On the board, I drew an arrow from HIV to AIDS. I wondered if it was "age-appropriate" to talk about condoms, whether this would create the furor here that it might in rural America. But these kids, whatever their sexual orientations, needed to know how to avoid HIV transmission in a country where youth were at risk. I asked Ohno-sensei for permission. Again, a hesitant yes.

A hesitant yes in Japan can mean no. It was possible that I was to interpret his reluctance as a polite way of ending the lesson. The line was blurry: speaking about queer marriage was okay, but speaking about sexual health was not? Uncertain of where exactly the boundaries were, I decided to play my *gaijin* card and take his permission at face value, as foreigners are so gauchely wont to do.

"There are two easy ways to catch HIV," I began. "What are they, do you know?"

The students stared blankly. Ohno-sensei translated, but they were still puzzled.

"Here's one," I said. I pretended to inject a narcotic into my arm, simulating bliss. Ohno-sensei forgot his hesitation and clicked into role-play mode, as I passed him the pretend needle. He injected himself and feigned an amusing high. The students laughed.

"We took drugs with the same needle," Ohno-sensei explained in simple English. The students nodded, getting it. I drew a needle on the board and an arrow to HIV.

Now I had their attention. In both English and Japanese, I said, "Here is another: *not using a condom when you're having sex.*"

The students nodded again, looking surprised and interested. There was an atmosphere of maturity in the room. In this slower-paced "step-class," kids who usually didn't pay attention were rapt. Ironically so, since it was perhaps not an acceptable conversation to have at their age level. Especially not in direct interactive terms, with a young, foreign, possibly radical teacher—in a public school, where the high esteem accorded to the *sensei* class made the reputations of Japanese teachers as sensitive as those of politicians.

To emphasize the point, I drew an X through the condom on the board, and an arrow from this to AIDS.

"So please, everyone," I said as I turned to face them, "always use a condom!"

It was a public-service announcement that had been on the tip of my tongue since we'd begun singing "Born to Love You." Ohno-sensei, shifting his feet, translated what I'd said. I was curious about the amorphous cultural context of this interaction and reflected that I might never know what was going through his head.

Later, I received a hint, when Ohno-sensei told me that he had given the same lesson by himself to the other third-year classes. It didn't seem to be an accident that he hadn't taken me along. I understood that I wasn't to bring it up, but I was relieved that it had received at least some attention. It is critical that AIDS education receive emphasis in Japan's public schools. Acting like a positive corollary of the virus, the meme may spread. Hopefully, it will overtake the virus, and condom usage will become the norm before HIV infection has a chance to dent the demographics.

Having raised the meme in the first place, I had again the feeling of being a fortuitously placed cog in this system. I reflected that living in Japan can be discouraging at times. In the notoriously conservative *inaka* of Ehime, foreigners are often regarded as irredeemably different. A lingering reminder of the ideology that prompted the country's two centuries of isolation, the term *gaijin* translates as "outside person." This thinking seems entrenched within the education system that operates public schools and maintains the JET Programme: English teachers function as class jesters, whose currency hinges on their ability to keep the class entertained with their unchanging, irreversible otherness. In contrast with Vancouver, where international cultures seem to maintain distinctiveness while integrating within the larger, culturally diverse Canadian metascape, in Japan it feels futile for me to try to turn Japanese, as the Vapors' 1981 song suggests, especially when my employment hinges on difference. No matter how Japanese I become, the color of my skin and the nature of my employment will undermine my credentials.

But, in spite of the sometimes intense isolation, lessons like the one on Freddie Mercury and the one in which I spoke about my parents' queer marriage make me happy that I am here. I am able to make a positive contribution in Japan just by existing in my rural town as a living, breathing example of diversity; and the ways in which I am different from the generic *gaijin* model of otherness are received by my neighbors with curiosity and interest. (So are my similarities with people here.) My subversive contributions may turn out to be negligible in the overall scheme of Japanese pedagogy, but I'm doing my bit for the educational mandate of internationalization. And after all, it is for this, as the Ministry of Education and Cultural Affairs tells me, that I am here—for the gentle tug and push of boundaries. For the voyage over cultural lines that is emblematized in the crossing of the Pacific to teach English.

But soon after the Freddie Mercury lesson came a new challenge: the implementation of "school lunch." School lunch does not offer vegetarian options—or any options at all. So I was to continue to bring my own lunch to school and eat alone at my desk, while the other teachers sat around a table of plastic trays at the end of the long office we share, chatting together.

Again I was on the outside of the social group—an omission that can result in ostracism. I doubted my special diet, my uncompromising individuality. I doubted myself for speaking up about AIDS and condoms. Between my odd eating habits and my sex-positive, openly queer politics, I felt like a footnote in the Japanese teachers' room. I couldn't gauge the parameters of acceptability, and My Amazing Foreign Novelty had worn thin. Already physically distinct, and mediocre in Japanese proficiency, I didn't need another reason to feel outside of the group.

So one day, while eating alone at my desk and reading the copy of *Maclean's* that my mother had sent from home, I decided to bridge the cultural chasm. I showed friendly Higashi-sensei the photo of my married mothers in the center of the magazine. I had already explained the oddities of my family to her.

She actively and enthusiastically expressed her interest, as one does in Japan when someone makes an effort, and in the midst of this enthusiasm, she invited nearby Takeda-sensei to have a look.

I was obliged to explain who the two people in the photo were: my parents.

"Your parents?" he asked with interest, in Japanese.

"Yes," I answered. Pointing to Jena-mom, I said in Japanese, "This is my mom." Pointing to Joy-mom, I opted for the factually correct yet somewhat of a cop-out "This is my mom's wife." It seemed more comprehensible.

But it was met with silence. "*Eh?*" he finally ventured.

"My mom," I explained again simply. "And my mom's wife." I watched his face. It had gone from excited to see my parents in a magazine to pained confusion. He didn't understand but didn't want to be so rude as to say so.

"Your mom," he repeated, pointing at Jena-mom. I nodded. "And your mom's—"

"*Tsuma*," I finished for him. The word for *wife* was giving him difficulty.

"Wife?" he asked. "Not your mom's husband?" He was carefully hinting that I had mixed up the Japanese terms for "wife" and "husband."

"No, not her husband," I said delicately. "Her wife." I looked at the photo. It was plausible that Joy could be mistaken for a man. I guess.

"Your parents?" he asked again.

"Yes. My birth mother. And my adopted mother."

"Oh!" he said, getting it. "Birth mother … *To … Jaaa, kanojo wa oba ni naru sooo,*" he proclaimed. Joy had become my "aunt": an older woman who is not my mother.

"No, that's incorrect," I said politely. "Mother, and *mother.*"

"*Ehhhh?*" he said, confused again. "You have *two?*"

"Yes, I have two!" I confirmed with a pleased smile. To make it absolutely clear, I added, "They're married."

"*Ehh?*" But now Takeda-sensei looked uncertain again. "Married? *Ehh?*" Cautiously, he looked at Higashi-sensei. "Same-sex love?"

"*So, so, so!*" I erupted excitedly. "Yes! Same-sex love!" I was pleased to have registered as intelligible and elated to have recognized *doseai*, the word for "queer love."

"Oh, is that right! That's complicated, eh?" He was smiling.

"The *explanation* is complicated," I conceded. Not my family. My family is just my family.

I explained briefly that my moms had helped to change the law in Canada. He nodded politely, seeming to have heard. Or maybe he was just overwhelmed. Then he asked the inevitable questions about what had happened to my father—the more important issue. Had they divorced? The relevant *they*, of course, being my mother and father.

Politely, I gave him the truncated version. "My mother and father were never married." I left off with a serious face, and looked down at my desk. This was a subtle way of letting him know that I had begun to feel like a sideshow exhibition, reluctantly exoticized, and the show was over. The boundaries that were being pushed were now mine, and it made me uncomfortable. This dissection of the Life of a Foreigner was no longer part of my work; it had become personal.

Nodding, Takeda-sensei went back to his own desk. "Ah, ah, ah. Probably I've understood. Interesting!"

And I went back to my lunch alone. Glad of it, for once.

Explaining the intricacies of my personal life, and being met with incredulity, can be exhausting. It puts me in the position of "other" in a way that is discordant with my intuitive sense that I am fundamentally a subject. Like any minority person anywhere, I forget that I am a novelty. I forget to be surprised by my family, taking them for granted. I don't feel as if they should have to be explained. Who else has to draw up a chart to indicate the whereabouts of a parent they never knew, whenever they make a new friend? Why is it difficult to recognize, in Japan or Canada, that two women and their kids make a complete family?

Indeed, we do.

While in the past it has sometimes been fun to shock people with the details of my lineage, in *inaka* Japan, the elision of queer identities and the extremes of disbelief have been turning the mission tedious.

But perhaps confronting this disbelief, tugging gently at it and expanding the boundaries of awareness, is the point of Life as a Foreign Object. The point of grassroots internationalization. To smile and be gentle about it every time someone doesn't understand; to stomp and holler clever retorts every time someone is nasty. And maybe someday my children won't *need* to explain why they have two maternal grandmothers. (Or hell, maybe four.)

In the end, in *Six Feet Under*, Ruth does share an intimacy from her past with Robby, and the two enjoy a laugh together. But Robby is staunch that he isn't going to tell her his coming-out story—because he hasn't got one. Sidestepping disbelief and messy confrontations, he has opted for self-protection instead, leaving a part of his story unwritten. Like queer people throughout Japan, he was faced with a choice between becoming a Foreign Object and elision. He chose elision.

As I eat lunch alone at my desk, listening to the rhythmic trill of cicadas in the summer heat, and thinking back to the omission in the lyrics of "Born to Love You," it occurs to me: probably I understand his decision. Maybe once in a while, it's just easier not to divulge. Easier to tuck away the story of your life, fold up the pages, and gently hide *Maclean's* away in the drawer of your desk. To focus instead on the way the light strikes your palm through a glass of *mugicha*.

Growing Up in Shanghai

Marion E. Jones

Upon finishing my BA in development economics at the University of Toronto, at the tender age of twenty-two, I embarked on a grand adventure that set the course for much of the rest of my life. It was a year when I finally broke out of my chrysalis, the conservative, serious rigidities of late 1980s Toronto "preppydom" and emerged as a vibrant butterfly, or perhaps merely a better-adjusted human being. Such metamorphoses are rarely smooth and painless, but in the end, they are invaluable.

Lesson 1: The Road Less Traveled Leads Away from Woulda, Shoulda, Coulda

I had spent my summer working at Statistics Canada with Dr. Ed Pryor, then director general of Census Division. I had applied to study in Shanghai, at Fudan University, before going to graduate school, but as the summer wore on, there was nothing forthcoming from the Chinese government regarding my study plans—a fate worse than death for a triple A-type personality. This was 1988, and there remained many vestiges of the Stalinist bureaucracy in China. I started to panic and orchestrated a place in graduate school at Carleton as a fallback. When at last the nod came from China, the letter informed me that I had two weeks to get to Shanghai or lose my place. I hesitated! Looking back, I cannot believe that I almost did not leap at the chance when it came at last. This was where Ed Pryor's mentorship was vital. Unlike other influential forces in my life urging me to follow through with graduate school, he encouraged me to go, saying that graduate school would always be there, but the opportunity to study in Shanghai comes only once, and that if I passed up this opportunity I would regret it for the rest of my life. His was the voice of reason; truer words have rarely been spoken. I rushed to finish up my summer work and prepared to move to Shanghai for a year. To this day I have never looked back. This was the start of an amazing year of transformations, at the end of which I now had the strength to follow my convictions, weighing carefully advice given, but free to follow my own head and heart. It helped me persevere in both my doctoral studies and the topic of my dissertation, and at the same time opened the doors to those opportunities. My life is richer and more rewarding, and thanks to Ed Pryor, free from regrets about missed opportunity. The lesson was quickly learned as, on the strength of my Shanghai experience, I went to graduate school in England—Cambridge and London—instead of Carleton.

Lesson 2: Perseverance Bears Rich Rewards

It was cold and wet in Ottawa that late August, and I was exhausted when I boarded the plane to Shanghai—tying up loose ends in Canada and preparing for a year overseas had robbed me of sleep the last two nights. My fatigue, the wall of heat and humidity, and the smells of sulfurous coal and human waste that washed over me as I left the plane in Shanghai made it seem as if I were passing through the looking glass into another world—and so it proved to be.

It was quite an adventure getting from the airport to the University. Although I was armed with one year of Mandarin Chinese and on paper should have been at least bare-bones literate, nothing had prepared me for the challenges of Shanghai dialect, or even Shanghai Mandarin, after a summer's neglect. It was only by proffering my official piece of paper that I managed to communicate with the taxi driver at all. Thank heavens that Chinese characters do not alter between dialects, merely their pronunciation, and that most people were literate in China, including my taxi driver.

It took two hours, and an alarming share of my disposable income, to travel by cab from the airport to the main gates of the university, during which time the sun set. The suffocating heat abated a little. The driver had no idea how to find the foreign students' dormitory—apartheid was alive and well on Chinese campuses in those days—and the police stationed at the main gate were not very helpful. Finally, we arrived at what was to become my home for the next nine months: an annex off the northeast corner of the campus, surrounded by factories and their employees' concrete apartment blocks.

The last glimmer of twilight hugged the horizon, and the gates to the compound were securely locked. The gatekeeper informed me that he did not have my name on his list and therefore could not admit me no matter what my fancy paperwork from Beijing might say. I was looking at a night on my luggage in the dirt outside the gate, surrounded by impersonal concrete, off the map of central Shanghai, with no food, no shelter, and no access to a bathroom. Things were grim, and my accumulated sleep deprivation was catching up with me: despair was setting in. But humanity triumphed in the face of bureaucracy. The gatekeeper relented. No longer a heartless official, he became the kindly, elderly gentleman he truly was. He let me in the gate and led me to a room where I could crash for the night. The room had only a box spring, no mattress, and a thin cover made of toweling. The wooden struts that gave the box spring its substance were visible through the material, like a ribcage. I deposited my bags and went in search of some sustenance. I was starving.

The canteen had closed, and the night had settled in like smoky black velvet—there was an alarming lack of streetlights in this part of the city. But there were people around. A well-established foreign student, who was holding court with some newbies on the steps of the male student dormitory in fluent Chinglish, dashed my hopes of finding grub—the hand waved in some general direction out of the gate was not helpful enough. I returned to my room, ate one of the two plums I had spirited off the plane (saving the second one for breakfast) and settled down to sleep, wondering where I was, why I was here, and what had possessed me to travel halfway around the globe. I longed to be back at home in the comfort of Canada. It was the first of a number of bad moments that first week. But I pulled myself together and made a conscious decision to stay the course, transform the unfamiliar and foreign headwind into a wind at my back, and face new challenges with an open mind.

The following day, after I had paid tuition, rent and deposits for futon, bedding, mosquito net and holder (complete with spider mites), enameled metal plate, bowl, cup, and a pair of chopsticks, I started to settle in. Life was looking up. Within a week, I had made some good friends, had a bicycle (the equivalent of car ownership in Canada), and the means to cook for myself on the single gas ring down the hall. This latter was not easily achieved with steel and aluminum products, including kettles and pots, still being rationed by the state, and new products were only purchasable with an old trade-in or a state marriage certificate, neither of which I possessed. Adjusting to a new culture was difficult at times: there was the meal with weevils in the rice, and a pork chop like shoe leather in the canteen; and the sweaty bus ride down-town to register with the Canadian Consulate—this polite Canadian let five cramped buses leave the Wujiaochang station before she could push her way onto one, and then she was not sure whether her clothes were wet from her sweat or that of others, or that her body was the same shape on exiting that it was when she first got on. But I was reminded that my life of comfort in the West was a privilege, not a right, and realized that I had slipped into taking it for granted.

After the despair of that first evening, the only moment of doubt and regret occurred in the Canadian Consulate after that first trau-matic bus ride downtown. The sudden oasis of familiarity and com-fort afforded by the air-conditioned consulate, where people were kind and understanding, and spoke French and English (a veritable slice of Canada in the middle of Asia) triggered an emotional volcano of sobs and tears. I suddenly realized that I was experiencing culture shock. The kind people at the consulate offered invitations to tennis and barbecues to perpetuate a sense of the familiar and to ease my transition. However, I quickly concluded that the answer was not in re-exposure to the safety of the familiar but rather in wholeheartedly embracing this new, and at times adverse, reality. Cowering in my cocoon was not an option: this butterfly had to fly—no matter how turbulent the flight.

From that day forward, I have had many wonderful experiences and formed numerous strong friendships that have extended beyond my year in Shanghai to the present on the road less traveled. I have moved around from continent to continent and am now always excited by the prospects of the new and unfamiliar and perhaps rather too eager to shed the old and familiar. Life is never dull on the poet's "road less traveled," and I have discovered that I often meet the most remarkable, lovely, charming, and friendly people there.

Lesson 3: Don't Judge a Book by Its Cover

I started life with principles of tolerance and inclusion, and although I always approached people on an equal footing, I was often quick to attach to or dismiss people based on relatively little data. My newfound friend Michael set me to putting those principles into practice. My first exposure to him had left me completely unimpressed. Michael was the well-established student holding court the night I had arrived at the dormitories, and his Chinglish affectations and lack of assistance that evening had done little to endear him to me. It was only weeks later that I associated this person with my friend Michael. By then our friendship was firmly formed, and I could only laugh at the narrow escape that I had had from my prejudices and misgivings about people. Instead, with Michael, I share a friendship that has spanned four continents, our respective families, and most of two decades.

I have forgotten just what event first introduced us as friends, but I am sure that it was associated with food—shopping for food, cooking together, or eating out—all being a chief source of entertainment, and at times frustration, but always a means through which to explore Shanghai and ourselves. I met Michael through Sandy, a wonderful hall-mate from New York who had just returned to Shanghai after a year in the States and had shared Michael's first year in China. The three of us, through our common love of food, music, art, and culture, and the very dark sense of humor we shared, were soon the closest of friends. To the outside observer this seemed improbable, as we superficially appeared to have little in common, what with Michael's Oscar

Wilde persona, Sandy's punk image, and my preppy style—I got over it! Our friendship went deep: it was forged in the crucible of the Shanghai renaissance of 1988-89 and its reformation, which culminated in the events of May and June 1989.

Sandy, Michael, and I explored the delights of Shanghai by bicycle, inventing synchronized bicycle riding, a new Olympic sport, no mean feat in Shanghai traffic, learned about arbitrage and black market currency dealing, the antiques and treasures of art deco Shanghai and beyond, and became adept at negotiating the systems—political, cultural, and economic. Thanks to Sandy and Michael's generosity with their previous experience in Shanghai and our mutual curiosity and sense of adventure, we made many friends and acquaintances with other expats and Chinese—these latter relationships being highly controlled by the police and the neighborhood committees. Michael and Sandy were both endlessly generous with their knowledge, their friendship, and their sense of humor. Without them, my understanding of China, Shanghai, and myself would have been far poorer.

Together, the three of us calculated that foreigners in Shanghai in 1988 were only about one-tenth as plentiful as they had been in the 1930s, while the Chinese population had exploded in the interim. This made foreigners relatively rare. As a result, people keen to practice their English or learn about us peculiar foreigners relentlessly pursued us wherever we went—the cheery chorus of "Hello—disco—fuck" followed us wherever we went. Such encounters took place everywhere, even while we were riding our bicycles, using the washroom, or stuck in traffic. After the hundredth such encounter one day, the three of us started communicating in mock Swedish, which seemed to put people off for months. However, one day, I was approached by a distinguished elderly gentleman in the Bank of China, who said to me in perfect English, "Excuse me, do you speak Swedish?" He was hoping to find someone with whom to practice his Swedish. We laughed about this for some considerable time to come, and had to discover other polite ways to dissuade people. Three years later, while pursuing my fieldwork in rural China some 125 miles inland from Shanghai, I routinely had twenty to thirty women watching me pee, commenting on the color of my pubic hair; one entrepreneurial restaurant provided me with free meals in exchange for selling tickets to local people who watched me eat and commented on my chopstick technique. Little did I realize during my Shanghai days the level of invasive and unwanted attention that life yet held in store for me. Black humor, play-acting, and sarcasm are to this day the foundation of my coping skills, particularly when traveling or working in developing countries, but they are tempered with patience, compassion, and understanding—the Buddhist virtues. One of the cruel ironies in my life is that sarcasm has no place in Chinese because of the tonal nature of the language. Without the requisite sarcastic vocal intonation, exclamations of "*Tai hao le*" "Oh, how marvelous" to some adverse situation just does not work and instead yields some very strange looks.

Lesson 4: All's Well that Ends Well, or, How I Got My Email Address

In Mandarin "*hulihutu,*" pronounced *hooleehootoo*, can be used to describe a situation or a state of being. If you are being pulled in fifteen different directions at once, then you are *hulihutu*. It is a Buddhist term and should be thought of as the polar opposite from being on the verge of achieving nirvana. It is the source of my email address and causes my Mandarin-speaking friends much merriment.

An illustration of this comes from Christmas dinner. Shopping was still quite challenging in Shanghai back in 1988–89. It took Sandy, Michael, and me four days and some collective two hundred miles by bicycle to procure the fixings to make Christmas dinner. Our Chinese friends had insisted on helping in this process, so we entrusted two young men with the task of finding the four chickens that we were going to stuff and roast as a turkey substitute. They arrived with scrawny frozen chickens that looked exactly like the classic rubber chickens of comedy fame ... plucked, heads and feet still on, innards intact, and rigid as boards. In the interests of intercontinental cooperation, we took what they provided with thanks. They resided as gag shop chickens in my "freezer"—the bicycle basket suspended between the laundry lines outside my window—until Christmas Eve when we rented the large ovens in the kitchen and prepared Austral-Anglo, Canadian, and Chinese stuffing and dealt with the chickens. Fortified with Australian "champagne" and glugwine, provided by two travel-writing Swedes who were consulting us on the trendy Shanghai bar scene, we turned our attention to the chickens. I do not remember who had the idea first, but the next thing I knew we were having a puppet show with the chicken heads, speaking in perfect Chinglish and concluding with a macabre chicken foot cancan.

On Christmas Day we invited ten foreigners, including the glug-wine Swedes and a Norwegian, an Italian and an Italian Swiss, a Kenyan, a Saudi, and ten of our Chinese friends to gather at the apartment of a Canadian friend several miles from campus, where the Chinese friends could attend freely. We had planned dinner for twenty: however, all of our Chinese friends, in true Spring Festival style, had brought at least one friend each, and in the end thirty-five people gathered for the festivities. We prepared mashed potatoes and gravy, carrots, and *cai xin*—cabbage hearts in garlic—and heated up the chickens and the stuffing in the friend's toaster oven one at a time, no other oven being available. The vagaries of Chinese wiring meant we had to run the toaster oven in the bathroom. The Chinese all forswore the chicken, potatoes, and gravy—with an oath of *TAI XIANG!* "TOO STINKY!" The cheese and crackers we offered as hors d'oeuvres had suffered the same fate. The thing that saved the day was Michael's mother's fruitcake, largely because it had been laced with at least a quart of brandy.

In addition to the fruitcake, we consumed far too many varieties of Chinese alcohol— some of which were really only best used as floor strippers—and danced late into the night mixing Western, African, and Chinese pop music and using a bamboo broom as a limbo bar when required. Despite my being *hulihutu* in performing a veritable "loaves and fishes" miracle with the dinner, a good time was had by all, and my culinary apoplexy a complete waste of energy. I am only apoplectic now when the situation truly demands it, but I certainly wear my email address with pride!

Lessons Learned

The year did not contain a single moment of catharsis or eureka, but as running water erodes stone, I experienced a steady wearing-away of old rigidities, patterns of behavior, and preconceptions. During my year in Shanghai I feel that I emerged from a chrysalis and was truly liberated from the constraints that had kept me from experiencing a richer, fuller life. So often when the options were either to cry or to laugh at myself or the situation in the face of *hulihutu,* I chose laughter over frustration—-and still do every time. As a result, humor is an important coping mechanism for me both in China and everywhere else and has become fundamental to a happier healthier life.

These four life lessons—to take the road less traveled, to persevere, to avoid snap judgments (particularly negative ones), and to laugh, laugh, and laugh again—have been invaluable to me in my daily life, professional life, and travels. I learned many other daily lessons in patience, tolerance, and perspective while living in a developing country and experiencing an economy in transition; they have been invaluable to me during ensuing events and travels. From the chaos of China in May and June of 1989 to my travels in Southeast Asia, the travails of my fieldwork in rural China, and the challenges of reintegration into Canadian and British society, I feel that I was—and am—far more able to cope with new challenges, integrate into different cultures, and befriend people than I was before my year of personal growth in Shanghai, under the tutelage and friendship of Sandy and Michael.

Indelible Gifts

Anne M. Gasso

 At twenty-two I set out to travel solo around the world. It was no whim. I felt a visceral need. I didn't know what to expect; I only knew dimly that I was compelled to look deeply into the mirror of the world in search of a greater understanding of my place within it.

Eighteen years later, memories from my wanderings still rise unexpectedly to greet me: images as vividly etched on the screen of my mind as any archival photograph. Sunrise on the Ganges River in Veranasi; mist rising slowly, as golden reflections danced on the early-morning waves. Or the head-shaking improbability of being flashed by the one Indonesian who crossed my path as, on another early morning, I made my solitary way to the train station along the streets of Jakarta.

But it is my encounters with the world's women that are most indelibly seared into my soul. Images of certain faces return like waves lapping gently, unceasingly, on the shore of my heart. I turn these memories over like well-worn beach pebbles, searching for their secrets and their meaning. Each time I relive one of those shared interludes, a new facet of the experience is revealed, a new discovery worthy of quiet contemplation. And with each remembering, I feel the person that I am expanding yet again, reaching for the fullness of who I am yet to become.

India

On that first voyage, I traveled by train across northern India. Approaching the city of Veranasi, my companions and I were befriended by an earnest young man in an immaculately pressed dhoti. After politely inquiring about our origins, destination, marital status, and such, he invited us to his home for a meal. Invitations of this kind were a serendipitous gift of travel—we were honored and touched to visit people's homes and experience first hand a brief glimpse of their reality.

On the appointed day, we made our way to our new friend's house. It was a humble dwelling of mud-covered brick, consisting of several rooms, their floors swept clean and the sparse furnishings selected with care. A shady veranda provided refuge from the intensity of the afternoon sun. It looked out onto a beaten-earth yard where a small hedgerow masked a water ditch. The family waited to welcome us. We were greeted by three generations of female relatives: our host's mother, sister, wife, and infant daughter.

His sister, like him, had beautiful, expressive dark eyes, but while his expressed a guarded interest in his guests, those of his sister burned with passionate curiosity about the foreigners who had mysteriously appeared in her life.

The frankness of her gaze captivated me. I did not speak her language, nor did she understand a word of mine, but we communicated. To this day I can still feel the eloquence of her brown eyes. Her brother clearly thought it was beneath him to use his hard-won English skills to translate women's talk, but through cajoling and persistence I drew her story from him. She was about to be married to a man she did not know or love. That was all that I needed to hear. I understood what she was so desperately trying to say with her eyes. I instantly felt her fear as my own. Through this connection I sensed the fierce conflict within her between a duty to family and the promptings of her heart. I imagined myself trapped in such an existence. Rebellion would be harshly punished. She had no choice but to submit to the will of her elders.

On that gentle afternoon in the Indian countryside I wanted to do battle for her. The naive and idealistic young woman in me wanted to rescue her, adopt her as my sister, bring her back to Canada. To change her destiny.

Looking into her face, I began to cry. A rent formed in my armor of self-centered delusion as I understood that my power in the world had limits. I had met a soul sister, but she was trapped in a prison-world of inflexible beliefs, customs, and laws, and I could do nothing about it. I lacked the key to set her free.

To this day I continue to unweave the tapestry of that memory. Something arrogant and unbending cracked open in me that day. The unexpected jolt of my reality crashing into another's threw my beliefs into disarray. My heart wanted desperately to save her, but my mind balked at all that helping her would entail. I felt too young for such responsibility. And in the end, I did nothing.

In the following months, I sometimes agonized over my decision, but then the kaleidoscope of travel would swirl me away, and my moment of contemplation and doubt would pass. I do know that I never realized the extent of my freedom until I met her. That was her biggest gift to me—a gift that I continue to unwrap, one layer of subtlety at a time. Does she still remember my sapphire eyes, I wonder, as I recall the directness of her intense andradite stare?

Thailand

Several months later, shortly after arriving in Bangkok, I found myself bouncing along dirt roads, fording streams, and venturing ever deeper into the verdant jungle of western Thailand. My friend Rob, a doctoral student at McGill University at the time, was studying tin deposits near the Burmese border. Through a fortuitous cascade of events I was traveling with Rob's assistant across the countryside en route to an unexpected reunion.

I showed up just as Rob was finishing work at one mine and preparing to move on to the next one, which was tucked into hills at the end of a tortuous, deeply rutted dirt road. We arrived late in the day. It was a family-owned operation, and my presence was an unexpected development for Rob's hosts. He disappeared with the patriarch, and I was left in the care of the women and children.

Much discussion ensued, and then the mine owner's eldest daughter was given the task of putting me at ease and making me welcome. She led me to a private corner of the courtyard and showed me the bath. Bathing is an art in Southeast Asia, and is deeply nurturing and cleansing to more than just the skin. Water is scooped from a large earthenware urn and sensuously poured over the body. The ritual is meditative and soothing. As I bathed, my clothes were replaced with a worn sarong. When I emerged, my freshly laundered clothing was hanging in a corner of the yard still warmed by the rays of the late afternoon sun. The bath settled me, allowing me to forget my travel-weariness and relax into the strangeness of my new setting.

In the kitchen, four generations of women were busy preparing the evening meal. A grandmother motioned me to her side to help with some vegetables. No sooner had I sat down than a pair of mischievous sparkling eyes peered into mine. I smiled, and giggles erupted from one of the youngest and liveliest members of the household. She had been playing with a doll and helping her great-grandmother until I became her distraction.

My blond hair hung loose down my back; the temptation was too great for my little friend. As she began to stroke and then braid my hair, I became the center of attention. A brush materialized from a pocket, many hands touched my hair, and my stylist began to remove the tangles. Someone took over from her, and I soon had smooth French braids curling back from each temple.

I had never before experienced this form of kinship—the grooming and meal preparation rituals shared by the women of a clan. It was a brief glimpse of a world so different from my own that I could only perceive the ripples on the surface; the underlying currents swirling within the depths of the river were beyond my reach. However, something within me remembered this timeless and orderly way of life. I understood that something intangible but invaluable had been lost in the mobility afforded by modern Western life. I could feel the attraction of this ordered existence in which everyone knew her place and role, yet I was content to sit on the edge of the stream, safe from any strong currents, and peel vegetables.

That night I slept with the mine owner's daughter and her infant son. The intimacy of sharing a bed was startling. Shocking. She smiled timidly at me as she turned out the light. I lay in the dark, listening. The son slept, but I could sense that she was still awake. We lay together, two women breathing steadily in the night, unable to engage in the casual conversation that slowly softens the edge of strangeness until mutual ease is created; we did not have that luxury, we could not communicate. I had the uncomfortable feeling that I had plunged into the deeper flow of the powerful currents of this woman's life. I wondered whether she felt the same. Or had she navigated this territory before? We each thought our own thoughts and slowly disappeared into sleep.

My brief immersion in the women's world of the tin mine seemed to have reawakened some ancestral memory lodged deep within my bones. I felt the comfort and refuge that this life offered. Where respecting your elders, knowing your place, doing your chores and bearing your children was all that was expected of you. There was no drive to invent, to forge, to accomplish, to succeed. There was no anxiety about what to do with your life.

By the purely capricious fortune of my birth, I had been offered many more choices. So many that at times I was overwhelmed by the array of options available to me. I wondered whether it would not have been easier to be born into a system where my destiny was predetermined, where the path from A to B was well worn and well marked. But then I remembered the young woman in India and the spell broke. I may not always have a clear picture of where I am headed in my life, but I make my own choices. The mine owner's family embraced me with their welcoming warmth, the laughter in their kitchen, and their generosity. My time with them was a delight in many ways, but it also renewed my gratitude for the opportunities that my life affords.

Argentina

Many years later, now a veteran solo traveler, I met another woman who touched me with the kindness of her spirit.

The day was perfect for driving. My work as a geologist had taken me into northwestern Argentina, and I was traveling to a remote camp to meet a colleague. I was moving through one of my favorite landscapes. The Argentine Puna is a geographical anomaly: a broad, high-altitude plateau, windswept, and beautifully desolate, buttressed against the shadow of the Andes. The closeness of the earth to the sky sharpens contours and accentuates the blueness above. The sun shines unfiltered on volcanic dreamscapes and fantastic vistas that appear to continue to the four corners of the earth. Exhilarated by the freedom of driving and intoxicated by the beauty of the land, I sang at the top of my lungs as my Land Rover flew along dirt highways.

A small volcano rises to the right as the road approaches the town of Antofagasta de la Sierra. Its dark basaltic flows spread out over the sand, broken and agonized where they ceased their forward exploration, too tired and too dense to push on. Distracted by the view, I was into a curve at high speed. In a heartbeat, my expanded awareness came rushing back to the present.

The Land Rover was suddenly flying sideways on two wheels. It bounced once on the passenger door, flipped onto the roof, and cut a deep gouge in the desert floor as it slid to a full and abrupt stop.

Adrenaline surged; emotions had fled, cowering in some dark, safe corner of my being. Hanging from the seat belt, I was unhurt. The door wouldn't open. I crawled out a back window. The Land Rover was destroyed. Information came to me in small bits: I could see Antofagasta in the distance; I had not passed another vehicle all morning; one of the spare tires had escaped down the hill.

I was wondering what to do next when a truck groaned its way to the top of my hill. Three men were sitting shoulder to shoulder across the bench seat. They seemed as surprised to see me as I was them, yet they quickly got to work. Two of them attached a heavy chain to the undercarriage of the Rover and used their truck to flip it upright. Then they left. I drove slowly into town with the wind whipping my face through the empty space once filled by the windshield.

With adrenaline still flowing, I was an example of cool organization: calling the office, storing the truck in the police compound, and arranging a room.

Several years before, I had stayed in that same town with an older widow who rented rooms to travelers. Seeking comfort in the familiar, I sought her out again. As I sat at her kitchen table and told my story, she brought me strong tea and thick slices of coarse homemade bread along with a white dish of her quince preserves. She listened to my tale, horror and compassion chasing each other in her facial expressions and then said, *"Gracias a Dios,"* "Thanks be to God" or "By the grace of God." The words struck, white-hot, to my core. Argentina is strictly Catholic. I had always doubted the existence of a god, but in that instant I realized that there exists a form of divine protection. I knew in my bones that some energy does look over us, be it God, Allah, the Great Mother, the Spirit Who Moves Through All Things or the Universe. Each of these is but a name which cannot come close to expressing the essence of what I felt. In that moment, I agreed with her and adopted the words as my own mantra, always said in Spanish, *Gracias a Dios.* I was still alive. I collapsed in tears.

The following morning I awoke stiff and still reverberating. After serving me breakfast, the widow invited me into the warmth of her kitchen. She was making fresh pasta for lunch; I was waiting for my colleague to come and collect me.

Our conversation was stilted at first. As I watched her clear away the breakfast dishes and dust the table with a handful of flour, we ventured shyly into the realm of shared experiences, into questions and answers. I remembered her nursing an invalid son on my previous visit. She slowly pushed flour into a mound as she told me of his decline and demise. The movement of her delicately powdered hands punctuated her words. Forming a well in the top of the dune of flour, she cracked fresh eggs into the crater. She asked me, what brought a woman like me, unmarried and childless, so far from country and family?

I tried to answer, and by the time she had mixed and kneaded the dough, we had abandoned the cool space of our strangers' inhibitions for the territory of love, emotions, and relationships. In that small kitchen, in a faraway land, we rolled out pasta dough and cut it into narrow strips, as cultural and generational boundaries dissolved in the candid exploration of our hearts.

As my body slowly relaxed, my mind was beginning to expand beyond the self-limiting belief structures that in the past would have kept me from opening to this woman. Normally my protective arrogance would have rushed me past such an opportunity to learn from another. Now, in my scrambled state, I welcomed the intimate contact, the compassion and the ageless wisdom of this kind soul.

We passed beyond the labels of being a young, single, overeducated Canadian traveler and a dignified Argentine grandmother of humble upbringing who had buried a husband and a son. We were simply two women sharing thoughts and feelings as we cooked the day's meal, as generations of women had done in the past.

I have a clear memory of her standing in the doorway, with her dark gray hair pulled back into a bun and an old beige cardigan buttoned over her faded floral print dress. As we said goodbye, tears came to the eyes of us both, and I thanked her for her compassion. Her gifts to me were priceless gems—I suddenly saw a universal pattern to our lives that spans cultural, political, and generational boundaries. I had been inspired to a newfound openness to possibility, and I was suddenly unafraid to speak of the grace of God.

My encounters with these women offered me insight into myself, my nature, my beliefs. Yet I can only hope that the inspiration flowed in both directions. I often doubt that my gifts to them were as rich as those I received. Thankfully, I no longer need the shock of intense experiences—a young woman's misery, a terrifying accident—to expand my vision and allow entry to others. I have learned that in venturing into the currents of relationship with women, I will touch and be touched, move and be moved, and that change is life and growth. I am no longer merely an observer; I am fully engaged in the intimate dance of existence. This is the sublime thread that now weaves together the tapestry of my travels.

Gift of Whimsy

Carole TenBrink

Kim played Bob Marley's "Freedom Song" on his tape player, and hot air from the open windows sheared across our faces as the rented sixties-vintage Chevy chugged along toward Vung Tao. We had been in Vietnam for just a few days but were already weary of Saigon's heat, noise, and thick polluted air. Leaving the city was like opening a door to our fantasy: rice paddies, white cranes, and water buffalo. The air was fresher and cleaner, our driver was sweet and congenial, and we sailed along like royalty.

I had long been divorced from my Vietnamese husband, Phu, but had been lucky enough to raise our son, Kim, in Canada in full contact with the tradition and culture of Phu's family. They were immigrants who had arrived in Canada in 1975 when Saigon fell, some time before Phu and I divorced. Now it was 1994, and Kim and I were in Vietnam for the first time, venturing into the countryside we had heard about for twenty years from Phu and his family.

We stopped in the seaside town of Vung Tao, called Cap St. Jacques in French colonial days. The place was an aging grande dame, way past her prime, but the beach was beautiful. We spent the afternoon there, and I took my first swim in the South China Sea. The day hangs in my memory like a crystal. Craggy boulders, big waves, and water as hot as a bath. Never mind that the beach was deserted, we still had to contend with the usual string of peddlers offering food, postcards, and beach chairs for sale. In such situations I try to turn opportunists into momentary friends. It's difficult, but not impossible.

Then I noticed a woman with an intense look on her face, different from the others. Her eyes sparkled—not with hopeful dollar signs, but with profound mischief. Never before had I experienced such strong magnetism, physically drawing me into another person's space. She was like a female Puck, just four feet tall and dressed in black peasant pants, a brown top, and a conical hat with a fitted knit cap underneath, covering her ears. We introduced ourselves. Her name was Huynh Lien. We beamed and beamed at each other, like two grade school friends wanting to jump up and down with delight. I engaged her in my "point and laugh" dictionary game, taking turns pointing to something in my Vietnamese-English phrase book. After a little banter, I tried, "*Thoi thiet ... nong ... tai lanh?*" Literally "Weather hot ... why ears cold?" In answer, she pulled off the hat and cap to reveal the shiny shaved skull of a monk. Suddenly, I understood the deep well of compassion and delight I'd been drinking in from her eyes. She was a spiritual searcher, too, I thought, but more advanced.

"*Dau chua?*" I asked. "Where is your temple?"

She pointed high up the cliff and looked at me with an expression I will never forget. She looked just like a bird, her head cocked and her piercing eyes gazing straight into me. We stood there together, a Western woman and an Eastern monk, two dots in a huge expanse of sea, cliff, and sky. Her face and hands were brown and weathered as if she spent her days in the sun and sea air. I'm a nature girl, too. My childhood home had been an unhappy and dangerous place, but I had found a deep sense of Mother Earth's protection in the outdoors, on the shore of Lake Michigan, where I would stand gazing straight west over open water.

My conversation with Huynh continued playfully. She wrinkled up her nose at me each time we achieved some form of humor. When she discovered I understood ancestor worship, she showed enthusiastic approval, making big thumbs-up signs with both hands. When she was listening to me describe something, she'd look *into* me, entranced, as if she could see into my soul. I'd never met anyone who lived so completely in each moment, so totally Buddhist.

Any Vietnamese friendship quickly leads to touch, and as we created more good fun with the phrase book, she moved closer and patted my thighs. In my swimsuit, their impressive size would surprise any Vietnamese, never mind the diminutive imp beside me. But Huynh's touch conveyed deep affection with not a hint of ridicule. Tears came to my eyes, as I remembered how Me, my Vietnamese mother-in-law, had patted my legs that way. I always sat close to Me at family gatherings to receive this loving gesture, the matriarch indicating to her clan that this is her special daughter-in-law, the one with the big sturdy legs. Huynh's identical confirmation of this part of me touched me deeply. We spent much of the afternoon huddled close together, in this grand expanse, her warm, leathery hands patting my legs and arms, and me caressing her shoulders and wiry back. She felt like a miniature twin sister, shorter and thinner, but a soulmate.

The year before this trip, I had gone back to Michigan to help my father after my mother died. The bad feelings of childhood trauma had erupted again. My trip to Vietnam was a gift to myself, and I had hoped it would bring me healing. It had brought me Huynh.

The warm sea breeze and Huynh's affection melted away my tension and the culture shock, noise, and pollution of Saigon. I felt smoothed out, brand-new, and boldly confident. Out tumbled a whole sentence of my broken Vietnamese. "*Toi thick di chua.*" I said. "I would love to visit your pagoda." If I couldn't enter the private nunnery perhaps she could show me the outside.

To my delight, she nodded vigorously. "*Den, nam goi chung toi,*" she said. "Yes, we can go at five o'clock."

We fixed a meeting place back up on the road, and she left. Kim wanted to join us. We spent the rest of the afternoon in the shade of scraggly palms drinking *ca phes*, Vietnamese sweet iced coffee. I wondered if Huynh really would come back, but at five sharp she was there. We began our climb up a steep dirt path between pagodas and homes jutting out from the cliff. The view at the top was breathtaking. The South China Sea stretched before us as far as the eye could see, and on our clifftop perch we seemed suspended in this great expanse. We were level with the sun, looking straight out to the west—like my beloved childhood spot, but much grander because we were so high up.

The altar room was open to the west, and the Buddha's altar was on the opposite wall. Kim and I observed the ritual of incense, prayers, and bowing, and were shown where to sit on the floor. More nuns joined us in a semicircle in front of the altar. Introductions were made, snack food and tea were offered, then came the questions and teasing and stories with much touching and laughter. I was amazed. We were a group of middle-aged women and one young adult son dissolving into silliness and high spirits before the Buddha. This was evening vespers?

As time passed the stories got better. You'd have thought we were drinking liquor, but it was only tea. Ut, also a mother of sons, looked at me and said, "I love you." I beamed at her and made a little prayer sign toward her with my hands.

Made reckless by Ut's effusiveness, I turned to Huynh Lien and said, "And I love you." We all laughed and fell over each other like a pile of puppies.

Kim sat respectfully in our midst, quite used to this affection and female giddiness, which was the norm in his Vietnamese family. When we calmed down, we turned to face the horizon where the sun was setting. Stillness came over us. My mind drifted and the water-sky horizon line worked its tender magic, filling me with a sense of safety and protection. Nobody could appear without warning from that direction. The infinity of the line always sends waves of peace through me. Now here in Vietnam I married myself to the same mysterious line I had known on Lake Michigan.

The sun sets quickly in southern Vietnam. In Saigon the change from daylight to nightfall had seemed inexplicable and arbitrary, like someone turning out the lights on a whim. Here we could see the miracle take place. At 5:50 p.m. the sky went rapidly from orange to pink, then purple. At 6:00, the sun slipped below the horizon, and by 6:10 it was dark, dark night.

We parted with an exchange of addresses, hugs, kisses and promises that I would *di ve*, come back. Kim wanted to take a picture of Huynh Lien and me, but the directress insisted we include the sign above the Chua's entrance. She also instructed Huynh to put on her saffron robes and "look dignified." Not easy for Huynh! To get the sign in, Kim moved down the steps and angled the camera. As a result, my keepsake photo shows me gazing fondly at Huynh who is barely suppressing a grin (which, I always remember, I could feel vibrating throughout her body), the all-important sign appears blurred above us, and my disproportionately large, lumpy knees dominate the center of the picture.

Huynh walked with us down the stone and dirt steps back to the road. Her gaze bored into me again. She gave me a fruit I had never seen before and described how to let it ripen and prepare it. Her gaze was still intense, out of proportion. It seemed too much, and I wondered, was this woman crazy? The fierce energy behind her eyes suddenly didn't seem normal. Disturbed, I couldn't follow what she was saying; I shrank away, unable to absorb her searing attention. Then the moment passed and I relaxed. She smiled sweetly at me and pure delight filled her face again. Like a fairy child, she pulled at my hand, dragging my reluctant bulk down the cliff to the waiting taxi. Kim scrambled behind us.

I don't remember the taste of the fruit, but I'll never forget Huynh's last gaze. I don't care if she moves between crazed and enlightened. I think she probably lives on the edge. Her intensity may spill over sometimes into bottomless fire where nothing is stable. But she pulls herself back. When I think of her, I sometimes fancy we are holding hands. She pulls me toward the edge, and I pull her back to safety; we are like two edges of crazed delight. What matters is the image that she gave to me of my own pure inner core, which I believe is like hers: impish, exuberant, lavishly affectionate, and utterly concentrated on the spirit inside each thing, each moment.

I tried to keep in touch, but it was not easy. She lost her home in a flood that year, and when she did receive my letters it was difficult to find someone to translate them. But I knew I wanted to find my way back to see Huynh again.

In 1998, I returned to Vietnam with my sister-in-law, Co Linh, and her husband, Chin. We went to Vung Tao, but the place had changed. The potholed path of a road was now slickly paved. Oil had been discovered offshore; money and tycoons had arrived.

I found the right path along the cliff, climbed up to the Chua, and called gently toward the interior. The directress appeared and we chatted until I could politely ask my burning question. "*Dau*, Huynh

Lien?" She smiled and motioned toward the interior, and out came Huynh. I stood up and we hugged each other. I'd forgotten how very small she was. She seemed to have aged twenty years in just four. The terrible flood in her village must have caused her tremendous hardship. I kept patting her arms and murmuring; it was so good to see her. Her eyes on me were like a caress. After we'd taken each other in, I asked her, "*Di, di* ... ?" pointing back down to the sea and waving my arms in a swimming motion. I wanted some time alone with her.

We promised the directress we'd be back soon and made our way down the cliff. I stripped to my swimsuit and dived in, and Huynh plunged in after me fully dressed and clutching a plastic container as a float. She bobbed up and down on her float, and I rode on the waves, got knocked under the water, and thrust myself back up to laugh with Huynh and search out our next ride. I will always remember her beaming face at those moments, with a deep sadness shadowed behind it.

After our swim, we sat on the shore and I tried to make conversation. It was difficult, because I didn't just want to exchange pleasantries as we had four years ago. I wanted to find out how she really felt. Were her home and family intact? "*Ya dinh, nuon*?" I tried. "Is your family okay?" She gestured, one finger down, "*Co chet*," she said. "One sister died."

So she had lost a sister in the flood. I gave her a gentle hug and she leaned limply into my side. We were so alike: soaring up with exuberance and plunging down into grief. We didn't have the language to communicate fully; there was no way to go deeper in friendship, so we contented ourselves sitting shoulder to shoulder on that beach, feeling our bond and the impossibility of doing anything about it. We gazed out to sea thinking our own thoughts until Huynh tapped her index finger to her watchless wrist and we started the climb back up to the top.

The directress gave me a tour of their modest grounds, a garden and a small building behind the pagoda. A funny feeling came over me there, as if a shutter had moved back, momentarily letting me see beyond the serene saffron robes to a middle-aged woman of pious demeanor but little substance and a slight desperation. In a flash, the shutter closed again. We were standing by the small shed when she astounded me by saying, "This, for sale ... For you."

"Me?" I stammered, heart pounding.

"Place for holidays ..." she went on. "Can put AC ... very comfortable."

I was dumbfounded. I had longed for such a place, looking west over open water, a view like the one that had given me solace as a child. To find it here in Vietnam, a country I loved, was just too much, and I couldn't take it in.

"Five thousand US dollars," she said.

"For me ... to buy?" I repeated foolishly.

"Yes," she said gravely. "Come join us in pagoda...."

I wandered around the grounds some more. Feelings I couldn't describe were pulling at my chest. There was longing, but also a sense of doubt about this community. I couldn't form any thoughts to speak. I went back to the pagoda for tea. The three of us sat quietly, watching the sun go down. It made me weep. My heart's desire was right there, in front of me, and I didn't know what to do.

"I will think it over. I will come to see you again soon" was all I could say as we parted for the night. A great gift was being offered to me, but I sensed trouble.

The next day Co Linh and Chin visited the pagoda with me.

Afterward Chin said, "I don't know. I'm afraid these women are flaky."

"Maybe you can just keep Huynh Lien as a friend. She is wonderful," said Co Linh encouragingly.

"There are difficulties with owning land here," Chin said. "The government, the person who's looking after it for you, everyone wants money for repair, for tax. And when you're far away, what can you do? Even looking after my parents' home with them still in it is a mess. I wouldn't recommend this."

"You're connected to us, always," said Linh. "You don't have to have a place in Vietnam to feel connected." She put her arm across my shoulder, and I gave her a hug. What they were saying meant a lot to me. There was a feeling of destiny to what had been offered, but somehow the feeling was not quite right.

A few weeks later, when I was teaching at Hue University, I got a letter in Vietnamese from the directress. A friend translated the mix of pat advice about Buddhist devotional prayers and practices and a repeated invitation to buy land. It read more like a greeting card than serious spiritual wisdom. I went back to my room and sat on the bed holding the letter in my hands for a long time. I felt the longing. The sunset view appeared before me and tugged at my heart. But the longer I sat there, the more I knew that I would not buy it, a postage stamp of land in a country run by fiefdoms. I felt sad but relieved.

Back home in Canada I realized the directress's offer had spurred me to accept with absolute certainty that my roots were deep in North America. In late middle age, I couldn't grow them again in Vung Tao. By the end of that year, I had made a decision and bought a little piece of land across the road from Lake Ontario. Its sunset views are different from those of the South China Sea, but they are spectacular, and they are mine.

I wander my deserted beach and think of Huynh wandering hers. I hope she's roving in health and vigor. Our bond will always be there. Huynh has become an image to me, an icon inside me that represents the carefree, puckish being that I was meant to be. She shines in me, reassuring me that I may yet become what my heart desires. May we both continue to walk on the edge and ride that horizon line.

Day and Night in the Horn of Africa

Cheryl Mahaffy

 Solitary trees march along the horizon, like a child's cutouts pasted against the sky. I will carry this image home from an intense three weeks in Ethiopia and Eritrea, abutting countries in northeast Africa. Like most of the memories I gathered in that July 1997 pilgrimage, this one has a flip side: behind the beauty lies the unfortunate reality that these silent sentinels are all that remains of the lush forests once holding back the soil against the rainy season's flash floods.

This trek to the Horn of Africa is spearheaded by Tigist Dafla, an Edmontonian whose family is originally from Eritrea but moved to Ethiopia while the two countries were still one. The initiative is Tigist's answer to a question that gnaws at many who, like her, fled during a thirty-year war waged by the government of Ethiopia against Eritreans seeking independence: *Should I return to help in the rebuilding? Or can I accomplish more from afar?*

Intent on exploring a wide gamut of grassroots efforts, Tigist has invited a diversity of women (and a few related children) to travel with her: social workers, a farmer, a nurse, teachers, communicators. That latter category includes me: writer, and thus scribe. Despite (or perhaps because of) my trusty diary, tape recorder, and interviewing skills, I feel somewhat the voyeur, or at least interloper. After all, it was my husband who grew up in the Horn with his missionary parents, not I; he who worked with Eritrean emigrants to ship a container of computers and books from Edmonton to the land he'd never yet had opportunity to revisit. Were he a woman, Peter Mahaffy would be the one crossing the ocean. That fact became all the more ironic near our departure date, when a spot opened up and we accepted a male, Daniel Aarons, to fill it.

After months spent preparing to rub shoulders with Africa and each other, we experienced the power of ancient rivalries when expatriate Ethiopians threatened to picket the Centre for International Alternatives (which has since been dissolved), whose Lorraine Swift coordinated our itinerary while Oxfam Canada provided overseas logistics. "How can a woman with Eritrean roots lead a credible tour through Ethiopia?" the expatriates demanded to know. "For shame!" Demonstrators and placards never appeared, but on departure day the threat prompted a wary scan of the airport crowd and reinforced a nagging sense of foolhardy innocence. Was I—were we—equipped to understand what we were about to see?

Touching down in Addis Ababa, Ethiopia's capital, we enter a land with no dusk; this close to the equator, the sun plummets from the sky. Walking in the light, we're suddenly groping through dark. I take it as a metaphor for the wild swings we will all experience as our pilgrimage progresses from abundance to drought, from hope to despair.

We lose hope in Addis Ababa, where each stoplight attracts a mob of insistent humanity minus legs, arms, money, and future. As myriad cardboard lean-tos flick past like frames in an all-too-repetitious film, I imagine my own family of five shifting to this life, where sharing a bedroom is the least of a daughter's troubles. The immensity of that leap fuels my sense of being surrounded by irreversible doom.

But then we leave Addis Ababa, driving dramatic, awe-inspiring highways to meet equally awe-inspiring people who are banding together, hundreds of thousands strong, to build sustainable works. Restaurants. Training centers. Mills. Wells. Poultry farms. Micro-credit circles. Day-care centers. And much, much more. The networks that for centuries telegraphed messages like lightning across the landscape now circulate care and generate hope. "Don't lose that!" I want to urge them, contrasting their energy with the suburban isolation inexorably paving over the barn raisings of my own rural youth.

In the city, we meet women (girls, really) pulled into prostitution on Addis Ababa's meanest streets—some by force, others hoping to escape early marriage, poverty, backbreaking household work. Then, just blocks away, we listen to other young women, fervent leaders determined to finish high school no matter how many gauntlets of taunting males and questioning parents line the way. Determined not to be included in the staggering 95 percent of females who do not complete high school, determined to be pilots (like a previous woman graduate), journalists, politicians, teachers.

We see premature newborns in the Addis Ababa hospital intensive care ward being saved with the most appropriate of technology: kangaroo care. Cuddled upright in a sling, each tiny baby receives warmth and comfort on mother's bare chest, an ear to her heartbeat. But we learn from their doctor that hundreds of babies perish for lack of something as simple as preemie formula; that more women and babies die here than almost anywhere else in the world. Such heartrending reality will prompt Kerry Pridham, the neonatal nurse among us, to dedicate her next several years to gathering and sending whatever she can beg, scrounge and buy—aided in part by intimate benefit concerts featuring her good friend Jann Arden. I applaud Kerry's energy even as I wonder whether yet another nonprofit is our best answer to death in Ethiopia.

The deaths are not for lack of knowledge. At that same hospital, the Black Lion, we meet editors engrossed in publishing the *Ethiopian Journal of Health Development,* whose reputation is international. It must be a paradoxical existence, I think as we leave the computers behind and wade through dark, stinking hallways where rivers of people wait to be treated. These doctors, with all their understanding of what needs to be done, fight a losing battle just to keep people from fouling their drinking water. In a land where less than half the population has access to basic health care, there isn't enough money, or will.

Of course, we Canadians put more than urine into our drinking water and call it progress. Daily, I'm struck by such ironies as we wander the Horn, recognizing imported habits and artifacts we cringe to call ours: a stark stirruped birthing table in a village clinic, ancient Canadian history texts on library shelves, garish advertisements. Yet in those very same communities, we see evidence of Canadian energy as a force for good. In the village with the birthing table, Hagersalaam, we meet a spirited preschool funded in part by Oxfam Canada. As thirty children sing lustily and recite their "ah bay çays," I marvel at the contrast between the bright art all around the room and the stark, bare walls we've come to associate with Ethiopian schools.

Now zipping past a Coca-Cola billboard through Addis Ababa's wild traffic, we pick the brains of Kathy Marshall, Oxfam Canada's presence in Ethiopia, a woman Tigist Dafla calls "More Habashat [Ethiopian] than me." Driven to pour her energy into a nation where bureaucratic wheels sometimes grind backward, she has detoured long enough to host this crew of naive Canadians—and not without reason. "We're trying to build linkages, to connect Mrs. X in Canada with Mr. Y in Africa," Kathy says. "If you just give dollars and Eritrea is bombed, you don't tend to care."

Our few hours at the Addis Ababa Fistula Hospital leave us wondering at both the depth of need for such a place and the miracles worked. Here, Australian-born surgeon Catherine Hamlin, and her staff repair holes in women's vaginal walls caused by tearing during long, painful labors. Leaking urine and feces, suffering women walk days, even weeks, seeking a cure for the damage that has turned them into outcasts, objects of scorn. I only wish we could apologize for the fact that our presence puts the women once again on display. Yet both watched and watchers know that visits like ours keep funds from World Vision Canada and other agencies flowing this way.

The very fact that Ethiopia needs a fistula hospital reveals another irony—the fact that the challenges faced here in the Horn are often ones North America overcame a century ago. New York had a fistula hospital once, when pioneer women birthed babies far from emergency care. "Fistula disappeared in North America around the end of last century because now you have plenty of roads and plenty of hospitals," Dr. Hamlin says. Ethiopia holds the dubious distinction of housing the world's only remaining stand-alone fistula facility.

Another day, another irony. The lights dim, the video begins and a beautiful little girl in blue wins our hearts, peering out from behind her mother's skirts with that shy preteen smile. Next minute, she is screaming, screaming as blood spurts from her vagina. The women behind the girl, holding her down, avert their eyes. The mother, far from stopping the pain, is causing it to happen. She has sanctioned this mutilation—this circumcision, if you can call it that—of her own child.

I sneak a glance around the room. Am I alone in feeling sick? Stomach sick and heartsick. I'm not alone. We're all intent on getting through this bravely, all the while willing it to *stop*.

And then it does. For us, at least. Daniel, our fill-in-the-gap traveling companion, has fainted. As others dash to grab wet towels for him, I splash water over my face, then—forgetting the rules for this journey—cup water from the tap, drinking to wash the image away. But it won't wash away. While we Westerners worry about drinking Africa's tap water, thousands of girls around the world each day endure a cutting that opens their bodies to infection, childbirth complications, even death. For them, this is not simply a video with stop, pause, and rewind. This is life minus clitoris, labia, perhaps vulva, minus space even for menstrual blood to flow. This is tradition so powerful that mothers bring their own daughters to the knife, believing it best. What force, I think, could ever persuade me to subject my two daughters to this?

Against the gut-wrenching reality that nine of every ten women here have endured this, what seems unspeakable torture, we despair. But our hosts call us back, gently, and hand us hope. They describe the twenty-six-nation push to end this and other harmful practices, while reinforcing traditions that enhance life. They tell of a church leader who was able to convince sixty thousand people of circumcision's crushing health effects, of a circumciser who switched to scrubbing clothes after facing the consequences of her previous career. Person by person, family by family, village by village, the custom of female genital mutilation is losing some grip.

We're back on Canadian time now, but our journey's not over. That's clear from the moment I roll jet-lagged out of bed to find Peter engrossed in my trip diary, one step closer to planning his own return to the land of his youth.

As I transcribe my notes and craft articles, adding my thoughts to various global-awareness events, I feel reconfirmed in a career decision only recently made. The tales of determined individuals accomplishing important things make me even more confident of the rightness of my own move from the safety of salaried public relations to live-by-your-wits freelance writing.

One article, a reflection on our encounter with female genital mutilation, is particularly hard to write. Seeking an informed reading, I share the piece with Tigist. Her reaction reminds me how lightly we skimmed over the surface of this other culture, how little I know of FGM's infiltration into my own culture, at home in Edmonton. Tradition carried from afar can calcify here, becoming even more rigidly adhered to, she tells me, and a heavy-handed response by law and society can send women even deeper into back alleys, where unsterilized knives breed infection and death. Africans transplanted to Canada need to hear enlightened and credible leaders from their own communities, she believes. At her invitation, I listen to expatriates who, like her, are seeking to build the trust that must take root if this tradition is ever to be ended. I applaud plans to connect the women we met in the Horn with women in Canada. I admire efforts to help physicians understand how they can help mutilated women cope with the special challenges they face in living and in giving birth. Vacillating between "How can this go on?" and "Who am I to judge?" I finally set the writing aside, unready to speak.

Tigist has answered her own question about how best to help, I realize. Confirmed as Canadian yet tied umbilically to the Horn, she's hard at work in her adopted land while staying attuned to the other shore. Doing all she can to support others like her, with roots in both continents yet not quite at home in either. Eyes open to the contrast, *be* contrast where you live: it's a restless solution that makes sense to me as well, feeling as I do somewhat alien in the have/have-not culture we Westerners have managed to create.

I recall a discussion with Beyan Atta, a journalism professor at Eritrea's Asmara University, with whom I was arranging to work during a sabbatical year that later became impossible due to Eritrea and Ethiopia's return to war. "Life here is paradoxical," he mused. "From one side, it looks hopeless, but on the other hand, there's reason to hope." That reality applies not only in the Horn, I see, but on our side of the ocean as well.

Andalusian Admissions:
Becoming my Mother's Daughter

Larissa L. McWhinney

The phone rang: it was my brother calling from Boston to say he had two free tickets on points to anywhere British Airways flew. He couldn't use them—he wanted me to go on a trip instead! Excitement surged through my veins like the first morning coffee. I was ecstatic with gratitude. Two tickets to anywhere: my boyfriend and I could use them for a romantic *tour du monde*. Perhaps he would propose to me in some fantasy location. I could almost see the diamond solitaire twinkling in a glass of French champagne.

But not so fast. My brother's voice interrupted my reverie: he was giving me only one ticket, not two. The second ticket was apparently for our mother. This was to be a mother-daughter trip, not a premature honeymoon. My sisterly thanks were suspended in disbelief: my mother and I alone on foreign ground? It would be a journey, all right, but not necessarily a holiday.

I love my mother dearly. And she me. But the prospect of traveling with her was daunting precisely because of how intertwined we were. I was only barely becoming my own person at the tender age of thirty-three, and it had taken crossing the continent from Toronto to Regina to initiate my quest for autonomy. Despite the distance, the tangled wire of the telephone still managed to connect us like an umbilical cord stretched across Canada's broad belly. We were too close to respect each other's differences, too close to see each other for who we were, too close for comfort. But despite my trepidations, turning down a trip abroad was not in my lexicon.

And so began our trip to Spain.

The turbulence began even before our departure. We barely made it to the airport because Mum had a fender-bender two hours before takeoff. I recalled the tale she often told of the gunwale-bender a few months before my birth when she, and I in utero, capsized in rapids and were whisked into a whirlpool. As our plane—which we had caught, just—etched an arc over the smooth Atlantic, I wondered if we would ever find calm waters.

We landed at dawn and took a bus to the centre of Barcelona, alighting in the crowded chaos of an urban Spanish morning. As we were dizzy from jet lag, everything blurred in a busy bustle. Locals hurried to work along wide, marbled arcades. Small cars lurched around the large plaza to the counterpoint beat of shouting, honking, and gesticulation. High-heeled businesswomen buzzed by on Vespas showing generous proportions of nyloned leg. Buff and tanned young men lounged on the steps of the central fountain, smugly surveying the orbiting scene.

I looked at my mother as she stood in the vortex of this matinal commotion. Her long, silvery white hair was characteristically swirled into a loose bun on top of her ever-erect head like a seeding milkweed. A few wisps were waving in the gentle breeze as she took in the new-ness of this Old World city with a soft smile and tired, but wide, blue eyes. She looked like a fairy: small yet proud, delicate yet strong, light of step yet surefooted, knowing, yet naive. I felt a surge of protective-ness: I felt maternal toward my own mother.

My concern was not unfounded. I had read up on Spain before our arrival and knew that we that we needed to be wary of pickpock-ets, scam artists, and muggers. Our Canadian candour and openness could get us into trouble—particularly my mother's tendency to rush to the aid of just about anyone regardless of their need or desire for help. (She has been known to stop on the sidewalk to assist complete-ly competent strangers park in spots big enough for a Mack truck). And it did: despite my insistence that we use small locks to secure the zippers on our handbags, my mother's trust in humanity persisted even after she was nearly pickpocketed by a teenage girl only moments after she had warned the very same adolescent delinquent that *she* should zip up *her* handbag because of thieves! On the other extreme, I was so wary that I routinely attached my purse to my chair with a bungee cord in restaurants so that it could not be nicked while I was obliviously enjoying my sangria. Mum and I were in stitches once when I got up to go to the toilet, reached for my handbag and began walking off with my chair in tow. So much for "when in Rome…"

So there we were: both well traveled, both accustomed to dealing with unfamiliarity, foreign tongues, and unusual customs, yet neither of us quite certain how to be strangers together. Seeing my mother in the whirring constellation of that first Spanish morning, I felt the need to take care of her; but I still wanted her to take care of me. Even though she is generally completely compos mentis, her occasional absent-mindedness unnerved me: her pre-departure rear-ender was a case in point. Was she entering her dotage? Perish the thought: I was still feeling daughterly; it was too early for my mother to get doddery. And yet being my mother's daughter seemed to entail enduring eternal maternal commentary: on my lack of sufficiently warm clothing (it was a particularly cold Spanish spring, but I was determined to wear my new, strappy sundress purchased specially for the occasion), on my insufficient appetite (I ate endless courses of *tapas*), or on my apparent predilection for red wine (I assumed it would be impolite to drink less than a half litre in response to Spanish hospitality). Ironically, my mother knew me so well that it was hard to be myself.

As the pressure mounted in the easily induced claustrophobia of the constant presence of a travel companion, I wondered how to respond maturely to the tensions of a mother-daughter relationship. Are mothers always mothers, as people say? Would she ever be able to accept me as an autonomous person despite my occasional regressions? And would I ever be able to respect her as a distinct individual without being embarrassed by her eccentricities? Perhaps our symbolic umbilical connection had become a Gordian knot that would have to be cleanly severed rather than gently disentangled.

The days in Barcelona were difficult. I didn't know much Spanish and felt uncharacteristically disinclined to make much of an effort. I concluded that my mother's unparalleled ability to communicate in Romance tongues resulted in my hiding in the wings rather than sharing the spotlight. I am an Aquarius, she a Libra—but we are both air signs, and we seemed to be invading each other's air space. She would sashay up to shop owners, restaurateurs, and even police officers to ask for shoes, food or directions, win them over in a single twinkle of her smiling eyes, and make me feel like the wing(wo)man. I started to feel like neither parent nor child but the jealous sister of a charming Cinderella. Was I actually envious of my own mother? Later when we were hiking in Andalusia, I wondered if she felt the same. I was a few paces ahead (my mother has an incorrigible habit of walking more slowly than her co-perambulator, even when he or she slows to her speed), when a group of construction workers whistled and hissed audaciously as I passed. When Mum caught up and went by the site, she confidently informed the workers, "I'm her mother," sending the wonderfully mixed messages "That's my daughter, and I'm proud," "Back-off or you'll have to deal with me," and "Hey, if you like her, this is where she got it from!" From the look on the construction workers' faces, they understood her perfectly.

I was relieved when we finally left Antonio Gaudí's city. It had great charm, and the tiny alleyways of the Gothic Quarter, where we'd stayed, were full of history and character. But my mother and I did not fare well together in this urban landscape of noise, nightlife, edginess, and chaos. Although I should have been appreciative of the fact that I had my own personal translator, my mother's gregariousness was annoying me. And I was even more annoyed at my own annoyance. Furthermore, looking out for her was becoming exhausting. I was always fearful that she might get pushed around by unruly crowds or step into oncoming traffic in her enthusiasm to get to yet another famous site. Maybe it was the landscape we were in. The blackened stone walls and dark narrowness of the Gothic Quarter were beginning to suffocate me. It was like trying to be born again. I was being squeezed through passages that were too small and crowded for me. It was painful. I wanted either the comfort of the womb or the freedom of adulthood, but not this liminal compression of my identity.

As soon as we began driving down the eastern coast of Spain I felt better. I was behind the wheel, which made me feel in control again—

not only of myself but also of my mother. I turned the tables: the car became a surrogate womb, my mother its precious, but involuntary, contents. She could no longer determine our itinerary: she could not lag behind, get engrossed in exclusive conversation with a local, or spend an hour contemplating a Picasso while I wallowed in boredom.

With a misplaced sense of power, I sped perilously down the *autovia* cognizant of my mother's obvious discomfort, while the bountiful, varied Spanish countryside expanded before us. I was surprised by the ruggedness of it all. Unlike France, Germany, or Switzerland, Spain was almost Canadian in its imperfect vastness. The mountains were jagged; the valleys were sloping. There was an undulation to the landscape that soothed my jarred nerves like the rocking of a cradle. It was a visual lullaby. I finally starting started to relax, and gradually released the puerile pressure on the accelerator, relinquishing my imaginary autocracy.

When we arrived in Granada we found ourselves a quaint hotel on the edge of the central square. Our room itself made me feel at home, with its two Juliet balconies and a beautiful view of the cathedral and plaza. This was the Spain I had conjured up in my overactive, romantic imagination—a cityscape that was familiar to me simply by virtue of its congruence with my fantasies.

In the comfort and relief of this home away from home, my mother and I held a truce and made peace. I had come down with a bad cold and stayed in bed for the day, grateful to have a view of *la vie quotidienne* in the square below as I convalesced. Ironically—or perhaps typically—being unwell was cathartic. Sickness was *terra cognita* that allowed my mother and me to transcend foreign ground. When it came to illness and healing, we knew how to relate to each another. Mum brought me freshly squeezed orange juice and tea from the local cafés along the plaza, and I gratefully received her care. Cradled in her kindness, my self-protective vernix was washed away and my Aquarian waters finally broke. In a pool of tears and through a labor of love, my mother and I talked into the night, addressing our frustrations and aggravations. I told her that what she did affected me as strongly as if we were still one, not two. She spoke of her discomfort with my infantilization of her, my bossiness and my over-protective, premature maternalism. And rather than just listening, we heard each other.

The honesty and openness of this exchange allowed a mutual rebirth. Instead of trying to become an adult by distinguishing myself from, or by controlling, my mother, I saw that I could become myself by allowing her to be who she is and letting her see me through her eyes. And I realized that I could perceive my mother's penetrating gaze as accepting rather than judgmental. In this *terra nova*, the symbolic cord that connected us no longer appeared as a knot or a noose. It was a spiritual connection that needed to be nurtured. It no longer epitomized the dichotomy of mother and daughter. It represented a psychic bond between two deeply connected and caring women.

As I recovered, my mother and I toured the sites of Granada with a deepened sense of purpose. Rather than gaze at my navel, I was able to look out and engage with the world. Side by side, we paid homage to the Alhambra—the stunning Moorish castle perched above the city, testifying to its Islamic past. The detailed mosaics along the walls and ceilings reflected the effort involved in getting different shapes and colors to fit together in a harmonious and symbiotic whole—nothing dominating, nothing receding. Later, in Córdoba, we visited the Mezquita, the elaborate mosque that was partially converted into a cathedral in 1236. Although the initial renovation was born out of the domination of one culture by another, the beauty of the structure now lies in its mediation between distinct histories, religions and architectures. The Islamic pillars and arches support Christian ceiling frescos and baroque side chapels. Muslim calligraphy accents Catholic iconography. The Mezquita honors the peaceful coexistence of distinct cultures, intertwined but not parasitic: Arabian nights meet the light of Christ. This was the landscape my mother and I needed: the uplifting vision of mutual coexistence—: a testament to human interrelations both personal and global.

As we traveled harmoniously on to Ronda, a spectacular, white-washed town perched on a precipice over a gorge in an almost African landscape of wide hills and stunted trees, the newspapers were reporting a disharmony of cultures and a regression of diplomatic coexistence: George W. Bush's imminent invasion of Iraq. That night we watched Spanish opposition members deplore their prime minister's support of America's new supra-UN foreign policy on local television, and my insufficient Spanish was no barrier to comprehension: the malignant message was transparent as U.S. and Spanish allies repeated history, invading an Islamic stronghold in the name of Christian values, flouting the hard-learned lessons of the Mezquita and Alhambra.

But as events degenerated internationally, my mother and I evolved interpersonally. In the rhythmic cadence of the Andalusian hills and vales we reaffirmed our unique *amitié*—that magical harmony of mother, daughter, sister, friend, accomplice, defender, self-extension, and distinct entity. She saw me both as the little child that she had nurtured and adored, and as a young woman—an adult—with my own idiosyncrasies and eccentricities. I saw her as a beautiful, enigmatic, energetic woman who forever embraced and engaged life, and whom I was blessed to call my mother. It was I who should have proudly told the cheeky construction workers, "*She* is my mother!"

My initial disappointment on realizing that this was not to be a romantic tryst with my beau complete with diamond solitaire on the banks of the Seine was now long forgotten (though I have since received such a solitaire—on the banks of Ontario's Elora Gorge). This journey was as intimate as any voyage could be, and in going the distance together, my mother and I reaffirmed a love that is close, not closed. Although I am no longer a child, I have become my mother's daughter.

> *For the pillars of the temple stand apart,*
> *And the oak tree and the cypress grow not in each other's shadow.*
> —Kahlil Gibran

Travels to Momostenango:
Every Day Has a Face

Gillian Steward

The old yellow school bus was packed. Bulky adults, some with children on their knees, filled every little seat. Others stood in the aisle, battered straw hats bumping on the bags and boxes spilling over the edge of the luggage racks. There were lumpy, sweaty bodies in my line of vision, but just beyond them I caught a glimpse of the red-and-black woven headdress of a woman looking out the window. She held her head in a queenly sort of way. Then she turned, and I saw a beautiful dark face with eyes set above high cheekbones; a long, elegant nose; gold bangles dangling from her earlobes. I was entranced. In love with Guatemala again.

The morning was still fresh and bright as the bus crawled and groaned up mountain switchbacks like an overburdened armadillo. We were heading for Momostenango, a highland town and Mayan ceremonial center set amid a patchwork of pine forests and sloping maize and bean fields. I had wanted to go there ever since reading *Time and the Highland Maya*, Barbara Tedlock's account of the training she undertook to become a diviner. A rigorous academic, Tedlock had immersed herself in the world of priests/shamans, more properly translated from Quiche, the language of the indigenous people of this region, as *daykeepers*. In the complex Quiche calendrical system, each day is not only part of a larger solar/lunar cycle but has its particular properties, or face. Since the "face of the day" will influence a person's actions, even her fate, the daykeeper is often consulted by members of the community on questions of illness, marriage, business, and agriculture, almost anything to do with everyday life, as well as deeper questions. The daykeeper casts crystals and red bean-like seeds and then reads the pattern. Only seeds from the tz'ite tree will do for this old ritual still regularly practiced in many parts of Guatemala.

I had found Tedlock's account of her intense training so compelling that I expected to see many other tourists on the bus to Momostenango. Surely, Momos, as the locals call it, had become a sort of pilgrimage center by now. But I was the only tourist on the bus. J'Val, my daughter, was with me, but she wasn't exactly a tourist. She had been in Guatemala for four months doing research for her master's thesis in anthropology. Nevertheless, to the other passengers we were both *turistas*—people from somewhere else who wore utilitarian traveling clothes, toted ponderous backpacks, spoke little Spanish, and had more spare change in their wallets than most Guatemalans earned in a month.

How could they know I was living a dream? I had loved this part of the world ever since I went to rural Mexico as a university student to work in a community development project; I was adventuring now in the same way, some thirty years later; the feeling of excitement and wonder and joy was as fresh as it was then—only twice as intense, because I was sharing it with my lovely daughter.

J'Val and I had been in Guatemala together before—in the spring of 1990 when she was just two years out of high school, traveling through the U.S, Mexico, and Central America with her best friend, Judy. Judy's mother, Shirley, and I made plans to meet them in Guatemala and spend a couple of weeks seeing the sights. We rendezvoused in the chaotic airport in Guatemala City just as it was getting dark, then hopped on a bus headed for Antigua, about an hour away. Salsa music blared from the loudspeakers and that bus was so jammed that we had to stand in the aisle, crammed together like beans in a burrito. It was difficult to see through the jumble of bodies, so I had no idea if we were careening down a narrow city street or a broad highway. But it didn't matter; the music seemed to propel the bus and the chattering people in it. It was a carnival ride, and all that mattered was the thrill of it all.

It was about eight o'clock at night when we finally arrived in Antigua and got off that carnival ride of a bus, collected our bags, and headed for the hotel. I had expected to see streets full of people shopping, walking arm in arm, taking the soft night air, just like in Mexico. But the streets were almost deserted. In Guatemala things were very, very different, J'Val told me when I remarked on it. "People don't like to be on the street after dark," she said. "And there are certain parts of the city that you simply don't go to at night … it's not like Mexico." My heart did a little flip-flop as I realized my daughter was watching out for me, warning me of possible dangers. She knew many Guatemalans were still living with the memories of death squads that came calling in black Cherokees with tinted windows.

In fact, all that spontaneous joy so evident during the bus ride to Antigua was at complete odds with the everyday reality of most Guatemalans, the majority of whom are indigenous Maya. During the 1980s, the Guatemalan Commission for Historical Clarification has reported, thousands of them had been brutally killed or forcibly removed from their land to resettlement camps by the armed forces under the direction of President Rios Montt, with the help of U.S. President Ronald Reagan, who provided military aid as well as the expertise of the CIA. The massacres had ended but the memories lived on.

When J'Val went back to Guatemala to do her fieldwork, five years after that first trip, the situation was still precarious. The army and police could still do anything they wanted. And there were droves of unemployed young men recently released from military service roaming the streets, looking for people to assault and rob. Once again, J'Val asked me to join her; we could travel together for a while. I knew it wasn't the safest place in the world, but memories of serene, soulful women wearing queenly headdresses atop their black, braided hair, their embroidered blouses tucked into long woven skirts, of women sitting like birds of paradise amidst the hurly-burly of crammed old school buses, drew me back.

So here we were on yet another old school bus, this time headed for Momostenango, so busy talking, catching up, that we didn't notice we had entered a town until the bus lurched to a stop in front of a row

223

of shops and houses. It had been raining and the streets and crude sidewalks glistened with red mud. Some of the passengers pushed past us to get off the bus. At the same time, boys with thick slabs of hair as black as obsidian thrust baskets of tamales and other goodies through open windows screeching like mynah birds as they peddled their wares. Other boys scrambled to the top of the bus to unload the bags and boxes belonging to the departing passengers. Through the window I could see small heaps of weathered suitcases and grotty, damp cardboard boxes waiting to be picked up and taken home.

Suddenly the bus went quiet, quiet enough that when a man a few rows behind us laughed lightly and then muttered *mochila*. I heard the word as clearly as if he had been sitting next to me. I didn't know what it meant, but J'Val did. She leaped to her feet and pushed through clumps of people still standing in the aisle behind me. She was shouting something at someone, and when she got to the open hatch door across the back of the bus she jumped down to the ground, still shouting. I was stunned. What on earth was going on? Should I get up and try to help her? Why was she making such a scene? I hated scenes. Especially when I was in unfamiliar territory. People could turn on you so easily if they knew you were completely out of your element. Perhaps if I just sat still everything would calm down.

I looked through the window and saw J'Val berating the terse young man I had seen organizing cargo and taking tickets when we set off a few hours earlier. She was taller than he was, and much louder, and she had drawn everyone's attention to the undeniable fact that he had been about to steal the backpacks that lay at his feet. Our backpacks. They were supposed to stay on the bus with us, but she had been traveling in Guatemala long enough to know that it wasn't a mistake. She stood her ground and then picked up one of the backpacks, hauled it inside the bus, and dropped it in the aisle next to me. Then she went and got the other one. The other passengers silently watched her every move. No one said anything to her, or me. She sat down and said that as soon as she had heard the word *mochila*—Spanish for backpack—she knew what was going on and what she had to do.

I could tell that she was still angry. I was in awe of her quick, decisive action. We hadn't been in mortal danger; our cash, travelers' checks and passports were in small, wearable body packs under our jackets. Being stranded in a remote part of Guatemala with nothing but the clothes on our backs and our money pouches would have been very inconvenient, but we would have lived to tell the tale. But then I recalled that many of J'Val's field notes and interviews were in her backpack. That would have been an irretrievable loss. And besides, why not *do* something about it? J'Val had done what was necessary. I wasn't sure I would have been able to muster the same courage even if I had known what was happening.

But then who really knows what a person is capable of when faced with real and immediate danger? J'Val had had a truly terrifying experience shortly after arriving in Guatemala this time around, and her ultimate reaction was to feel renewed determination to continue her work. She had been running with Neil, a young American friend, on a road on the outskirts of Antigua when a car pulled up beside them and two men with guns got out and forced them into the bushes beside the road. One of the men put a gun to J'Val's head. The other knocked off her friend's glasses and then demanded his money belt. Neil was on the ground on his knees. He gave them the money belt, his camera, everything he had, as J'Val watched, terrified, a gun at her head the whole time. Then the man came over to her, pointing at her waist. She thought he wanted her to take off her pants so he could rape her. But he wanted her money belt and the small rainproof shoulder bag she carried her field notes in. She threw them down. J'Val never knew whether the men meant to kill them because at the sound of a bus rounding the corner the men leaped into their car and drove off. J'Val and Neil ran to the roadside and flagged down the bus. It stopped, they got on and the bus rumbled out of there.

When I heard about this dreadful encounter over the phone a few hours later, J'Val was breathless, still reeling with fear and panic. I could imagine every second of the hellish scene, and it frightened me, though I tried to offer comfort. I asked her if she wanted to come home, if she wanted me to come to Guatemala, but she said she didn't want to abandon her work; she had gone to Guatemala for a reason and wasn't about to be deterred by a couple of gun-toting bandits. I would have done anything to protect her. I knew how hard it would be for her to get beyond the trauma of those few minutes, and for me to live knowing the danger she had faced and might face again. But her courage impressed me, and I realized she had made the right decision.

In Momostenango – which means "town of altars"—the indigenous men wear slacks and shirts instead of the more traditional woven kilts that men still wear in other parts of highland Guatemala, and the women have stopped wearing the traditional *huipil*—the intricately woven blouse for which this region is famous. The effect of this, as Barbara Tedlock notes, is to make the town appear dull and ordinary, like a poor town anywhere. And that is indeed what J'Val and I found when we finally arrived there in the evening. Momostenango looked dirt-ordinary. No colorfully dressed people on the street corners or at the market. The only hotel was quite run down, and the man at the front desk showed no interest in us even though we wanted to stay the night. But we ate well and slept well and awoke refreshed and ready to explore Momostenango.

Two blocks from the hotel we discovered a steep hill. Here, we started to climb the cobbled street, past walls of adjoining little houses with tiled roofs and dark, shadowed doors and alleyways. There were shops too, some selling candles and copal incense, for at the top of this hill were some of the many altars, and shrines, of Momostenango. Where the cobblestones ended, we found ourselves amid pine trees, brush and grass. When we reached the crest of the hill, we saw that it had been worn almost bare by the feet of devotees coming to pray at the little rock shrines blackened from decades of incense smoke. There were people praying there now, so we found a spot under a tree a respectful distance away and quietly sat down to watch.

The shrines looked like little, sooty ground ovens or hearths with rocks built up and around a vacant center. A man was sitting on the ground directly in front of one of them. He had built a little fire in a piece of potsherd and was burning copal. He threw sweet-smelling *aguardiente* (a popular liquor) and white petals into the fire and the heart of the shrine all the while chanting in Quiche in a low voice. He seemed completely focused on his prayers, oblivious to everyone and everything around him. A woman with long, shiny black hair was praying at a second, smaller shrine. Her voice rose and fell, wafting away like the smoke from the incense she was burning. The flames of the votive candles she had lit flickered in the breeze. Were they day-keepers? There was no way for us to know. They weren't casting crystals and red tz'ite seeds. And I certainly didn't want to interrupt them to ask. An old man arrived in the clearing and set about making another fire/altar in front of the third shrine. He saw us sitting under the tree but said nothing, just went about his business.

We sat and watched for about half an hour. It was wonderful to be up on that hilltop above the town, with green slopes beyond and the sun dancing up the blue sky while people prayed, praising their gods and ancestors. For a few brief moments I felt the prayers rising through me too, as praise for the beautiful world and this wondrous day.

The route we took down the hill was different, rock strewn, rough, and muddy. We had to keep our eyes on the ground and step carefully. About halfway down, I saw something red among the rocks. So I stopped to see what it was. Red tz'ite seeds lay across our path. I squatted and picked them up, one by one, thirty of the bean-like, orangey-red seeds. Had someone dropped them? Thrown them away? Had they fallen from a daykeeper's bundle as he or she walked down the hill? I just knew I couldn't leave them on the ground. I wrapped them in my bandana and knotted it to keep them secure. Later, J'Val and I divided them up.

Nowadays I keep them in a small purple velvet pouch that J'Val brought home after she finished her fieldwork. I don't know how or why they came to me. But each time I open the pouch and spill them into the palm of my hand I see those people praying on the top of that hill in Momostenango, and I remember that each day has a face, different from the day before and the day after, and that according to the Quiche, no face is totally positive, or negative, in its possibilities. Even days that are dark with foreboding are threaded with moments of light, and days full of light are threaded with moments of darkness.

SOURCES

Guatemala: Memory of Silence. Report of the Guatemalan
    Commission for Historical Clarification, 1999.
Tedlock, Barbara. *Time and the Highland Maya*. Albuquerque:
    University of New Mexico Press, 1992.

From Thailand to Japan

Christina Owens

 On the road into the Thai jungle, just before our timelines got all out of whack and my dad went crazy, I sat in the back seat of a double-cab mini truck and reminisced about home. Staring out the window, I watched glimpses of mid-country South Carolina slip by, rusted tin roofs, barns, sparse roadside produce stands. There's even a vine that has the same idea as kudzu: cover and conquer.

Unruly nature, rubbish, and stretches of red sand line the road and surround the houses and stores. These weedy expanses could be South Carolina, all the spaces in between the red brick houses and the trailer parks of my youth. I carry this landscape around inside me and transplant it to all the faraway places I go. Replace the rubber tree plantations with pines and this could be my dad's own pickup truck. South Carolina is inside of me and I am in all those spaces in between.

It was Christmas Day in Khao Sok National Park. I trekked down muddy, leech-infested trails, headed for a waterfall that didn't exist. Musician John trailed behind, microphone and MD in hand, capturing the stereophonic call and response of cicadas. Pure screech looping to staccato, changing in timbre, tone and pattern every fifteen minutes. Clockwork: the cicadas have cut the day up into pieces, allotted each species a quarter-hour slot to call out to each other. "I'm here. Where are you?" Day after day. They are a natural time-telling device.

This was my second Christmas away from home, my second Christmas with John and Michelle. We sat across from each other at the picnic table, took pictures to commemorate Christmas dinner 2002. Pineapple smoothies stood in for Aunt Doddie's fruit trifle. We had pad thai instead of potato salad or turkey. Two Americans and an Australian, all of us living in Japan—this was our escape to breezy Thailand, where we happily had our toes sucked by leeches all day, then tucked ourselves in to the sounds of Thai karaoke at night.

The local bar was a hut decorated in colored lights. Bing Crosby's "I'll Be Home for Christmas" drifted over to us as we fell sleep. Carrying home(s) inside makes everything more poignant and ripe with meaning.

In the jungle there was no Internet access, no phones for international calls, and no holiday greetings. I didn't learn about my father's madness until two days after it occurred. In this world where madness is an event, a newsworthy happening, I was two days late knowing about an incident in my own life. Technically, he went mad on December 26, Eastern Standard Time. I have tried to straighten out the wrinkles, read the cicadas, and pinpoint what this means. Where was I when he manifested his madness? What was I doing? Our parallel timelines slip and slide past each other and never come to an agreement. The distance is too overwhelming to understand.

December 26, Thai time, I was on a group tour through a lake towered over by limestone cliffs, going through a jungle leading to a cave. Hiking in a staggered line, we came upon bamboo collapsed in on itself, a jumble of chopsticks; tree vines like a jungle playground. My mind wandered to memories of all the beautiful places I've been— the Isle of Skye, the Yorkshire dales, Yosemite, the Olympic rain forest, the whole Iberian Peninsula, Spain and Portugal. How lucky I've been! These were my thoughts at the moment.

At the entrance to the cave, Michelle, John, and I found ourselves sadly unprepared, no flashlight in hand for personal exploration. Relying on the guides, we followed their dancing beams, caught glimpses of stalactites and stalagmites and bats suspended from the ceiling. We waded through acidic guano streams and the water got deeper and deeper. A sparkling quartz toadstool took over the path and edged us next to the wall. One of the stalagmites demanded our attention, a giant almond on a throne.

The water perilously deep now, the guides stopped, pulled out a black plastic bag and requested all cameras and non-waterproof materials. We descended into caverns, climbed down rock cliffs into deep pools where the water was over our heads. There I was, inside a dark cave, rock climbing and swimming between two sheer rock faces. It was all my childhood daydream adventures come true. Michelle yelled something about the Goonies movie, and I was aware simply of being blessed, of having come so far from childhood and seen so many things.

My childhood was what some people might call challenged, challenging. My parents divorced when I was young, my mother too strong to deal with my father's abuse. My father got custody and filled my head with his own paranoia, the intricate rules of conditional love. It's a typical story. I worshiped him and, in return, he kept me on a pedestal: I was the perfect child, the only woman truly deserving of his love, the key to his middle-class dreams, the first family member to go to college, the lightning rod for his hoarded sensitivities and vicarious needs.

I didn't see my mom for ten years while I was growing up. She says she couldn't deal with his manipulative spite. He says she abandoned me. Madness is not an event. It's a path. As you walk along it, the walls close in around you and everyone, even your prized daughter, becomes a potential traitor. My dad had been on that path for years.

I got the first emails in Surat Thani. Two-liners from a family friend, "Call home ASAP. Your father needs your help." Another posted four hours later, "We had somewhat of a crisis here. Things are under control now. I'll write more tomorrow." It was all too far away to imagine the scenario.

My father, locked in his house, two hundred police officers and an all-terrain tank on a standoff in my front yard. He held my step-mom hostage all afternoon. She lay on the floor, her arms and legs were tied together with red bandanas. Once the police were outside he threatened murder-suicide, but somehow she got away. As she ran through the yard, into the waiting throngs, he shot a gun over her head. It was three more hours before he gave himself up. Three more hours of his suicide threats and tearful telephone calls from my granddad, my aunts and uncles. That's what the family friend had been asking me to call home to: my dad at the peak of his madness.

Two days late in the knowing, I read the news in an Internet cafe in Bangkok. The blinking cursor became therapeutic. It pecked out words slowly, seemingly on its own, only to delete them again. Two

231

steps forward, three steps back. Michelle and John waited for me upstairs, in a room with matching cots and blank white walls. I sat down across from them, got lost in my own silence for a while. *Dissociated shock?* I wondered. *Perhaps my face is the same color as these walls. Sheer white ghost.* "I have to decide which is best for me, a night of solitude or a night of escape."

On the night I learned of my dad's madness manifest, I went to a "pussy show" in Phat Phong, Bangkok's famous sex district. Woman after woman trudged on stage to showcase her particular talent: pulling razors out of her pussy, smoking cigarettes, blowing out candles with her pussy, writing a letter, guiding Ping-Pong balls, shooting darts into balloons. It was the most methodical, unsexy "sex show" I had ever seen. You could tell time by it.

We left for Cambodia the next day. I got email updates throughout my whole trip, Siem Riep, Angkor Wat, Phnom Penh. Exploring one of the Seven Wonders of the Ancient World during the day, I sifted through police updates and emails at night. A part of me lived only in the Ethernet, the spaces between computers, the emotions that connected Cambodian computers with home.

The South Carolina inside me was inescapable. The whole trip was cast in its prisms, double meanings and unexpected poignancies. As I hiked through the forest, on the way to the River of Lingas, the signs read, "Don't stray from the beaten path," and I took the danger of mines as a metaphor for family. The blind man who gave me a massage in Phnom Penh had my father's rough, knotted, strong hands. At the Killing Fields and Tuol Sleng Museum, I took a closer look at death. Everything I did, everything I saw, was overlaid with the knowledge of my father in a police standoff, threatening murder-suicide, manifesting his madness after all these years.

After my second Christmas away from home, I returned to life in Japan, where in every room in every hotel and inn there is a free tea set kindly provided: cups, saucers, electric kettle, porcelain teapot and green tea. On Christmas morning 2003, I woke up at seven and ate instant cheese grits out of a round Japanese teacup. One packet of grits fits snugly into one little cup. The hot water from the electric kettle was just the right temperature, and the chopsticks I carry in my purse passed decently for a mixing spoon. My mother, the care package supplier of these Southern treats, would be proud.

This was my third Christmas away from home. I was traveling through the countryside of southwestern Japan, alone this time. In the past year, I had communicated with my father only once, while he was in F-lodge at the state mental hospital. I don't remember what we said. I got lost somewhere in the spaces between his apologies and his accusations.

Giving life to his paranoia, I soon arranged a meeting between one estranged woman and another. My mother and stepmother converged on his abandoned house and worked together to divest it of my things. With that transfer of property, I finally "gave up" an identity: father's daughter. Are you your father's daughter or your mother's daughter? Should you sit and contemplate or go to a pussy show? False dichotomies mock the reality of my life. In my reality, I contemplate *while at* the pussy show. I'm not on his side or theirs. I'm on mine.

Christmas morning 2003, tummy full of instant grits, I boarded a bus for Hagi, land of samurai revolutions, abandoned temples, and expensive pottery. My first photo of the day was of a Jizo statue alcove, the baby Jizo in his mother Mary's arms; Jesus and Mary come to visit Buddhism for the day. Two and a half years in Japan and this is the first time I've seen Jizo with a mother. In temple picture number two, there was Kannon, the goddess of mercy, with little babies gathered around her feet. Temple three was falling to pieces, occupied by an avid collector of junk, all of which was strewn throughout the yard. There was a yellow 1970s Citroën parked just inside the stately main gate. Here was a gritty look at the downfall of Zen. No samurai, no feudal system, no castle, no Zen.

The castle had been dismantled more quickly by the revolution. Now it's a forgotten park of bamboo forests and unkempt trails, signs, and paths that drift happily off into nothing. They got me lost, had me clambering up hills and climbing through underbrush in a dress. I laughed at it, the unmarked paths and myself, both so very un-

Japanese. Thus unaware, I stumbled out of the forest onto a grassy bluff. Pounding waves, rocky cliffs, and wind ripping through my hair: Christmas surprises.

At the end of the wandering, I trekked back to Mrs. Sakai's inn. Mrs. Sakai is a seventy-year-old with rheumatism who sits alone in her land of eccentric collected souvenirs. She has a Totoro cuckoo clock, a stand-up antique phone, wall hangings from Africa, placemats of Impressionist paintings, a stuffed deer head on the wall. Mrs. Sakai wears a beret and has two pet cats who live in the house with her. The whole inn smells faintly of old cat litter. She can talk for hours.

She told me of her years growing up in Korea, during the occupation, how they were taught to speak elegantly, using the word *go-kigen-yo* for good morning, good afternoon, good evening, goodbye and good night. When she came back to Japan after the war, everyone thought she was an uppity little girl. That was when she learned to be strong; that was when she had to live in a tiny house with twenty people.

Now, her head is still full of classic Japanese. Smiling, nodding elegantly, she pronounced that one word, *classic*, repeatedly, in English. Until nine years ago she was a high school teacher of *classic* Japanese. Since retiring, she's been plagued with rheumatism. She told me that it gets worse with rain and snow, that five years ago she could barely move around at all. Back then, she couldn't sleep for the pain. She would lie awake all night, alone, her body hurting, and that was when she realized: the new metal power poles, they sing. The old wooden ones don't, only the big metal ones. They sing to each other and there are all kinds of other sounds too, sounds of the night. "It was a night symphony, an orchestra just for me."

Sometimes she would sing to herself at night too, play accompaniment to the orchestra. Whatever old song popped onto her lips, she'd sing. One night, she began a song and old momma cat swiped a paw at her face. "You don't like this song? Well, how about I sing another one?" The new song, fast and upbeat, had momma cat purring and cuddling in no time. Then she realized, the first song was sad and the second one wasn't. Even her cats are wise.

Christina Owens

I sat with her, thinking of the wisdom I had garnered, the wisdom I had yet to see. Me, the granddaughter of sharecropper tenant farmers, school janitors, and cotton mill workers. Now I am the daughter of an incarcerated man. Seven years in prison. While I traipse through the world, through jungles and caves, Buddhist temples and abandoned castles, my father is behind bars. I wonder if he sleeps well at night. Has he found a goddess of mercy, a symphony of the heart to see him through? Does he ever listen to the singing of metal power poles calling out to each other, "I'm here. Where are you?" When he's sitting alone by himself, or wandering the prison grounds, what is it that reminds him of home? My heart goes out to him. Can he hear it?

My mother was not home when I called her on Christmas night. I knew where she was though—over at her elderly neighbor's house, having her own estranged celebrations, separate from family and tradition. She disowned her own father years ago. I'm not sure if I follow in her footsteps. I'm still living in those spaces in between, using Japan as a hiatus, a cauldron for slow, contemplative change. From the pay phone in front of East Hagi Railway Station, I left a message on my mom's answering machine. "Merry Christmas! I'm just finishing mine. I hope you have a good one too!" After hanging up, I went back over to the inn and received my Christmas present for the day, a fruit mousse tart, courtesy of Mrs. Sakai.

Yukon Odyssey

Aprille Janes

 Steering my Hertz rental out of the Whitehorse Airport parking lot, I wasn't surprised to find myself missing my father. He had dreamed of exploring the Alaskan Highway but never had the chance. My eyes filled with tears. If only he were still living and could share this with me. But I had come here following my own dream involving a different kind of road, a more inner journey. I wanted the Yukon undiluted by the presence of other people. I traveled alone by choice.

Turning south, I headed for the Lewes River Farm B&B. On my arrival, my hosts told me I might see moose feeding down by the water and cautioned me about hiking because of bears. An eagle soared overhead a few moments later. I'd found the right place for my base camp.

After I unpacked, the river called me outside. Pink fireweed flaunted its color along the edge of a spruce forest, and the steep slope behind my cabin with its thick layer of sphagnum moss felt as spongy as a feather bed. It provided the delightful sensation of bouncing my way down to the Yukon River, where I dipped my fingers in the water, conscious of the history in this place. Sitting on its sandy bank, I studied the far side and imagined the Gold Rush Stampeders crowding this watery highway in 1898. There was no boat traffic today; the river flowed empty of visible life. I rested there a long time, letting the present moment take root in my memory and become part of my own history. This was when I felt my journey begin.

I came to the north seeking a short sabbatical from the responsibilities of being a wife, mother, friend, career woman, and all the other roles I filled. I was claiming a time and place of my own. Being in complete control of where I went and what I did was every woman's dream—or at least every woman I knew.

I wanted to shed a little civilization, but letting go was harder than I expected. Little habits, absurd in this wilderness setting, kept surprising me. By southern Ontario standards, I was in the middle of nowhere, but I had still locked my car door when I arrived. That sense of humanity pushing in on me was like a heavy cloak, and I'd worn it without feeling its weight. Until now.

I also took for granted the sound of humanity, a steady hum that went unnoticed until it stopped. Seated on the deck of my cabin that first evening, I didn't hear one man-made noise except for an occasional plane overhead. Instead I heard the wind approach from the mountains, cross the river, and rush among the treetops. A bird called close by, and something squeaked from an overhead limb. I had been sitting so quietly that the wild things felt safe picking up their conversations again.

After 11 p.m. the sun still lit up the sky. I was hyper-aware of my unlocked cabin door and I couldn't doze off. I tried but finally gave up, got out of bed, and secured it. My brain kept saying there was no one out there for miles, but a slight paranoia kept whispering, You never know. Finally I fell asleep but at 3:30 a.m. I woke again, disoriented by so much light when my world should have been dark. Although the sun had shifted, adding a pink glow to the sky, I was uncertain which way was east.

Writing in my journal eased me through my first morning as I recovered from jet lag. By the afternoon I felt more in synch with this new time zone, so I went hiking in Miles Canyon. I consciously needed to slow my revved-up life to a walking pace. I wanted to feel my feet hitting the ground. Somehow, I felt it was important to leave a footprint that said I'd been there.

But I also wanted to feel safe, and Miles Canyon was a well-traveled path. I'd been told that bears avoid busy trails and had no more desire to cross paths with me than I did with them. I hoped it was true and tried not to think about any other possibilities. Even so, I turned back earlier than I intended, feeling suddenly vulnerable despite the other hikers I passed along the way. Or maybe because of them.

My reaction to that first "day without night" surprised me. At first it felt as if I'd found the center of the universe, a place where the sun orbited around me. But reduced to one small speck in a vast land, I made the trip back from Center of the Universe to Humble in about ten seconds.

The next day I headed for Skagway and discovered that distance is relative in that huge territory. A sign posted at the turnoff from the Alaskan Highway declared "White Pass Railroad—Next Left." I signaled and made the turn, but it wasn't just around the corner as the sign might have implied in Ontario. One hundred fifty miles lay between me and the White Pass Railroad. Later I discovered that he true Yukoner measures distance by hours of driving, not miles.

Historic markers and scenic overlooks along the way tempted me to pause and visit. Here in the Yukon I had no deadlines and no appointments to meet. I indulged in the luxury of time. At my second stop, a strong sense of déjà vu surprised me. It took me a moment but I soon realized why. My daughter once asked me to paint a watercolor from a photograph she had taken on this very spot looking out over Emerald Lake. I delighted in my sense of connection with her. It also reinforced for me how important it was to be mindful of detail. Painting that picture made this place part of my experience before I ever set foot here.

In Skagway, I boarded the White Pass Railroad. We chugged along one of the Gold Rush routes, surrounded by staggering beauty as the train climbed high into the mountains. Portions of the original Trail of '98 were still visible. People and horses had labored here, making multiple trips to get the required ton of supplies through the pass. It seemed ironic that of all the thousands who were drawn here by the lure of gold, only a handful found any wealth. The ones who made the real money catered to the miners' needs and vices.

After the spectacular train trip, I impulsively boarded the ferry to Haines with my rental car to take in some coastal scenery. Too late, though, I realized my mistake: there was no road back to Skagway from Haines. I had a choice; at least a two-hour wait for the return ferry coupled with a two-hour drive from Skagway to Whitehorse, or a four-and-a-half-hour drive from Haines.

As it was already 6 p.m., I felt as if I was facing a marathon after an already long day. With no one to "rescue" me, I grabbed a quick supper, got behind the wheel and started driving, planning to sleep in the car if I needed rest. Scanning the radio stations for company, I discovered only dead air. Up and down the dial I searched for intelligent sounds until I gave up and switched it off. With no music or voices on the radio, no other vehicles, and apparently no towns along this stretch of road, I felt completely alone, like the hapless star in a science fiction movie. The world had ended, leaving me as the sole survivor.

In the next two hours I did pass a few cars—and two bears. Just on the verge of worry, I drove into a small town and gratefully filled up on gas and bought a Coke. As I drove on, I finally started talking out loud to keep myself alert. The very emptiness of the landscape lent clarity to my strange conversation with myself, an interrogation of my past.

A teacher of mine once referred to that thing fueling our need to write as "the wound of grace." My mother, suffering from manic depression, inflicted my wound. She had withheld, or just couldn't give, the love and approval her children needed. My adult self had forgiven her for the unhappiness of my childhood but part of me still tried to please her—or anyone.

Over the years, the word no had vanished from my vocabulary. My boundaries blurred and weakened, and critical advice from anyone I respected or admired crushed me. Thinking about these things now on that lonely road, I found a peculiar objectivity.

Before I left home, my daughter lent me *The Secret Life of Bees* by Sue Monk Kidd. In the book, an older woman tells the young protagonist, "You have to find a mother inside yourself." That line had stayed with me since I'd read it, and now I understood why. Unconditional acceptance had to come from inside. I could now choose to give this gift to myself. With this insight, my spiritual awareness also made a major shift.

I had walked away from a strict fundamentalist religion a few years before when I realized it recreated the same abusive relationship I had known as a child. Trained to obey strict rules and respect traditions, I was subtly taught that God couldn't love me unless I placated Him. In the quiet of my car as the scenery rolled by, I recognized the huge gulf between God's reality and man's attempt to control by guilt. I'd been looking at Him through distorted lenses. I hadn't recognized the unconditional acceptance He also offered.

It was a lot to absorb, but convinced I'd stumbled onto something, I wanted to take it deep into my being. I needed to wrap my heart around these new ideas. This was a new foundation on which to build a different life, moving away from rule keeping and approval seeking to acceptance and a genuine relationship with myself, with God, and finally with those around me.

I carried this new awareness with me through the rest of the trip. I lost patience with all the chatter and hype about the Gold Rush. I was surrounded by the Yukon's natural splendor, while everyone I met seemed focused only on its history. Like a woman pining for an old beau, they were rejecting life and the present, growing old with memories of the past.

The next morning I drove to Whitehorse and purchased an art journal and watercolor pencils. Retracing my trip down the Skagway highway, I again pulled into those same scenic overlooks and, with new eyes, sketched the incredible scenery as I practiced Emerald Lake's lesson of mindfulness. I had always loved to draw, but in the past had been too self-conscious to work in public. People would look at what I was doing; it was too visible, too available for judgment, my mother's critical voice too loud in my head. Now that voice was silent, and the only person I wanted to please was myself. My drawing became a form of meditation. The joy of the process was enough in itself, and I reveled in my release.

I lost track of time sitting in a quiet field sketching an abandoned trading post. The midday sun was warm, and the only noise was the faint buzzing of insects in the grass. After about an hour I wondered if this was such a good idea; I didn't want to surprise any bears. Suddenly, from behind me, an arctic ground squirrel popped out of his hole with a shrill whistle. Startled by this surprise ambush, I jumped and whirled around, spilling pencils and notebook on the ground. He scolded me and disappeared. I laughed at him, but he was right. It was time to move on.

Stopping on a whim or because a particular slant of sunlight attracted me, I rediscovered the childhood joy of taking all the time I needed to study the clouds, a leaf, a mountain, or a bird. The Yukon granted me that indulgence once again. Intoxicated by the splendor of mountains and the uninhabited spaces, I felt greedy to see it all.

On Sunday I drove three hours to the Tlingit Cultural Center and was disappointed to find it closed. Not wanting to just turn around and go back, I explored the grounds around the unoccupied building and along the lakeshore. Impressive totem poles lined the front walkway, so I decided to make some sketches.

As I sat in my car with drawing materials, one of the Tlingit elders, an older woman with a weathered face, came by and greeted me. I asked her about the symbolism of the totem figures, and she explained that contrary to what most people believe, these poles are not religious symbols but rather a method of preserving culture and heritage. The poles honor deceased relatives, celebrate family histories and important events and preserve the stories of their community. They are sacred because they commemorate a rich tradition and remind people of who they are.

As I listened to her, I realized I might never have learned this if the Center had been open. I also received two other great gifts from this experience—the knowledge that writing out my own stories is a sacred trust and the reward of accepting changed circumstances without judgment or expectation.

Toward the end of my time in the Yukon, I made my way to Kluane National Park. Rain clouds cloaked the spectacular mountains, creating vignettes of glaciers swathed in shrouds of fog. Mist veiled the peaks, weaving intricate designs along the ridges laced with dark trees and rocky crags. Hours later, the dramatic drive around Kluane Lake brought me to Burwash Landing.

Exploring the remarkably sophisticated natural history museum that seemed built at the end of beyond, I suddenly felt a long, long way from the people who mattered to me. There was no one to share this remarkable place and experience with, and it struck me just how far away from home I was. Like an elastic band stretched taut, I sensed every one of the thousands of miles between us. Somehow, by defining my own boundaries, I'd acquired a new appreciation for the important people in my life. It seemed I had to get away to recognize the value of what I possessed. It was time to think about home.

I checked into an area B&B, but my desire for new places had vanished. I felt uncomfortable and edgy. After half an hour of trying to relax, I gave up, repacked my things, got back in my car and headed for Whitehorse. The sight of my now familiar cabin on the Yukon River welcomed me three hours later.

I fell asleep with my door unlocked and the windows wide open.

I put twelve hundred miles on my rental car over the course of that week, but on my last full day the need to be on the move evaporated. Daydreaming in a comfortable chair with my feet resting on the top rail of the deck, I listened to the forest sounds, wrote in my journal, and savored the warmth of sun on my face. The soft breeze tousling my hair carried the faint scent of spruce.

On my last morning in the Yukon, I sat in the airport with my boarding pass tucked in my carry-on bag and gazed out the large windows, trying to memorize the mountains and clay hills surrounding Whitehorse. My heart felt tight and uncomfortable, caught between the tug of home and my desire to stay.

My odyssey offered me the calm of unpopulated places and the inspiration of extraordinary natural beauty. Undistracted, I saw with my own eyes and heard my own voice again. I uncovered parts of myself that had been buried under childhood scar tissue, lost in the hurry and noise of society and the busyness of my life. I went north looking for solitary time mixed with a bit of adventure. I also found acceptance, renewed my spiritual life, and deepened my appreciation of family and friends. I fell in love with the Yukon and hope to return someday.

A surprising conversation that I overheard in the Moose Café on my first evening in Whitehorse summed up the experience for me. One fellow was bemoaning his difficulties writing a jazz concerto for strings. His companion offered, "It's like following a new road. You just explore, and sometimes you make an interesting discovery, and sometimes it's a dead end. But every road teaches you something."

Calle 55:
Notes from the Canada-Mexico Writing/Photography Exchange

Shelley A. Leedahl

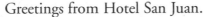

Greetings from Hotel San Juan.

It's 5:40 a.m., my windows are open to the morning, and it smells like rain. In my three and a half weeks in Mexico it has rained only once, but it was a downpour, a baptism, and one of the Canadians—Rosalie, a photographer—danced in the puddles like a child, happy in her feet.

We dance a lot here—in the streets, where a different band plays salsa or merengue on each block and people of all ages manage to *become* the music; in clubs, where we might hear the same songs five times a night and no one would dream of complaining; in our rooms, if Laura (pronounced La-ora), easily the best dancer among us, offers an impromptu salsa lesson. Shoes are kicked off, beds pushed aside. Another *buen día* in Mérida.

When I see myself in photographs or catch a glimpse in the mirror, I wonder, *Who is this woman, smiling all the time?*

I left my husband and teenage children in autumn-dreary Saskatoon, where the cool weather mirrored my disposition. I left a manic schedule that included numerous school tours, leading creative writing workshops, editing, freelancing, and the simultaneous writing of my next two books. I left the absolute drudgery of washing floors, doing endless loads of laundry, cleaning the dog's kennel. I left exhaustion and bitterness. Just surviving each day was so much work. And even though I rarely took time off, I only ever had just enough money to pay my bills. Clearly, I was adrift. This Mexican adventure was a life raft.

In order to make the separation complete, I told my family I would not be contacting them in the month I would be away, except by very occasional emails.

This two-part *intercambio* (exchange), sponsored by the Banff Centre of the Arts and FONCA (Fondo Nacional para la Cultura y las Artes), integrates countries, disciplines, and cultures. Next year: six weeks in Banff. Before I left Canada, a producer at CBC Radio called to ask if I would phone in weekly reports from Mérida. Absolutely not—if I was not going to be speaking to my family, I was certainly not going to speak to anyone else.

And then Mexico happened. *Is* happening! It's real! And I will never be the same.

The Canadians (five photographers, five writers) arrived on October 15, 2002, in a city in ruins. Mérida, the Yucatán capital, a high-spirited city of one million, is recovering from the aftermath of Hurricane Isadore, which struck three weeks ago on September 23, devastating roads, buildings, trees, and lives. An estimated 500,000 Yucatecáns are homeless. Three died.

The beautiful city I had toured many times via the Internet was not the city I arrived in, yet as I piled into a taxi with three other Canadians, I had the distinct sense that for the first time in my thirty-nine years, I was home.

This is my second visit to Mexico. I have also enjoyed brief visits to the Dominican Republic (1987) and Venezuela (1997). My euphoria in Mérida is similar to emotions I experienced in those other countries. I am beyond joy. I am floating.

The Canadian participants rendezvoused in the hotel lobby that first evening. The ten Mexican writers and photographers—mostly from Mexico City but others from Mérida, Mazatlán and Comalcalco, Tabasco—were not around. This might have been a good thing. I was disoriented enough as I settled into my hotel room—two single beds with bright orange quilts, a fan, a dresser with an elaborately carved mirror frame—and met the other Canadian artists.

Our initial meeting with the Mexican contingent occurred, perhaps symbolically, on a dark street. We introduced ourselves and shook hands as if in a receiving line—*mucho gusto, encantada*—then dined together in an outdoor café with music, roaming street vendors, begging grandmothers, and Spanglish weaving together the multicolored threads of our first of many surreal nights.

From my landing in Cancun and bus ride to Mérida until this moment, as I'm scribbling these notes, I have remained in a state of hyper-acute sensitivity. Colors and images are vibrant; every sound, even the constant drilling in the streets, reaches my ears as music.

I sat between Laura and Gerardo—two young photographers, part of the Mexican half of the *intercambio*, and recognized as among the finest of their generation. I don't remember the conversation, but we raised our glasses—*salud*—and smiled *frecuentemente* (often).

Although about half of the Mexican participants speak good or excellent English; the others speak little or none. I had decided before I came that I would I speak as much Spanish as possible. I've studied Spanish off and on since 1987, and arrived with at least enough for *conversaciones breves*. I know how to conjugate. I possess a decent vocabulary. Yet I tremble and inadvertently close my ears when anyone speaks Spanish to me. *Un problema muy grande.* A full-fledged phobia. I manage well in restaurants and stores, but discussions among this group of brilliant, educated, and predominantly young intellectuals quickly rose to levels I had no words for—sometimes, I feared, in any language.

Why does this happen? I want more than anything to be able to comprehend Spanish. Maybe I want it too much. I'm so afraid of failure that I can't even hear. I cannot imagine having arrived here with no knowledge of the language, as some of my associates have. At least I can *speak* Spanish, even if I understand only a morsel of what's being said.

Mérida, rebuilding.

There is much to do. Trees as wide as Volkswagens have been plucked from the ground. Branches litter the sprawling city. There's aluminum roofing dangling in treetops. Concrete's tumbled, windows are smashed, but nothing I see compares with the ruined streets. It would be easy to die here: to avoid toppling into a crater is only half of it. *Cruzando* (crossing) a street without getting smeared—by bus, car, or screaming *ambulancia*—or crushed by the *muchedumbre* (crowd) on the narrow sidewalks, or dissolving in the oppressive heat of the *mercado* (market) where you writhe shoulder to elbow to knee with other shoppers, are blurrier matters.

Yet I feel safe. Safer walking alone on the streets at 2 a.m. than I would feel in my own neighborhood at dusk. There is a strong police presence, which helps, but also a general feeling that no harm can come to me here.

Mérida is cosmopolitan and ancient, garishly rich and desperately poor. Founded in 1542 by the Spaniard Francisco de Montejo (a popular beer is among his namesakes), it was once a large Mayan city known as T'ho. After the Spanish conquest—a particularly long and bloody battle depicted in numerous murals inside the Palacio de Gobierno—the Mayan temples and palaces were dismantled and the stones used as the foundation for the Cathedral of San Idelfonso, located in Mérida's main plaza. Spanish and French colonial architecture, as well as Moorish influences, are evident throughout the city, especially along Paseo Montejo, the elegant, tree-lined street that runs like a long vein toward the historic heart of the city.

Mérida is clowns with colossal balloon bouquets. It's horse-drawn carriages; soldiers on parade; lovers on park benches; shrieking sirens; little girls primped up like princesses; road repair crews; schoolgirls in tartan skirts, blouses white and crisp as sails; Spanish-speaking Mennonites selling cheese; shoe shiners; street musicians; salsa dancers; sprawling markets. I see newspapers and sweets sold on street corners; vendors pitching *hamacas* (hammocks), fans, Panama hats; beggars with physical deformities; bats as big as pigeons; Mayan women in traditional white dresses with elaborately embroidered flowers at the neck and hem; live outdoor theatre—magic. How can *any* season in Saskatoon compare with all this?

The Yucatán is rich in Mayan tradition. It's dotted with *ruinas;* some three thousand *cenotes* (sink holes); *pueblos*, low and high jungle; almost deserted coastal villages; un-Americanized beaches; thin dogs; plazas with centuries-old *catedrals* on one side, government buildings on the other. *Tiendas, restaurantes, parques, panaderías, lavanderías, peluquerías, mercados, escuelas, papelerías, universidades, cantinas, museos, galerías,* and *casas* (stores, restaurants, parks, bakeries, laundries, barber shops, markets, schools, stationers, universities, cantinas, museums, galleries, and houses) at both ends of the economic scale fill in the gaps. Stores that sell material and Christmas wrapping paper are big here. As are saints.

Although I am not Catholic, I am spiritually moved by the outward signs of faith the mostly Catholic Mexicans exhibit. People of all ages genuflect and kiss their hand when they pass cathedrals. I spend a fair amount of time in cathedrals, too, feeling like a little girl. I am in awe of the beauty of elaborate architecture; burning votives; old men on their knees, praying. I try to pray, but I am so overwhelmed I'm unable to concentrate. Perhaps this is prayer enough.

In the small towns—we've visited several—you see folks riding three-wheeled, canopied bikes with a seat in front for passengers or packages. I have seen ladders transported this way; even a boat floating sideways down a street. My experience in the Yucatán has been perpetually hallucinatory. I am in a constant state of "pinch me." I keep expecting to wake up, hoping I never do.

When I mentally set Saskatchewan beside the Yucatán, it's impossible to fathom that the two exist in the same world. Everything I have experienced here—from the meals to the weather—is so radically different that it might be another planet.

The structure of this exchange is that there is no structure. For some this has been incredibly frustrating; for others, myself included, it's been one of the highlights. What is meant to happen is collaboration and the creation of art. But how to begin?

In the first few days, in the lavish Teatro Mérida, the photographers gave slide presentations and the writers spoke about their work. I recited a poem, "Vestidos Sencillos," ("Simple Dresses") that had come to me, in Spanish, back in Saskatchewan. I said, in Spanish and English, that my being in Mexico to write and collaborate with Mexican artists was the dream I had been having my entire life. On the stage I felt a surge of emotion, and I could not avoid tears. Maleea, a young poet from Victoria, also cried during her talk. We have become very close friends.

The presentations required lengthy translations, and afterward we left en masse to eat. For twenty-two people to dine together in Mexico can take what seems like a lifetime. The Mexicans were very helpful, suggesting what we might order, naming the free appetizers as they arrived, plate after plate, demonstrating the proper way to fold tortillas. Will we be as generous when they come to Canada next year? They've made maps to help us locate economical restaurants, offer Spanish lessons, assist us at the bank.

But we are twenty-two. Every little thing takes so much time and I like to be quick and decisive. By the third day I only wanted to be alone. Too much talking, too much waiting, too much standing around. And the heat! I swim through the air, and my clothes fuse to my skin.

I'd had enough of *el grupo*, and found refuge in *el parque*—think pavement, not grass, a few huge trees with trunk bases painted white—on the corner near our hotel. Except when I'm touring, I am a woman who spends much of her time alone. I require absolute silence to think and write and even, I believe, to adequately recognize what I'm feeling. My teens and husband are usually gone all day; the quiet and solitude are blissful.

Here, in *el parque* with the setting sun, I watched couples congregate and, oblivious to anyone else, make as much love as is physically possible when fully clothed and seated (or semi-reclined) on a public park bench. They sank into each other's arms and eyes, trailed fingers through hair, kissed as though enacting the lyrics of one of the popular songs I've learned to dance to: "I want to eat your mouth and never breathe again."

From those early evenings sprang the idea for my first collaboration. I asked Gerardo to help me interview and photograph couples on park benches; back in Saskatoon I will fabricate stories for each of them. We had to wait several minutes for our first passionate couple to come up for air. "How long have you been together?" I asked. "*Dos horas.*" Two hours? They'd just met via the Internet. In Mexico, all is not what it seems.

There were many more meetings in dark, airless restaurants with *el grupo;* we have finished with them now, for which I am thankful. I often found the presentations academic, and then there were questions and the necessary translating. I was anxious and frustrated. The small rooms felt claustrophobic. When it was my night I clipped it short. The heat. We chalk many things up to the heat.

At night, with the fan whirring above me, I sleep without dreams. *Dormí como un angelito.* (I slept like a little angel.)

Music is the current that runs through everything here. It's prevalent in stores, streets and *parques*, and I was going slightly *loca* with my desire to dance and no one to dance with. Finally, on the fourth night, a small group of us went out to a Cuban club, and as we danced we could almost hear the ice shattering around our feet. After that night there was much more dancing—as long as I live, I will never forget Azul Picante, an unadorned second-floor club with a live band and a small, wizened woman selling paper towels in the washroom.

Many tight friendships have followed.

I've connected with Maleea and three Mexicans—Juan José, Andrés (fiction writers) and Gerardo (photographer). We are *la familia*. As the days melt into each other we explore the Yucatán together in rented Nissans and cluster in sidewalk cafés. We talk about living as artists in Canada and Mexico. What's different, what's the same. (Here the artists rely heavily on the generous prizes and grants available.) We speak mostly Spanish. We eat. After I'd eaten all I believed possible of my fish in a fly-infested market in Progreso, the nearest coastal town, Andrés asked if I was done and proceeded to devour the head. We take our photos together. We translate each other's work. We laugh all the time.

One evening, after a day of traveling from beach to beach, the five of us landed in Sisal, and I reached one of the peaks of my life. After dinner in a beachside restaurant, we moved closer to the water. It was phosphorescent, otherworldly; the sky was exploding with stars. There was a slight breeze, the music of waves, and a collective awareness that poetry was being made. I don't know how long we stayed there, together but alone, as time lost all meaning.

The Canadians take turns being sick. Maleea says we spend the first two weeks arriving, the last two trying not to leave.

The photographers work harder than the writers. We scribble impressions—mine in three notebooks, on a laptop computer I balance on my knees (there are no desks provided), on scraps of paper, napkins, the palm of my left hand—and soak our experiences up for future reference. The photographers need to get it on film now.

By the end of the second week there are several collaborations in progress. It's all an exchange; there is no way to do this wrong. At times some of the participants get hung up on the end result: tentatively a book. They worry about the format, the theme, the constriction of pages. I don't worry. I don't yet know what shape my exchange-inspired work will take. I live each day in Mexico to the fullest. I learn, sweat, dance, and trip; I record more impressions, and take photographs, and try to freeze time.

I don't attend everything—there are dinners, exhibitions, day trips—and I don't form a personal relationship with every one of the participants. There are a few I have scarcely spoken to, others who will be lifelong friends.

One of the women has become depressed. I empathize, yet selfishly make no effort to be helpful. I am at the other extreme here. I don't want anything to interfere with the perfection my life has become.

There is much more to tell—the jungle, ruins, the Day of the Dead, flamingos, a badly taped Doors cassette, walking in shadows, swimming in a punchbowl (for snakes), the hours of just being together and not saying anything at all—but now it is almost ten-thirty, and time to eat.

I will say hello to Faosto and Ebam at the front desk as I leave my key. I will step onto Calle 55 and swim again through the thick morning heat toward a breakfast of yogurt *con fruta y granola*. I will hold a cup of *te negro* in my hands and try not to think about the few days left. I will attempt, again, to convince myself. This is real. This is real. This is real.

It is hard not to feel a profound sadness, as well, for I have learned a painful truth: I do not miss home. Here I am happy right through to my bones, with these people I hardly know at all. I want each member of my family back home to experience this elation in their own lives, however or wherever it might occur for them. It doesn't seem fair that it is mine alone.

As some people feel they were born in the wrong body, I feel that this place is where I was meant to be. I could lose the map here. But not yet. I am too responsible. I have commitments. I have a great big life in Canada to walk back into, and the people there who love me haven't heard my voice in weeks.

Separate Spheres

Lynn Cecil

Standing at the shore's edge, I watch the warm turquoise water of the Atlantic Ocean approach in powerful crests, then break into foam before retreating. I close my eyes and sigh deeply, as I feel again the strange pleasure of traveling without my husband and two young children, as if I have shifted identities, abandoned roles that defined me, confined me. I am distinctly aware of my environment, of being alone, of feeling younger, freer, than I have felt in years. I have left the safety and complacency of my daily familial life and have, through two airplane flights, slipped away into another sphere of existence, separated by space, geography, and time.

Above me, the sky is a deep cerulean blue, a color I know that my photographs will not capture. I wade into the water, lie on my back and float. This moment refuses to be stilled, will be one that I remember as fluid motion, simultaneously drawing me in and away, like the ocean that holds me, rocks me back and forth beneath the sun. I ride the swells of water that unlock forgotten memories in my body, and I relax, the deep cold of a Canadian prairie winter dissipating from my thoughts like the dissolving foam at the shore. Housebound for weeks on end with wind chills outside dipping to temperatures to as low as negative fifty-five degrees Celsius, I had felt like a prisoner of weather chained to a monotonous daily routine. I began to feel sorry for myself, as if the life I had once willingly and gratefully chosen had become a trap. I had everything I had ever wanted—a husband, two children, a home, a career in teaching that was on hold while I cared for my children, evenings free to write and paint—and yet, I was often overcome by a sense of longing, a need for more—or perhaps less. Somehow, in becoming a wife, mother, homeowner, teacher, writer, and artist, I had lost a sense of who I was. I felt like a missing person, a person missing to myself. I was unhappy, restless, starving for change, for a chance to get away, to travel in search of the person I once was, so many years before, when I was barely defined by roles.

The June sun, almost directly overhead, is so brilliant, so hot that I feel warmed from the inside out. I experience a sense of peace that I have not felt in years, as if my fears and anxieties, duties and obligations, parameters and roles have melted away in the heat. I had felt selfish at first, for suggesting it, even more selfish when my husband agreed it would be good for me to get away alone. "Go to Bermuda. Visit your brother—really, we'll be fine—go and have fun." *Have fun?* Sure, if I could overcome the guilt of leaving my family behind, if I could believe that I might actually deserve having a week on a sub-tropical island to myself—then I could have fun. Friends who are also wives and mothers encouraged me to go, their voices and eyes full of envy at the idea of escape—glorious escape.

Leaving wasn't easy. I think briefly of that moment when I hugged and kissed my children and husband goodbye at the airport, how my children's faces crumpled into tears as they told me they would miss me. I kept my own tears hidden until the plane was airborne, when it would be impossible to turn back, then the tears had flowed freely and I felt first a sense of fear—all the *what-ifs* plaguing my thoughts—then a sense of emptiness, an emotional tabula rasa. As the Saskatchewan prairie landscape receded from view, I dried my eyes and made the conscious decision to enjoy this trip—I was going to be away from home for nine days whether I had fun or not: why waste such an opportunity for personal renewal on feeling sad and guilty?

There are a few other people near me at the beach, yet they remain distant, separated by their own lives, their own reasons for being there. I am comforted by their presence, but aware of how disconnected we are, how I feel no need to have my life overlap with those of strangers at this moment. I am conscious of being a tiny speck in the vast spherical landscape of the earth, and think of movies in which a camera zooms out from a single person, expanding far into the universe, offering a view of how minute and seemingly insignificant one person seems. Saddened at this thought, I feel a sense of hopelessness. For a moment I feel that nothing I do as an individual matters, that I am nothing but a number lost in the tabulation of the earth's billions of inhabitants. But then I remind myself that there is also the return, when the camera focuses back down to earth, moving back to the person, as if affirming that the individual, too, is important.

I look far out to the horizon, try to comprehend the size of the earth, its place in the universe. I try to picture first a map, then the earth itself, as if I am hovering over it, trying to minimize the distance that separates me from my family simply by being able to see two places at once. I think of the many landscapes I have visited, others I hope never to experience. I feel deeply privileged to live in a country where people have choices, freedom, rights. I am acutely aware of living in a segment of time that has been separated from my usual reality, of being given a second chance to appreciate who I am and, in doing so, to appreciate all that I have and what my place is in this world.

I have no real schedule here, no routine, no obligations. If I want to swim, I swim. If I want to read, I read. The ocean is like memories, washing over me in waves, lulling me back to my beginnings, the other spheres in my life space, to who I once was—a carefree, inquisitive person, enchanted by colors, the energy of weather, people, life itself. There are moments when I feel like a child again, thinking of stories my parents told me, of how we swam together in the Caribbean Sea just weeks after my birth. I vividly remember living in Nouméa, New Caledonia, and playing with my younger brother in the Pacific Ocean, as our sister, still a toddler, splashed at the shore's edge with our parents. Several years later, while living in Florida, we played together in the Atlantic Ocean. On my twenty-second birthday, I spent the day at Peggy's Cove with a close friend, longing to swim deep in the cold Atlantic but instead staying on the rocks taking photos of scenes I would paint years later. I am drawn to oceans, to their beauty, the flux of energy and power in their motion, their hidden depths, the life they contain.

Here, at Elbow Beach, I am overly conscious of the need to savor the experience, allow the rocking of the water to enter the memory of my body and mind. When I emerge from the water, I feel free, adventurous, deliciously rejuvenated, as if I've been released from a winter cocoon, or a deep sleep, my body physically invigorated from playing in the surf, my spirit refreshed. As I prepare to leave the beach, I cast one last lingering look at the water: I crave going deeper, want to dive and swim along the ocean's floor, view fish and seashells, breathe underwater as if I were a part of the ocean itself.

The following day, I find myself on a dive boat speeding out to the first of two dive sites over two separate shipwrecks. My brother surprised me with the gift of this excursion the day before when I arrived back from Elbow Beach. There are maybe a dozen people participating in the dives—two are being tested for their open-water dive rescues and will recruit the rest of us to act in scenarios between our dives. The diving instructors are gregarious, their wit sharp, their laughter contagious. Despite feeling seasick—I can experience motion sickness on a swing set—I am excited, thrilled to be diving again.

Stride jumping from the stern of the boat, holding my mask and regulator against my face with my hands, I feel a sense of exhilaration. My seasickness is gone the moment I hit the water. I descend slowly, plugging my nose every few seconds, and swallow, allowing my ears to equilibrate. It's been eight years since I dove in Barbados, fifteen since my first open-water dives in the St. Lawrence River. I breathe calmly, my vision narrowed to the view in front of my mask.

I hover over the wreck of the *Montana*, just thirty feet below the water's surface. The ship hit the coral reef and sank in pieces in December of 1863, a fate that befell many ships. Their underwater remains make Bermuda a prime diving area. Once a Civil War blockade-runner that traveled to Bermuda, England, and North Carolina, the *Montana* now lies quietly embedded in the Atlantic Ocean, its broken body covered in brain coral, a stunning exhibit in a wide-open underwater museum. I wonder if anyone survived the disaster, if the bones of the crew are trapped in the hull below me. Yet I feel detached from the emotion that surrounds this wreck—I won't allow it in. To do so would be dangerous, disorientating in such an environment. I am reminded that the ocean, though gentle today, can become suddenly violent, its unpredictable nature turning on those who ride its surface, and I shiver despite the warmth of my wetsuit. Yet I am not afraid. I feel completely calm beneath the water, as if this is where I belong. When I was younger, insecure about so many parts of my life, water became my sanctuary. I would swim length after length in pools, sometimes for hours. At night, I often would dream I was flying away—always *away*—in liquid air.

Our second dive is over the *Lartington*, a freighter that crashed on the reef in 1879. Many of its parts—the boiler, the bow, the stern, and propeller—are still intact and identifiable, as if mummified in the salt water. I dive with one of the instructors over the wreck to a clearing on the ocean floor where we sit and feed an inquisitive parrotfish a worm. I look up through water that is so clear that I feel I can touch the surface even at forty feet below. I lie back, watch the sunlight streaming through the water, sift sand and tiny shards of pink shells between my fingers. I stay close to my dive partner, almost choke when he grabs my bare hand. No one else is within sight. I remember I'm not wearing my rings.

The water feels cooler now against my skin—I had removed my wetsuit between dives, wear only my bathing suit. I am distinctly aware of the distance that separates me from my family, how our lives continue to be lived independently. I wonder if my children are thinking of their mother, so far away, breathing from an oxygen tank beneath the ocean's surface, awkwardly holding hands with some stranger who knows nothing about her, about them. I realize that I am feeling detached from my family, not just physically but emotionally. In this new sphere, this new environment, I start to reconnect with nature, with ocean waters, with the essence of what formed me. I drop my diving partner's hand as if stung, swim by myself.

That evening, like every evening since arriving in Bermuda, I feel a need to write about the day in my journal, record my feelings, describe the events, knowing that all too soon I will leave this island paradise. My days seem almost surreal, as if I am living someone else's life, have borrowed it for a while. When our sister flies in from Canada to join my brother and me, it's like a family reunion, but one for siblings only, without parents, spouses, or children. It is as if time has stilled and we are back on one of the beaches of our childhood, yet, paradoxically, time has made us older, given us our independence, allowed us to choose what parts of the world to visit, where to make our home. I begin to feel a connection with my brother and sister that I haven't felt since I was much younger. Over the years I have often felt like I an outsider, as if the separate spheres of our lives barely overlapped. We talk and talk, share stories and secrets that are spilled, opened. We form our own sphere, one in which we are paradoxically the same, yet different. I hope that it will strengthen our relationships with each other, that we will plan another trip like this together soon.

Throughout the rest of the week I take black-and-white photos of Dockyard, a former British naval base; enjoy an enchanted afternoon swimming with dolphins; explore several more of the beautiful beaches; spend evenings dining and dancing with my sister, brother, and his friends. I am increasingly aware of being a unique individual, undefined by roles, unrestricted by schedules not my own, simply experiencing life. I feel more in control of my life than I have felt in years.

Then, strangely, the night before I leave the island for home, I feel a sudden and unexpected shift in my mindset, as if the emotional distance that disconnected me from my family has suddenly shrunk, like a map folded to connect two points. I find myself longing to be at the airport, to be on the first of two planes home, to be home. I feel anxious, restless. I crave the moment when I will enter the airport and hold my children, kiss my husband. I laugh at myself, knowing that I have changed, that I am more at peace with myself than I have been in a very long time. I feel that I can now embrace the life roles that I have chosen rather than being confined by them. I also am newly aware of the need to keep separate but overlapping spheres in my life, and of the need to break away at times, to remember who I am when I am defined by no one but myself.

Contributors

Catherine Bancroft is a social worker in Toronto. She is a social activist and currently works with women survivors of trauma. She has traveled and lived in Zimbabwe Africa, and has traveled throughout parts of Asia including Korea, Japan, Taiwan, Thailand, Nepal, Cambodia, Myanmar. Her initial idea to create a women's travel anthology was sparked by the impact of her travels on her spiritual journey. Her vision of the anthology has been informed by what she has learned from her interactions in the "developing world."

Sharon Butala has published fifteen books of fiction and non-fiction, including her newest release *Lilac Moon: Dreaming of the Real West* (2005 HarperCollins Canada). She has twice been nominated for Governor General's Awards: for fiction in 1986, and for non-fiction in 1994. She was nominated for the Commonwealth Prize for fiction, received the Marian Engel Award in 1998, and was made an Officer in the Order of Canada in 2002. Her travels, mostly done after fifty, have included East Africa and Haida Gwaii.

Charlotte Caron recently moved to Winnipeg, where she occasionally leads workshops and retreats. Previously she worked at St. Andrew's College in Saskatoon. She enjoys feminist spiritual communities, writing, and playing Scrabble, as well as watching birds. Her forthcoming book, *No Fluttering Angels' Wings: Loss and Hope in Women's Lives,* follows three award-winning books as well as numerous articles focusing on ritual, living with chronic illness, loss, and feminist spirituality.

Lynn Cecil is a writer, editor, teacher, university instructor in English literature, and visual artist who loves to travel and scuba dive, especially in hot places. She began traveling in the Caribbean at four weeks of age, and has since developed a passion for water and travel. Often, her paintings and her writing are inspired by her travels, most recently by her trips to Bermuda and Spain. Born in Montreal, Lynn has lived most of her life in London, Ontario, and has also lived in several other Canadian provinces, Florida, and the South Pacific. Currently, she lives in Regina with her husband and two children.

Amy Coupal is an avid traveler and teacher. Some of her favorite travels have been to Honduras, Brazil, Portugal, Japan, Thailand, Malaysia and of course Papua New Guinea. Amy lives in Toronto with her husband and travel partner, Brad. She is currently pursuing her M.Ed. and works in the education sector. This is her first published piece.

Lorna Crozier's *Inventing the Hawk,* won the Governor General's, the Canadian Authors' Association, and the Pat Lowther Awards for poetry in 1992. Her most recent book is *Whetstone*. She has published essays in such publications as *Dropped Threads*. Recently the University of Regina awarded her an honorary doctorate for her contribution to Canadian literature. She is a Distinguished Professor and the Chair of the Department of Writing at the University of Victoria, and she lives in a house with a huge garden, the writer Patrick Lane, and two fine cats.

Janet Greidanus lives in Edmonton and is the mother of six adult children and the grandmother of eleven grandchildren. As a young woman she began a career as a nurse, but followed a different path when she returned to university as her youngest child started grade 3. She is now a certified chaplain who companions bereaved children and teens and is a counselor of college students at the King's University College. She is also a student in the Doctor of Ministry Program at St. Stephen's College and has just completed writing her dissertation about young children and their storied experiences of loss and grief. She and her husband have been married for thirty-seven years and enjoy traveling together. Most recently they have discovered the fun and challenge of kayaking around Vancouver Island's west coast. Although she has been writing stories and poems since she was a child, this is Janet's first publication.

Jane Eaton Hamilton is the author of six books, most recently the Ferro-Grumley nominated short-story collection *Hunger*. She has won many contests for her writing, including the 2003 CBC Literary Competition. She is also a photographer and her web site may be accessed at http://www.janeeatonhamilton.com. Jane and Joy joined the court case for same-sex marriage in 2000. The nineteen couples from across Canada were victorious in 2003. Jane and Joy married on June 28, 2003.

sarahmaya hamilton has been published in several Canadian magazines and poetry anthologies. Her first poem was published when she was eleven, and fourteen years later, in 2003, she was shortlisted for the CBC Literary Awards, in Poetry. She is proficient at the circus art of spinning fire and meditates daily in her home in Nagahama, Japan, next to a river that flows backward. She loves her moms, who live in Vancouver.

Ellen S. Jaffe grew up in New York City and lived in England before moving to Canada in 1979; she now lives in Hamilton, Ontario. She has been writing since childhood, teaches writing in schools and other settings, and has also worked in theatre. Ellen has published two books, *Water Children,* a collection of poetry, and *Writing Your Way: Creating a Personal Journal,* and her poems and fiction have been published in several Canadian journals. She has received awards from the Hamilton and Region Arts Council and other organizations. She has one son, born 1980, and enjoys journeys to various places and dimensions.

CONTRIBUTORS

Aprille Janes is a freelance writer whose articles appear in many publications. Her short stories and poetry have been included in various anthologies. When she's not traveling, Aprille facilitates creative writing workshops and retreats. You can find out more by visiting her website at www.ajanesinc.com.

Marion Jones is a development economist living and working in Regina. Combining her love of mountains and travel, she researches how tourism can or cannot be used for sustainable community development in fragile mountain environments and among indigenous peoples in China's southwest. Other activities include a sustainable development project in Nepal, social welfare research on the Canadian Prairie, ice climbing and mountaineering in the Canadian Rockies, and pioneering ice climbing in Sichuan.

Jeananne Kathol Kirwin is an Edmonton, Alberta, wife, mother of four, and lawyer. Her childhood dream to become a writer was rekindled during her family's one-year sailing sabbatical. During that time she penned a variety of pieces, among them bi-weekly missives sent by email to family, friends, and a growing audience back home. Those emails and that journey formed the basis of Jeananne's book-length work of narrative non-fiction, which has recently been accepted for publication by Borealis Press under the title *Greetings from Cool Breezes*. Jeananne continues to write and publish in the creative non-fiction genre. One of her travel pieces was shortlisted in a recent CBC Literary Awards competition.

Shelley A. Leedahl's most recent books include *The Bone Talker* (a children's book with illustrator Bill Slavin), *Orchestra of the Lost Steps* (stories), *Tell Me Everything* (a novel), and *Talking Down the Northern Lights* (poetry). She also works as an editor, freelance writer, and creative writing instructor, and frequently reads in schools and libraries across the country. She received a Fellowship for the Hawthornden Castle International Retreat for Writers (Scotland) and has attended numerous Canadian writing retreats. Next up is the Hambidge Center, in Georgia, US. Shelley lives in Saskatoon.

Alison Lohans, born in Reedley, California, has been writing since early childhood and was first published at age 12. She immigrated to Canada in 1971 and moved to Regina, Saskatchewan, in 1976. She is the author of thirteen books for young people and has published numerous shorter pieces. Alison has won awards for her writing and has served as Writer-in-Residence at Regina Public Library. Her most recent book is *Waiting for the Sun*.

Holly Luhning grew up on a farm in rural Saskatchewan. She is a graduate of the University of New Brunswick's M.A. program in English and creative writing. Her first book of poetry, *Sway*, was published by Thistledown Press in 2003. Holly is studying toward her Ph.D. in English at the University of Saskatchewan.

Jan MacKie, a fourth-generation Canadian, lives in Toronto, Canada. She spends her time balancing her work as a textile artist with her job as a program coordinator for Spiral Garden and Cosmic Bird Feeder (integrated, outdoor art, garden, play programs) and the joys of remaining connected to a grown family and large community of friends. Her interest in creating healing spaces in collaboration with others has taken her to Colombia, Sri Lanka, and now to the Palestinian Territories. She is delighted to have her writing included in this anthology.

Cheryl Mahaffy lives in Edmonton, Alberta. For her and her busy family of five, travel figures large in the bits of leisure time they can snatch, whether they are pondering antiquity atop the Great Wall of China or screaming down Rocky Mountain backcountry ski trails. Words that Sing, her independent writing business, is now at work on Women Building Alberta, unearthing the stories of women architects who have contributed to our built landscape. Editors have termed her a lateral thinker, to which she replies, "Fine by me, as long as that doesn't imply lying down on the job. Writing is hard work."

Chris Marin is a multi-media artist and jewelry designer who lives with her Dalmatians and her husband in a house on top of a cliff overlooking the ocean in West Dublin, Nova Scotia. Their two daughters work, travel, and study nearby and afar. On her trips to Peru, the Quechua mountain people inspired Chris. They still live lightly upon the land out of deep respect for the earth. Their way of life, *Ayni*, meaning "today for you, tomorrow for me," is a philosophy close to her heart.

Christine McKenzie is a curious journeyer, popular educator, and activist who has worked in the development industry in Latin America and the Caribbean over the past ten years. Christine is indebted to those she writes about here, who taught her so much as collaborators in her participatory research Masters work.

Larissa L. McWhinney grew up in Toronto and was educated at the Waldorf School. She received an M.A. in philosophy and bioethics from the University of British Columbia and is currently completing a Ph.D. in the same discipline at the University of Toronto. In 2001 she moved to Saskatchewan to work as a policy analyst on the Romanow Health Care Commission. She now lives in the Queen's City with her husband and teaches at the University of Regina.

Elaine K. Miller's travels include extensive biking in Europe; a women's tour in China; a safari in Tanzania and Rwanda; Peace Corps work in Zaire, Peru, and Honduras; an exchange fellowship in Argentina; interviewing of Latin American editorial cartoonists for a videotape project; and directing a study abroad program in Mexico. Her videos on gender issues in editorial cartoons are in distribution with First Run Icarus Films. Her M.A. and Ph.D. in Spanish are from Indiana University and UCLA.

CONTRIBUTORS

Christina Owens is a misplaced Southerner who has lived in the Pacific Northwest, Britain, and Japan. Before moving to Asia to teach English, Christina worked as an advocate for immigrants, refugees, and domestic violence survivors in the U.S. Soon to be a graduate student in cultural studies at the University of California-Davis, Christina still lives between places, with no husbands and no cats.

Angèle M. C. Palmer lives in London, Ontario, working toward an M.A. in counseling psychology at the University of Western Ontario. Angèle has traveled extensively, starting from age eight, accompanying her family on their business travels. Journeying with friends or solo, Angèle has covered land as far east as Taiwan, Singapore, Malaysia, Thailand, and Australia, to Europe, much of the U.S. and across Canada.

Linda Pelton is a social worker in Toronto, Ontario, working as a psychotherapist in an eating disorders program and in private practice. She worked for ten years with Ojibwa-Cree in mental health in the most remote, fly-in, northern Ontario communities (another life-transforming experience). Her love of Mexico began when she spent a summer as a teenage volunteer in an isolated Mexican village teaching language and math skills.

Alison Pick's novel, *The Sweet Edge*, has just been released by Raincoat. She was the 2002 Bronwen Wallace Award winner for most promising unpublished poet under thirty-five in Canada. In 2003 Raincoast published her first book of poetry, *Question & Answer*, which was shortlisted for the Gerald Lampert Award for best First Book of Poetry in Canada and for a Newfoundland and Labrador Book Award. The title section of the book won the 2003 National Magazine Award for Poetry. Originally from Kitchener, Ontario, Alison spent several years living and writing on the Prairies and now divides her time between southern Ontario and eastern Newfoundland.

Anne M. Sasso is a Canadian geologist and writer. Her geology career has taken her to areas of the world rarely visited by travelers. Her articles about science, travel, and spirituality appear in many mainstream magazines, including *Outside* and *Backpacker*. Anne is currently working on her first book, "Postcards from Lima," about her experiences living and working in South America.

Amanda Stevens has been writing since childhood and published her own 'zine as a teenager. She studied English at Simon Fraser University and after graduating spent a few years wandering across Canada, down to California, through the United Kingdom, and way down to New Zealand. Amanda recently moved back to her hometown of Kamloops, B.C., where she works in community development and food security. She is using her thumbs for cooking, crocheting, and gardening until her next hitchhiking adventure.

Gillian Steward is a Calgary-based journalist and visiting professor at the University of Regina's School of Journalism. She has traveled extensively in Mexico and Central America with her husband, Terry, her daughter, J'Val, and on her own. In 1993 she prepared a documentary about the Maya—*Living at the Centre of the World*—for the CBC Radio program *Ideas*. She has also written newspaper articles about Mexico, Guatemala, and Nicaragua.

Kathie Sutherland lives in Fort Saskatchewan, Alberta. She writes poetry, fiction, and creative non-fiction and is dedicated to exploring human spiritual connections through the written word. Kathie has recently completed a collection of stories about growing up military and continues to enjoy writing personal opinion essays for the "soft market." She has recently taken up scuba diving with her husband of twenty-five years, enjoys her growing relationship with her two adult daughters, and finds inspiration in her two lively grandchildren.

Carole TenBrink is a published poet with one book to her credit. In recent years she has turned from poetry to prose for the pleasure of writing all the way across the page. Raised in the United States and active in the anti-Vietnam War movement at university, she became disillusioned with her native land and moved to Montreal with her Vietnamese fiancé, who was, in effect, a draft evader from the South Vietnamese army. Carole became a Canadian citizen, a college teacher for many years in Montreal, and has recently moved to her rural retreat in Prince Edward County, an island in Lake Ontario, in order to write full time. Carole has enjoyed a forty-year association with Vietnamese people through marriage, friendships, and two teaching stints in that country. Her piece included here is from an as yet unpublished manuscript tentatively titled "Pagoda High Above the Sea, a Memoir of Connection to Vietnam."

Jody Wood is a partner, daughter, sister, and a devoted caretaker to one cocker spaniel and one kitten. She is a native Calgarian now living in Eastern Passage, Nova Scotia. She has a great love for travel and has visited many places, including Indonesia, Great Britain, France, Holland, Cuba, and Mexico. She takes great pride in having traveled Canada from coast to coast to coast. "Lautan" is her first published piece.